ORIGINAL PORSCHE 911

Other titles available in the *Original* series are:

Original AC Ace & Cobra
by Rinsey Mills
Original Aston Martin DB4/5/6
by Robert Edwards
Original Austin Seven
by Rinsey Mills
Original Austin-Healey (100 & 3000)
by Anders Ditlev Clausager
Original Citroën DS
by John Reynolds with Jan de Lange
Original Corvette 1953-1962
by Tom Falconer
Original Ferrari V8
by Keith Bluemel
Original Honda CB750
by John Wyatt
Original Jaguar XK
by Philip Porter
Original Jaguar E-Type
by Philip Porter
Original Jaguar Mark I/II
by Nigel Thorley
Original Land-Rover Series I
by James Taylor
Original Mercedes SL
by Laurence Meredith
Original MG T Series
by Anders Ditlev Clausager
Original MGA
by Anders Ditlev Clausager
Original MGB
by Anders Ditlev Clausager
Original Mini Cooper and Cooper S
by John Parnell
Original Morgan
by John Worrall and Liz Turner
Original Morris Minor
by Ray Newell
Original Porsche 356
by Laurence Meredith
Original Porsche 924/944/968
by Peter Morgan
Original Sprite & Midget
by Terry Horler
Original Triumph TR2/3/3A
by Bill Piggott
Original Triumph TR4/4A/5/6
by Bill Piggott
Original Vincent
by J. P. Bickerstaff
Original VW Beetle
by Laurence Meredith
Original VW Bus
by Laurence Meredith

ORIGINAL
PORSCHE 911

PETER MORGAN

PHOTOGRAPHY BY JOHN COLLEY
WITH DAVID FETHERSTON, DIETER REBMANN AND IAN KUAH

EDITED BY MARK HUGHES

This edition first published in 1995 by Bay View Books Limited, Bideford, Devon, EX39 2PZ England

Published by MBI Publishing Company, 729 Prospect Avenue, PO Box 1, Osceola, WI 54020-0001 USA

Library of Congress Cataloging-in-Publication Data Available
ISBN 1-901432-16-5

On the front cover: A Carrera 4 from the '993' period in striking Speed Yellow. Poly-ellipsoid headlamps were the most obvious distinguishing feature of the 1993–98 '993' models—the fourth-generation 911s.

On the half-title page: Another Carrera 4, this time in ever-popular Guards Red.

On the title page: A 1973 2.4E shows early deatils of Porsche's styling refinement for the 911—matte black intake grilles and a spoiler make the front look purposeful.

On the back cover: This 1971 2.2T shows off the Fuchs forged alloy wheels that are so characteristic of the early 911s.

Photograph Credits: All photographs were taken by John Colley except for the following: David Fetherston, pages 11 (lower), 12 (upper), 13 (bottom), 14 (lower centre), 15 (top & right), 17 (bottom), 19 (bottom), 23, 24, 25, 28 (lower), 31, 52, 53 (top), 56 (top two), 58 (centre), 59 (top), 60, 61 (top), 68, 70, 71 (top & bottom), 73 (bottom), 76, 78 (right), 103, 104, 110 (bottom), 111 (top), 112 (centre), 113 (top three), 114 (bottom left), 115 (top left & bottom), 117, 118 (bottom), 122 (bottom); Dieter Rebmann, pages 7 (top), 8–9, 10, 12 (lower), 14 (upper centre & bottom), 33 (upper), 40, 42, 48 (lower), 95, 106 (bottom left), 112 (top), 125, 140; Ian Kuah, pages 1, 7 (lower), 126, 129 (top), 131 (top), 133, 134 (top & centre), 135, 136, 137; James Mann, pages 127 (bottom), 131 (bottom); Jerry Sloniger, pages 54 (top), 105, 106 (top), 109; Peter Morgan, pages 54 (lower), 94 (lower), 115 (top right), 119 (top).

Typesetting and design by Chris Fayers & Sarah Ward

Printed in Hong Kong

CONTENTS

INTRODUCTION

I can still remember the moment well. I was in my mid-20s and I made a habit of scaring my girlfriends with an old Lotus Elan, the car to have in the mid-1970s if you knew about sports cars and, like me, did not have much money. I spent most of my Saturdays under the Elan and I learned almost everything about keeping one running. It was on just such a Saturday morning, as I was walking back from the local car parts store with my usual collection of replacement electrical bits and pieces, when a wonderful sound came from behind and rasped by. It was a brand new 3-litre Carrera in red. It looked fantastic, with its big rear wing and the sun glinting off its curving roof line.

This was my initiation into the 911. For some reason I had not really taken Porsches seriously until then as a car to own, but from that moment I knew that I would have to have one. In 1978 I bought my first Porsche – a 1973 911T. After the Elan, of course, it did not really handle at all, but that six-cylinder engine was just incredible – if only for its noise. And suddenly I found I had time on my hands on Saturdays, much to my girlfriend's delight!

But it did not take long to realise that early Porsches rust quite badly, and this poor old T was already bubbling nicely. I had learned that unless you wanted to spend all your time restoring paintwork, you bought a 911 that had been made after 1975, when the factory started to galvanise the cars. I moved on up the Porsche ladder, learning more and more about 911s. I came to appreciate the reliability of that six-cylinder engine, the build quality of the body and, of course, what not to do when you find yourself going into a corner too fast...

Driving an early 911 quickly is a real skill. I confess that even today there are times when I still lift off into fast bends in my current 1972 911S. The last time I did that was at a racing circuit on my first drive of the car after a winter lay-off, and as I pirouetted on the grass I found myself laughing. This car lets you know who is boss – which is one of the factors behind the enduring 911 legend. Yet driving a 1990s 3.6 Turbo – a car directly descended from the earliest 911 – you ask how it can possibly be related. Most drivers would never get near the limit of the Turbo, and you would have to accompany a factory driver to understand the real limits of the modern car's handling and braking. The technology is absolutely astounding – these 911s are many miles distant from the early generation.

Today's 911 engineers and technicians are the metaphorical sons of the original 911's designers, and the older generation can only gasp in wonder at how the 911 has developed over the years. But get into a discussion with any of the original 911 development team and the enthusiasm bubbles out: their eyes sparkle as they tell the old stories, perhaps waving their arms around as they recount how they steered their way out of another wild 911 tail-slide. These guys are part of the reason the 911 is still with us: they created a philosophy for a sports car whose longevity no-one has been able to better.

A grouping of faster 911s. In the foreground is a 1991 Carrera 2 RS, to the right a 1973 Carrera RS and in the background a 1987 Carrera Club Sport.

And philosophy the 911 now is. Porsche's Chief Designer and head of the Weissach Styling Department, Harm Lagaay, says that 911 is not just a number, but that it represents a car concept – a package of engineering and styling – that is eternal: "No matter how many changes the car goes through, the philosophy of the car, namely the way it drives, the seating arrangement, the rear-engined drive and so on, that is forever."

Asked which styling cues make up the 'original' 911 line, Lagaay responds: "The cues are in graphic and form. The graphic things are the shut lines of the bonnet, the doors and the engine lid, the drip rails and obviously the graphics of the side windows. The forms are the convex and the concave of the shoulders – the more you go to the rear the wider the shoulder becomes. There is obviously the silhouette of the car and the front fenders, the front lid being lower than the front fenders and the headlamps being dominant. There are lots of smaller cues too, like the engine lid grille."

Those now-immortal three numbers, 911, have come to signify the benchmark by which every other sports car is measured. Just as it was 35 years ago, sports cars are still all about excitement and speed. And this the 911 provides in abundance.

The objective of *Original Porsche 911* is to set down as authoritative a reference on 911 specification as is feasible. I have covered the first 35 years of 911 production, including a very brief specification of the 1998 model 996. I have deliberately avoided the racing 911s. I have tried to answer all the specification questions that I have asked myself over the years and had not been able to find. I have had to leave out a lot, but it is down at the cotton-bud level of detail (to use a concours analogy) that the sifting has occurred. Option lists are an example: I have not

"The styling cues of the 911 are in graphic and form – the shut lines of the bonnet, the doors and the engine lid, the drip rails and obviously the side windows" – Porsche designer Harm Lagaay.

Turbos are used to being described in superlatives. These views show the spectacular 360bhp version of 1993 (top) and its 408bhp successor of 1995 (above). Latter view shows the profile that every schoolchild knows simply as 'the Porsche'.

been able to include the full worldwide option list for every year, especially where models are similar, but the lists presented give a feel for what is right and what is not. I apologise to those who feel I have omitted the option list for 'their' year.

The subject of specifications and their accuracy makes dedicated enthusiasts become emotional, especially on the early cars, but I would suggest that maybe we should not get so serious about this. In the 1960s and early 1970s, Porsche's attitude to new component introduction was simple. The spirit of control was there in the form of the programme changes from year to year, but on a detail level this pattern was often broken. When a new part or modification was considered, the engineers would first try to break it, say by thrashing a car around the Nürburgring or on a drive down to Sicily for the Targa Florio. Parts that survived usually found their way into production fairly quickly, so it was quite normal to see changes being rolled into production at any time of year as new stock became available. On the other hand, it was just as likely that an old parts bin would be used up if later stock (especially of trim) was short.

It is important to keep these thoughts in perspective with the early cars, and these sorts of differences make older 911s interesting to the knowledgeable. What we should be concerned about is the importance of originality, and that is quite different. For obvious reasons, a good original car is worth more to a collector than a good rebuilt one. This book cannot help you tell an original car from a rebuilt one,

Four cars show the evolution through the ages in a splendid photograph by Dieter Rebmann: 1964 911 (bottom left), 1973 911T 2.4 (bottom right), 1984 Carrera 3.2 (top left) and 1993 Carrera 4 (top right).

but I hope it will give you the information to understand the general specifications from year to year.

If the shape of the 911 is still with us after 35 years, everything else has changed, even the factory in which the cars are built. In 1989, for the start of the Carrera 4, the new body assembly factory opened in Zuffenhausen, finally replacing the old Reutter plant that had been with the company since the early 1960s. There is a sort of legend going around among long-time Porsche employees that maybe just somewhere there is a single screw that has quietly stayed on the 911 parts list since 1963. It's very unlikely, especially with the introduction of the all-new 996, but it's all part of the folklore surrounding one of the world's most famous cars.

This book is the result of a significant amount of personal research, but I could not have produced it without talking to a large number of people. Among those at Porsche in Stuttgart, I must mention Klaus Parr, Olaf Lang, Michael Schimpke and Harm Lagaay. Claire Titcombe and James Pillar at Porsche Cars GB, and indirectly others at Porsche Cars North America, were also helpful.

Many authors have preceded me in writing about the 911, but those I would like to compliment on their work as a valuable reference for this effort are Tobias Aichele, Bruce Anderson, Jürgen Barth and Lothar Boschen, Dean Batchelor, Michael Cotton, Paul Frère, Dr Thomas Gruber and Georg Konradsheim, Karl Ludvigsen, Dominique Pascal, Jerry Sloniger and the many hard-working contributors to *Porsche Panorama* (USA), *Porsche Post* (GB) and *Christophorus* (Germany). I must also record my appreciation of Britain's *Autocar & Motor* magazine

OWNERS OF FEATURED CARS

IN THE UK

Richard Baker (1965 911); David Cocker (1967 911S); Patrick Amos (1971 911T 2.2); Mark Waring (1971 911S 2.2 & 1973 Carrera RS Touring); Anthony Minshull (1972 911T 2.4 US); Nancy MacLean (1973 911T 2.4 Sportomatic); Dave Gray 1973 911E 2.4); the late Tony Knapp (1975 911 Carrera 2.7); Peter Hatfield (1977 911 Carrera Sport 3.0); Sue Baker (1979 911SC Targa Sportomatic); Peter Foskett (1982 911SC Sport); Andy Frost (1984 911 Carrera 3.2); Terry Davison (1987 911 Carrera 3.2 Cabrio Turbo-Look); John Colley (1987 911 Club Sport); Roger Wynne (1988 911 'Anniversary'); Mike Flannery (1989 911 Speedster); Ian King (1990 Carrera 4 Targa); Mike King (1991 Carrera 2 Tiptronic); Alan Stein (1976 911 Turbo); Robin Duckitt (1989 911 Turbo).

IN THE USA

Ernie Wilberg (1967 911S); Terry Zaccone (1968 911L Targa); Joe Hartman (1974 911 Carrera 2.7); Brian Carleton (1980 911SC Weissach); Jim Boyden (1986 911 Turbo); Carlsen Motor Cars Inc (1993 Carrera 2 RS America).

for providing such fastidious road tests over the years. The draft manuscript was read by one of Britain's Porsche experts, and the gems of detail contributed by Steve Carr are highly valued.

I must also compliment John Colley, a 911 enthusiast who drives a 3.2 Carrera Club Sport, on his superb photography of cars in the UK. David Fetherston, Dieter Rebmann and Ian Kuah provided equally accomplished work from the USA and Germany, while some further shots were supplied by Jerry Sloniger and myself. We chose our cars very carefully and I would like to thank all the owners who persevered with us in the task – their names are listed in the accompanying panel.

Peter Morgan
Marlborough, England

THE 2-LITRE 911 (1963-69)

The cry was heard after the prototype 901 was revealed at the Frankfurt Motor Show on 12 September 1963: "It's not a real Porsche". By that time, the company had built up a solid reputation based around the 356, a car that achieved its performance through fundamentally lightweight design and simplicity. For some people, therefore, the company had lost its way with the 901, by building a bigger, more powerful and more luxurious car. Porsche's first entirely new model since the 356 had been launched in 1948, the new concept was happily accepted by the majority as a major step forward and customers clamoured for a production version.

But the Frankfurt Show car, the result of a concentrated and tortuous development programme that had started in earnest in 1959, was a one-off. It would be towards the end of 1964 before the company was ready to put the 901 into full production at its factory in Zuffenhausen, Stuttgart. In October 1964, the 901 became the 911 in response to Peugeot's trademark objections, and so the most famous three numbers in the sports car world were coined.

The small styling team, under the guidance of Dr Ferry Porsche's son Butzi, evolved a compact 2+2 shape that would prove to have a timeless profile. Combined with the rear engine location and a smooth aerodynamic profile, the 2+2 accommodation is the essence of the 911. The new car was unmistakably a Porsche, capturing accents from previous prototypes and from the 356 line, but it was also fresh. The windshield was more steeply raked than on the 356 and there was a larger glass area, but probably the single most distinctive styling feature was the gradual, yet continuous, curve of the roof from the top of the windshield to the rear bumper. It gave the car its excellent aerodynamic penetration and was at the same time attractive. The attention to detail was carried over to the interior and several features, like the grouping of the five large circular instrument dials, have endured throughout the course of 911 production.

The 2-litre cars were subject to massive development effort after launch. The best of the bunch are probably the 1967 models (with their elegant simplicity, especially in the US before emissions laws arrived) and the 1969 models (on which handling and braking were close to their best).

BODYSHELL

The 911 bodyshells carry alphabetic designators, which make the differences easier to categorise. The first models formed the O-programme, covering the cars from the start of production in August 1964 to July 1967. The chassis number of the earliest cars was carried on the left-hand door pillar, but by the start of proper O-programme production a second chassis plate was carried on the lock plate at the front of

EVOLUTION OUTLINE

Sep 1963	Presentation by Porsche of the 901 prototype at the Frankfurt Motor Show.
Aug 1964	911 with two triple-choke Solex carburettors, 130bhp, five-speed gearbox.
Mar 1966	Weber carburettors replace Solex.
Oct 1966	911S with 160bhp, Fuchs wheels.
Dec 1966	Start of Targa production (with soft rear window).
Aug 1967	Four-speed Sportomatic option launched; 911T launched with 110bhp (replaces four-cylinder 912); 911L launched with 130bhp (replaces 911); dual-circuit brakes introduced.
Aug 1968	911E launched with 140bhp (replaces 911L); 911S (170bhp) receives mechanical fuel injection; glass rear window for Targa; 911E and 911S have CD ignition.

The clean lines of the Porsche factory's own 1964 911 coupé. The first 911s had minimal flaring to their wings, giving the cars a very clean aerodynamic shape. Evident in this view is the Durant driver's door mirror, of 356 vintage.

A timeless profile that is unmistakably a Porsche, as shown on Richard Baker's 1965 model (top). Painted Slate Grey and fitted with steel wheels, this car was the fifth right-hand drive 911 imported into the UK. This view (above) of Ernie Wilberg's 1967 S shows the classic 911 roofline and the graceful double curve of the rear wing line.

the luggage compartment. The full chassis number was stamped on the bodyshell structure in the luggage compartment, on the left side to the rear of the fuel tank. The last four digits of the chassis number were also found on the doors (beneath the interior trim, under the opening vent) and on the bonnet and engine lid – this was a factory aid to ensure correct fit during assembly.

The layout of the 911 bodyshell was based around the rear engine location and the requirement to provide comfortable 2+2 accommodation for the occupants. Because the new Porsche was a luxury GT, it had to have satisfactory space for luggage too. With these major compartments defined, together with the essential wind-cheating profile and an ancestry traceable to the 356, the 911 shape began to evolve into its unmistakable form.

The basic bodyshell was a unitary design (with no separate chassis) with much of its strength coming from a stiffened floorpan, large box section sills (or rockers) and a stressed roof. Sheet metal box sections gave support for the engine and rear suspension. Bodyshell stiffness at the front derived from the assembly of the sheet panels, especially the sculpted inner wings and the front cross-member supporting the front of the fuel tank.

Compared with the 356, the new 911, surprisingly, was 61mm (2.4in) narrower externally (but with more interior width) and 152mm (6.0in) longer. The wheelbase was 111mm (4.4in) more at 2211mm (87.0in), aimed at giving the 911 a more comfortable ride. But compared with other sports cars of the time, the 911 was still a short-wheelbase design, the E-type Jaguar, for instance, having a wheelbase of 2438mm (96.0in). The 911, with its overhanging engine installation and relatively small distance between the wheel centres, would give the engineers considerable challenges over the years. It would be some time before 'development triumphed over design'.

The earliest 911s had a more efficient aerodynamic shape than any previous Porsche. It came in part from the narrower body and from attention to detail, like integrating the front and rear bumpers into the body shape. The original 901 was even better aerodynamically than the Abarth Carrera racer that was considered 'state-of-the-art' at the time. Of course, as the years passed the slippery shape grew more and more external bits and pieces, such as bumper overriders, external mirrors, wider wheelarches and even spoilers. I shall leave it to you to decide whether or not the engineers got the appearance right first time...

An open version of the basic coupé was announced in September 1965, and Porsche conceived for it another term that has become an industry standard. The open-topped 'Targa' went into production in December 1966, and featured a folding roof that stowed in the front compartment or behind the front seats. A zippered convertible-type plastic window covered the rear area on the first cars, giving a rather cheapened look for such a luxury GT model. The word 'targa' is Italian for 'shield' and this is appropriate for the function of the brushed-finish stainless steel roll hoop, but Porsche fans always refer to the factory racing success in the Targa Florio, the legendary Sicilian road race. This gruelling event was won more times post-war by Porsche than by any other marque, and the Porsche marketing people loved the association.

The Targa model was not a true convertible, but featured the first production roll-over bar. The roll-over bar, a wide-section hoop to which a removable roof section could be attached, acted as a stiffener for the chassis, which would otherwise have been weakened by the loss of the coupé's roof. In producing a convertible, the engineers wanted to avoid the usually significant weight increase that comes from additional chassis stiffening. They partially achieved their aim, because the lower body panels and undertray are identical to the coupé's, the rigidity coming in part from the roll hoop. The reality was that Targas came out some 50kg (110lb) heavier than the coupé. Targas would never be as rigid – and the early ones without the glass rear window were even more flexible – but the trade-off in handling was more than

Despite its lowered suspension and wider tyres, this 1968 911L Targa is a remarkably original car because Terry Zaccone has owned it since new and covered 320,000 miles – and the car has made over 2500 race starts! Note the US-specification sealed beam headlamps with their large chromed surrounds, the 1968-only side reflectors, and the 'new' Durant external mirror.

This Belgian-registered 1967 Targa – actually a four-cylinder 912 – shows off its satin-finish roll-over hoop and the style of Targa driving. The zippered rear window of early Targas may not have looked too permanent when in place, but it allowed virtually open Porsche motoring when removed.

balanced by the attraction of open air motoring.

The Targa was heavily marketed in the US, brochures showing the various Targa configurations (top on or off, rear window in or out) described with attractive names like Spyder, BelAir and Voyage. This model was truly versatile...

The development years immediately after the 911's launch were spent improving what *Road & Track* magazine termed as the car's 'animal oversteer'. This accusation had been levelled at the earlier 356, but with the 911 it went deeper. In his book *911 Story*, Paul Frère recounts that the problems stemmed from the fact that the early press cars were assembled by very experienced technicians and so had few handling defects. When the 911 went into production, the impossibly fine set-up tolerances specified could not be held, and as a result some cars handled 'like real beasts'. *Autocar* magazine was more restrained – and very British! – in saying that the car needed care in the wet. Even the factory's own sales brochure suggested that the 911 'was not a car for the novice'. The problem was seen at its worst if you lifted the accelerator when cornering hard – the result would more often than not be a view of the world rotating around the car.

The earliest style of horn grille was made of chrome-plated brass and mounted with four screws (above), but a cheaper design for the 1967 model year was secured by only two screws (right). Both cars have the European-specification Bosch assymetric (non-sealed beam) headlights used until the end of the 1967 model year, but the bumper styles differ because the later car, without overriders, has the wide rubber insert that was a new feature of the S.

Porsche's engineers needed to find more latitude in the handling and their attention focused on the rear-biased weight distribution and the relatively short wheelbase. The first, fairly crude, attempt to improve stability came in 1966, when 11kg (24.3lb) weights were added into the extreme ends of the front valence – a modification the engineers were not particularly proud of.

The A-programme models from August 1967 did not fundamentally address, in chassis terms, the handling issues inherent in the original models, so it was the B-programme models, launched for the 1969 model year, that produced the first big improvement. The wheelbase was increased by 57mm (2.2in) to 2268mm (89.3in), which had the effect of shortening the engine overhang and reducing the 'dumb-bell' effect in cornering. With a reduction in the weight of the engine casing included, the front/rear weight distribution became slightly less biased to the rear when it changed from 41.5/58.5 to 43/57, and handling was significantly improved.

The wheelbase extension was achieved simply by moving the rear wheels backwards in the bodyshell, without moving the engine and gearbox. This resulted in slightly angled drive-shafts, but this aspect was not considered to affect the durability of these components. Externally, the longer wheelbase cars can be identified by the larger distance between the rear wheelarch opening (at its front edge) and the cover over the rear torsion bar. The B-programme cars also introduced the first slight flaring of the rear wheelarches.

BODY TRIM & FITTINGS

As was the fashion of the time, the window fittings and other trim of the launch cars used chrome as far as possible. This included the wipers, which parked on the right side of the screen irrespective of market. It was not until August 1967 that black wipers, which parked on the left-hand side of the screen on left-hand drive models, were introduced.

The horn grilles, next to the indicators and either side of the front luggage compartment lid, were changed in mid-1966 from the original chrome-plated brass examples, which were secured with four screws, to a cheaper design that used only two mounting screws. Optionally, owners could also specify additional spot lights that mounted through special horn grilles. For 1969, the horn grilles changed again, to a narrower design that made room for enlarged indicator/side light assemblies.

For the 1967 model year, the chromed over-riders were revised and received a rubber trim. The pencil-thin rubbing strips along the edges of the bumper valences and on the trim under the doors were initially similar to those used on the 356C, but for 1967 the new 911S was launched with a wide rubbing strip, but it was only an option on the same year's regular 911 US models. The 1968 911S sill trim consisted of a wider vinyl strip fitted to a much larger anodised aluminium extrusion, which covered the whole sill area under the doors, from wheelarch to wheelarch (and over the torsion bar covers). When the B-programme cars extended the wheelbase, this extrusion was lengthened and the new trim was also fitted to the new 911E model. A year earlier, for the A-programme models, the gold-anodised script on the rear engine cover also changed, from the previous linked lettering and angled 911 designation, to more spaced-out lettering with the model type positioned just below the grille.

An electric sun roof was available as an option on the coupé from the beginning. There were external water drain slots above the top of the rear three-quarter windows on early cars, but the design was cleaned up at the start of the B-programme by running the drains down into the inside of the rear wheelarch.

Two other trim details – door handles and exterior mirrors – help the diligent 911 spotter to identify the early cars. The first 911s had simple outside door handles with push buttons that stood proud of the handle. A tooling change to the handle casting in 1967 was so minor that you have to inspect both handles side by side to see the slightly more rounded corners of the later version. The prominent push buttons were changed to a recessed type for 1968, and these handles became more wedge-shaped.

The external door mirror was an option. It started out as the same Durant-manufactured type used on the 356C, with a cone-shaped backing to the mirror. The new 911S was given a Durant mirror with a larger flange holding the glass in place, and this became standard across the range in 1968. However, the story does not stop there, as other mirrors were available as options. These included simple rectangular mirrors in 1967 (which became mandatory in some countries later, due to the larger glass area) and the sporty Talbot mirrors as used on the racing cars of the time.

By the start of 1968 a new Targa version was offered with a significant improvement. A large, curved, glass rear window replaced the soft convertible type and was a more practical proposition for owners who wanted open top motoring with civilised 2+2 accommodation. The glass rear window remained available as an option until 1971, after which it became standard in all markets. For the 1969 model year, Targa ventilation was improved further when air extractor slots were included at the sides of the stainless steel hoop (and unlike the coupé, the Targa's front quarter windows could still be opened).

The original style of tail badging had a gold-anodised finish for the linked-lettering Porsche script and the angled 911 designation.

The first 911s used a simple push-button external door handle (left). The tooling for this door handle was changed for the 1967 model year, the later version having slightly more radius in the curvature around the button. A new handle (below left), which protected the button and prevented the door being accidentally opened, was introduced for 1968.

This 1967 911S (with the early style of push-button door handle) shows off its opening rear side window. The plated-finish rear wiper was an option.

A detail of a 1968 Targa showing the 'soft-window' rear screen stowed and the tonneau in place. The position of the interior light in the roll-over hoop and the gold-anodised Targa script can be seen.

Rear view of an Austrian 911 (right) shows the complexity of the hand-assembled engine lid grille of the 2-litre cars. The manufacturing cost of the grille was later reduced by using pressed bars and welded construction. The 1967 911S (far right) shows the rubber trim introduced on the rear overriders for this model year – these items were previously in plain chrome. This model year was the last when the engine cover featured a distinctive central body rib under the grille.

The engine lid release on the 911 is to be found on the left-hand 'B' pillar. This feature is not so convenient for right-hand drive…

INTERIOR TRIM

To talk seats and Porsche at the same time is to talk Recaro. There is a history lesson behind this which goes back to the war years, when the original Reutter father and son were killed. The company was managed on behalf of the remaining family after the war and Reutter prospered, especially when it signed a deal in 1951 with Zuffenhausen neighbours Porsche to build bodies and supply seats for the new 356 model. Eventually, Reutter came to the point at which it had to decide on a major investment programme to cope with the ever-increasing volume of bodyshell business from Porsche. The investment would have been large and the family backed away, deciding to sell the coachbuilding factory in Zuffenhausen to Porsche, in 1963. The main Reutter factory remaining in Stuttgart became the hub of a new seat manufacturing business named Recaro.

The first Porsche-designed 911 seats were simple affairs developed from 356 experience. They incorporated adjustment only for fore/aft position and seat backrest incline, with the combined seat recline and locking lever at the door-side base of the back. The mechanism for these seats extended across the base of the seat back to operate on the inside seat back support. The seat back supports were chromed, changing progressively from the 1967 introduction of the reclining Recaro sports seat to a black-painted finish. Seat tilt lock levers were incorporated into the top of the seat back support from 1969. Early production 911s came with basket-weave vinyl seat inserts as standard in a range of just four colours, although hound's tooth material was an option. Leather was available to special order from the beginning, or from 1965 as an option.

No head restraints were fitted as standard to the original cars, but these could be specified as an

This 1965 car shows a typical early interior with leatherette seat coverings, a perforated pattern to the pleated seat panels, and a chromed finish for the backrest support frame.

Folding rear seats have always been a feature of the 911, the 1965-66 models uniquely having a small leather surround to the seat cushion. The seat belts are a later fitting.

option, the 1965-67 models using 356 items. These attached on the rear of the seat back, whereas the later restraints were mounted on bayonet type legs that entered through the top of the seat back. The early 356 restraints were only adjustable for height, but the later ones could be angled forwards or backwards as well.

Sports seats were available from 1965 and the history of these on the early cars is one of essentially adding more and more comfort. To start with there were the Recaro or 'Ferrari' types. The 'Ferrari' was little more than a padded bucket with only reach adjustment and no head restraint, and it is believed this seat was discontinued after 1966. The Recaro was a more comfortable, but non-reclining, seat with high side supports and an integral head restraint. From 1967 Recaro developed its version to include reclining, and it came in all the materials available for

Some of the interesting features inside a 1965 model (right). The lever ahead of the gear lever is the heater control, and the warm air outlet at the front of the side member can be seen. The early 911 logo and period Blaupunkt Bremen radio have an elegant simplicity. The early style of door panel was simple (below). A button to open the door was fitted to the front of the armrest, which on the driver's side had no pull handle. A small door compartment was unique to the 1968 model (bottom) and there was generally an improved finish to the door trim. The loudspeaker is a later addition.

the standard seats. By 1969 it was an even more luxurious affair with height and pitch adjustment.

The rear seats featured fold-down backs. When they were down, the parcel shelf that resulted provided a useful extra area for luggage, and the area under the shelf provided concealed storage spaces on the seats themselves. The seat backs were held upright by leather straps that attached to the rear wall by popper studs. The rear seat backs on the Targa were shorter than those used on the coupé. An interesting feature offered to Targa owners from 1967 (but discontinued after 1971) was a security box, formed by a rear parcel shelf that replaced the folding seat sections and offered two lockable compartments below. The same year, 1967, also saw the first attempt at installing air conditioning in the 911 for the US market.

The door trims on the first 911s featured an arm rest (with the door opening button at its front edge) below which was a pleated soft fabric pocket for maps. The passenger door had a pull handle, but the handle was omitted from the driver's door because it would restrict movement. The door panels changed in detail through to the 1968 models, when, after a unique 1968 pattern door featuring a rigid pocket under the arm rest, the design adopted the shape seen to the end of the 2.4 models. This used a rigid forward pocket and an opening compartment under an extended arm rest, which now had a flush-fitting (and safer) door handle mechanism in its side face.

The 911 began life with a velour interior carpet, which later became the more luxurious option for the higher-spec cars like the E and S. From 1967, a cheaper material termed Perlon (with an appearance like felt) was introduced for the basic models (the 911 and the later 911T). Until approximately, the start of the 1968 model year, you could have any carpet colour as long as it was dark grey.

Increased safety standards demanded that the original internal mirror, mounted centrally to the front roof section by three screws, was changed to a break-away type for 1968. That year only the mounting stayed on the roof section, but the following year the mirror was mounted directly onto the windshield glass by an adhesive pad. Few drivers of these particular models have not come out to their cars to find the interior mirror sitting on the floor of the car...

Heating, never a strong Porsche feature in the early days, was provided by ducting fresh air from around the exhaust system and piping it forwards through silencers in each of the sills. A mixer provided after each of the two exhaust-mounted heat exchangers allowed the driver to control the amount of hot air ducted forward to the passenger compartment or dumped to the outside. The problem with an air-cooled engine, however, is that heater output is dependent on engine speed. High engine speed

The interior of this European-specification 1968 model year 911S shows off the hound's tooth inlays on its leatherette seats. This car has two interesting features: there is only one head restraint (on the passenger side) and no radio is fitted. Compared with earlier cars, the heater control has moved from ahead of the gear lever to a new position, out of sight here, alongside the handbrake.

meant lots of heat, but low engine speed, in town traffic for instance, meant little warmth for the occupants. It was for this reason that a small fuel-driven heater was standard on the first cars and an option on A-programme and later left-hand drive cars to 1973. These supplementary heaters were fitted into a small cavity behind the fuel tank and were manufactured by Eberspächer. The fuel heater took air from a vent in front of the rear seats and generated hot air for defrosting.

Cabin fresh air ventilation was achieved by allowing air to enter through a small inlet carefully placed in the high pressure area just in front of the windshield, and expelling it through a line of almost concealed vents in the roof line above the rear window. An option to the full heater on the A-programme cars was an electric fan, which assisted circulation of cabin air. Heater output was controlled by a lever mounted just ahead of the gear lever. A-programme cars had an additional duct which directed hot air onto the rear window for demisting, while B-programme models offered an optional electric rear window demister in place of the earlier ducted warm air solution. The floor-mounted lever (just ahead of the gear lever) controlling the heater output was moved to the right-hand side of the handbrake lever at the same time. The new model's heat could be separately ducted to the windshield and the occupant's feet. Output was further enhanced by a three-speed fan under the dash.

DASHBOARD & INSTRUMENTS

The dashboard of the 911 is dominated by the familiar flattened oval instrument housing containing five large dials. A classic Butzi Porsche detail, the layout was a case of 'if it's right, leave it alone', so the dial area has remained largely unchanged in basic form over 30 years, and has always been the same for left-hand and right-hand drive.

The five black-faced dials reduce in size either side of the large central rev counter, which on early cars was red-lined at 7000rpm with a maximum of 8000rpm. To the right of the rev counter are a 250kph or 150mph speedometer and, at the end, a clock. To the left of the rev counter are the combined oil temperature and oil pressure gauges, and to the left again another combination gauge showing fuel level and (uniquely) oil tank level. In the 1965 *Hints to Drivers* handbook, this last gauge was described as follows: 'The small combination dial on the far left of the panel indicates fuel level and has a red warning light which is illuminated when the fuel level drops to 6 litres (1.6 US gallons). The same dial incorporates the oil level – there are in fact 9 litres of oil circulating in the lubricating system. The gauge only shows oil in the tank when the engine is idling. The method is much neater and does away with dirty hands.' Until 1973, this clever combination gauge was labelled in one language only, with the

Right from the start the dashboard featured the 911 trademark of five dials reducing in size either side of a central rev counter. The colours of the wood veneer (used for the 1965-66 model years) and the green figures on the dials (1965-67 model years) complement each other, and are accented by chrome bezels.

The dashboard began to change for the 1967 model year. The S was given a leather-rimmed steering wheel and basket-weave vinyl trim on the lower dash area, but the green instrument markings remained. Note also the new glove compartment lid with 'square' 911S lettering.

The markings on the dials changed from green to white for the 1968 model year, and chrome trim virtually disappeared from the dashboard. Interesting details include the large switch under the clock for the optional sunroof and the heavy grain lower dash that was also new for the 1968 model year.

oil level always denoted by the German word 'oel'.

The early 2-litre cars have an elegant simplicity in their instrumentation. The pre-1968 models had chrome rims on the five main dials which, combined with the green lettering and wood veneer lower dash trim of the 1965 and '66 cars, demonstrate automobile fashion of the time. From 1968 the dial rims became black, with white lettering on the black instrument background. For 1967 and 1968, brushed aluminium replaced the wood (no doubt inspired by contemporary racing car style) for the lower dash area on all models except the S. The 1967 S had the heavy basket-weave finish on the lower dash that would become used across the 911 range from 1969. The dash contained an opening on its top deck for the single speaker radio. The holes for this opening were integrated into the dash top until 1969, but thereafter the speaker opening could be accessed by a separate panel.

There were many variations to the detail of the main gauges from year to year and model to model, including warning lights for the fuel, oil (on models where no level gauge was offered), charging failure and handbrake application. For the B-programme, the turn signal and headlight main beam indicators were located on the rev counter. As the engine was developed, the peak revolutions red marking on the rev counter changed according to specification. The speedometer had a trip odometer for specific distance measurement.

The instrument layout generally has received considerable 'flak' over the years, one British journalist describing the switch gear as looking like a packet of boiled sweets thrown haphazardly over the dashboard! But most 911 drivers will tell you that once you know your way around, the switches are just fine. On the earliest models there were relatively few controls to find, but when accessories were fitted ergonomics did become questionable. There were two areas where accessory switches could be clustered – on the lower dash to either side of the steering wheel.

The lights switch was down by the driver's door side of the steering wheel, just to the outside of the ignition. Above that under the instrument cluster was the optional sunroof rocker switch. On the passenger side of the steering wheel, under the 'inboard' dials, was the fresh air control lever, and under this on the dash panel was the switch for the cigarette lighter. Other switches were grouped to the passenger side of the ashtray, above the radio if one was fitted. These might include switches for auxiliary driving or fog lights, the petrol heater switch and the hazard flasher switch (which found its way over next to the ignition switch from 1970). Until 1968, these switches usually had a small indicator light at their centre to denote operation. From 1968, the switch knobs for the American and certain other export markets changed to larger rubber-rimmed affairs, with symbols denoting function at their cen-

The luggage compartment, seen here (below) on a 1965 model with the central piece of carpet removed, housed the spare wheel and the fuel tank, both of which were recessed between the front wheels to allow a useful volume on top for personal belongings. Note the fuse block fitted at the top right. The battery is attached by a later fitting, the original rubber strap and plastic cover no doubt having disappeared long ago. The 1968 S had a soft-grain finish to its tool bag (right), but from 1969 the tool bag vinyl changed to a basket-weave. The chassis number plate is seen to the left of the latch, with the windshield washer filler on the right. The battery at top right has the correct rubber strap and plastic cover.

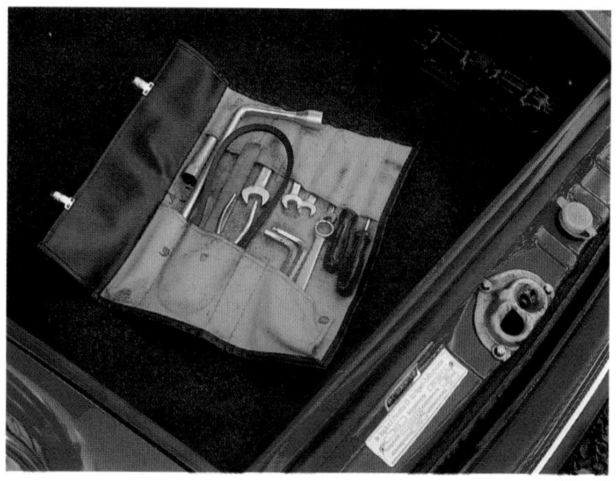

tres. The lever controlling the intake of fresh air from ahead of the windshield was replaced in 1969, by a new heating and ventilation control in the lower dash where the ashtray had previously been sited (the ashtray moved into the central kneeguard area of the dash). The hazard flasher moved next to the ignition switch in 1969, and from 1970 was changed to a red push button.

Until 1971, the model designation was mounted on the glove compartment lid. This script was originally an italic '911', but evolved to a block capital style for the 1967 911S. The lid itself started life with a wood inlay and a small central pull handle and separate lock, but in 1967 the handle was integrated into the whole of the top edge of the lid, with the lock slightly offset towards the driver.

The steering wheel is something that many people get completely wrong when restoring a car. As with the road wheels, it is relatively easy to switch steering wheels as part of a customising exercise, so it is important for the seeker of the 'original' 911 to know what is right for the car. All steering wheels were of 400mm (15.6in) diameter. The first 911s had wood-rimmed wheels, believed to have been made by VDM, with four black-painted spokes arranged in what *Car & Driver* described as a 'shallow X'. This characteristic pattern, another feature of the 911 to have lasted through the years, offers good instrument visibility and a place to rest your thumbs. The appearance of the wheel was updated after about a year's production, the spokes being coated in black plastic, presumably for better wear. From 1966, you could specify a horn 'butterfly' – so-called because of its winged shape similar to the wheel spokes – that replaced the previous central horn contact mounted in the boss; the first horn butterflys had a bright finish to the rim of the hub boss. A black plastic-rimmed (or hard rubber) steering wheel was also available, and was standard on the four-cylinder 912.

A leather-rimmed wheel with leather thumb-rests at the ends of the spokes was standard on the 911S from 1967, and optional on the other models. This wheel, which used a heavier design of horn butterfly that covered the wheel spokes completely, also became standard on the E from 1969, the year in which the wood-rimmed wheel disappeared altogether. It was also at this time that the two stalks behind the steering wheel were given a black look, the previous style of chromed stalk with a moulded top having been taken from the 356. The left-hand stalk was for indicators/headlamps and main/dipped beam, and the right-hand one for windshield wipers. A feature of the 911 was that there was a three-speed wiper system and an electric wash/wipe.

Luggage Compartment

It is difficult to get excited over things like luggage compartments on a car like the 911, but great care went into the compartment design to make sure that two people could pack enough belongings for a week's vacation. The shaped fuel tank of 62 litres (13.64 Imperial gallons, 16.38 US gallons), including a reserve of 6 litres (1.32 Imperial gallons, 1.59 US gallons), accommodated the spare wheel, with both of these set low between the longitudinally

The vertically-mounted fan distributed cooling air to the cylinder barrels more evenly than the 356's axial unit. The Solex overflow carburettors, seen on each side of the engine, were difficult to tune correctly and gave the engine a significant flat spot around 2500rpm. The later label (mentioning the 911S/911L) on the fan housing is incorrect on this 1965 model.

aligned torsion bar front suspension. This compact design resulted in a relatively large luggage volume. The washer bottle on the early cars does look like an afterthought, however, in its exposed position on the left-hand wing wall.

The first 911s benefited from the same square-weave carpeting in the front area as was used inside the car. Unfortunately this was replaced for the start of the 1966 model year by a cheaper felt carpeting called 'Perlon'. This initially came in three pieces (or more after the battery acid got to them!), but from 1969 a fourth piece covered the front area behind the latch panel. This carpeting was functional, but not very robust.

The vehicle chassis number, a strip of stamped aluminium sheet riveted in place, can be found on the left-hand side of the front lid latch panel.

ENGINE

The new 911 needed an engine with the power of the existing four-cylinder, four-cam Carrera racing engine, but without the noise and the complexity. But why the rear engine location when virtually every other manufacturer at the time was saying such a layout was obsolete?

The answer lies in a mixture of business risk and tradition. Porsche was a small company relative to the big names of the industry and all its experience as a manufacturer of sports cars lay with the rear engine layout. The 911 was also the first production Porsche totally to make the break with the VW parts bin, so everything was new. Design innovation, therefore, had to be kept within known boundaries, which meant that for the engine the opposed-piston (or boxer) layout was a requirement.

The six-cylinder 901 engine (the engine kept the original type number until the 2.2-litre version came along) was an elegant and 'leading-edge' production design in many respects, incorporating features that were usually only seen in motor racing at the time. These included dry sump lubrication, overhead camshafts and hemispherical cylinder heads.

The new engine was very over-square, with a short stroke of 66mm (2.57in) and a bore of 80mm (3.12in) giving a total capacity of 1991cc (121.45cu in). Firing order was 1-6-2-4-3-5. The individual cylinder heads, six in total, each contained one

The engine compartment of the 1967 S shows the coil ignition and the fuel pump mounted on the left-hand side. Emissions controls had yet seriously to restrict the 911's raw performance, power output for the S leaping from the regular 130bhp to 160bhp.

35mm (1.37in) exhaust valve and one 39mm (1.52in) inlet valve, with a centrally mounted spark plug. The plug aperture was fitted with a Helicoil insert, so that if the thread should be stripped for any reason the Helicoil – a coiled wire that formed an internal screw thread – could be replaced, rather than having to scrap the head. From the start of production the exhaust valves were hollow and sodium-filled for better cooling. On each cylinder bank, these were actuated through rockers by a camshaft contained in an aluminium housing. Each bank of heads bolted to each of these camshaft housings, which in turn bolted down to each side of the crankcase.

The cylinder barrels of the first prototypes were cast iron, but the first production models used Biral – a trade name for the process of sleeving the cast iron barrel with aluminium cooling fins. These fins and the cylinder heads were air-cooled by a vertically-mounted axial-flow fan, which improved on the old radial-flow 356 unit by distributing the air more evenly to both banks of cylinders. The alternator was mounted within this fan. Both fan and alternator were turned by a belt driven from the rear of the crankshaft at 1.3 times engine speed. The cooling air flow was ducted to the engine using a plastic-mounted shroud that covered the top part of the engine. Ducts in the shroud ensured that some of the air was directed to the barrels, the heads, the crankcase-mounted oil cooler and lastly to the fresh air inlets of the exhaust-mounted heat exchangers. This latter air was heated by passing it over the exhaust pipes from each bank of cylinder heads. From there the amount of heated air passed to the cabin was controlled by driver-operated flap valves just downstream of each heat exchanger. The complex exhaust system, with two complicated heat exchangers (one per bank of cylinders) each leading to the rear-mounted silencer, meant significant cost when replacement was due.

The pistons were cast aluminium with two compression rings and one oil scraper ring. Steel connecting rods ran in main bearing shells of lead-indium, the same material being used on the main bearings. The forged crankshaft, with seven main bearings, was fully counter-balanced. At its rear end, where there was an eighth bearing of smaller size, was a pinion that drove an intermediate shaft running at almost half engine speed – the ratio was 48 to 28 – in order to avoid unnecessary wear or noise. The ratio from the intermediate shaft to the cams was 24 to 28 via duplex (two-row) timing chains and sprockets, and brought the cam speed to exactly half engine speed. The intermediate shaft also drove the crankcase-mounted oil scavenge and pressure pumps. With a dry sump system there is no oil sump to act as a reservoir, so a separate oil tank was mounted in the right-hand rear wheelarch.

The timing chains were tensioned by spring-loaded hydraulic tensioners fitted into the rear chain cases. These tensioners, one for each cylinder bank, would prove to be a 911 Achilles heel over time. The tensioner was a mechanical spring, which forced a piston against the lever arm of an idler sprocket; this sprocket kept each timing chain in correct tension. The spring was encased in a small cup-shaped aluminium housing: the open top allowed engine oil to enter the assembly and, by a series of drilled holes in the piston, provided a simple form of hydraulic damping to the spring movement. These first tensioners were actually fairly reliable, but the oil could drain out of the tensioner in some situations. For instance, it was common practice to take the engine out if work was needed on the cylinders or heads, and then to turn the engine over to fit the heat exchangers. To overcome this drainage problem, a new sealed tensioner was introduced for the 1968 model year. This unit required filling and bleeding of air after assembly, and now the tensioner problem became one of unexpected failure of the sealed unit. Owners were soon able to purchase tensioner guards, small clamps that fitted around the piston shaft, that would prevent the piston from collapsing into the tensioner body and relaxing the all-important chain tension (which would, in turn, cause the cam sprockets to jump a tooth and potentially bring the valves into contact with the pistons).

The chain guide ramps were also targets for development. The effective, but complex, plastic-faced aluminium items were switched for soft black neoprene ones at the same time as the sealed tensioners were introduced. This change was accompanied by a cheaper idler arm, which did not have a bronze bushing. Studies would later show that this cost saving directly affected reliability.

By using a seven-bearing crankshaft, it was clear the designers were looking to future designs that would allow higher crankshaft speeds and more power. As Jerry Sloniger notes in an early text, 'all were plain bearings...Porsche had obviously had enough of roller bearing cranks' – a reference to the highly complicated layout used on the four-cam Carrera 356 engines. The original 901/01 engine delivered 130bhp (DIN) at 6100rpm, running on 98 RON fuel. It was quite a screamer by contemporary standards and notable for its free-revving character, thanks to the rigid design of the overhead camshaft cylinder heads.

The first production 911s used Solex overflow carburettors, but although these functioned like an injection system, they needed to be kept in very close tune. The Solexes replaced the triple down-draught types fitted on the Frankfurt prototype. Unfortunately they gave the new engine a significant flat spot around 2500rpm, and two triple-choke Weber 40 IDA carburettors quickly became the standard fit for racing. On the road cars, no other solution could be found to the Solex problem, so from February 1966, with the introduction of the 901/05 engine, the Webers were used.

Using experience gained from racing, the engine announced in July 1966 for the new 911S was coded 901/02. As a side note, 911 production engine numbering generally does not appear to follow any logical pattern, but this is because all the special variants made during development and for racing were included in the numbering. On the 901/02, the pistons had higher crowns and this lifted the compression ratio from 9:1 to 9.8:1. Increased valve overlap, bigger valves of 42mm (1.64in) inlet and 38mm (1.48in) exhaust, Weber 40 IDS carburettors and a new gas-flowed exhaust system resulted in a power output of 160bhp at 6600rpm. Internally, the engine was stronger with nitrided connecting rods and forged pistons. The new exhausts were used on the 901/06 engine for the 'Normal' cars, but their 10bhp power gain was eliminated by reducing the camshaft overlap, thereby slightly improving maximum torque. The weight of the 1965/66 engines (including the 911S unit) was given as 184kg (406lb) in workshop documentation.

The 911T engine, the 901/03, was introduced in 1967. With 110bhp at 4200rpm, this less-stressed engine had cheaper cast iron cylinders (as used on the prototypes) and a crankshaft without counter-balancing for the big end bearing carriers. The T used the same 42mm (1.64in) inlet and 38mm (1.48in) exhaust valves as the S, with the same porting. However, unlike the S, the compression ratio was restricted to 8.6:1, with less overlap on the valve timing. The steel camshaft rockers used on the higher output engines were replaced by cast iron items on the T, a modification that was incorporated across the range in 1968.

In July 1967, new engine variants were used for the T (901/13), the 'Normal' (901/07) and the S (901/08) engines to coincide with the introduction of Sportomatic transmission. These differed mainly in the mounting flange for the new transmission. Two more 911L variants for the US market had fittings for the unloved exhaust air pump (driven by a V-belt) on both manual (901/14) and Sportomatic (901/17) versions. Many a 1968 US 911 had its air pump removed, which partly cured that model's ten-

The 911L model was unique to the US and had a 130bhp engine that could be fitted with an exhaust air pump for emissions control.

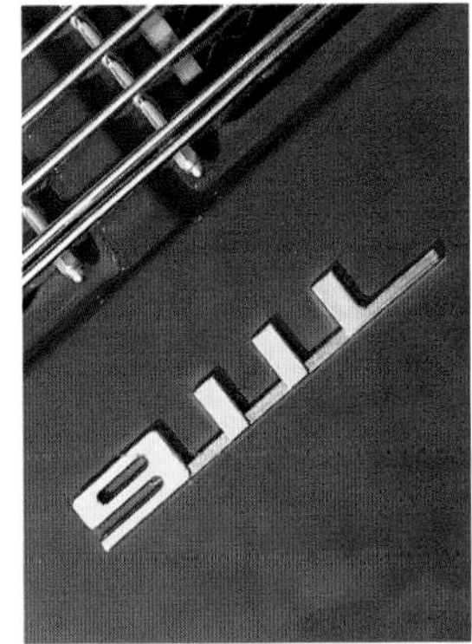

Beautiful triple-choke Weber carburettors adorn the 2-litre S engine. Another visual distinction of the S is the red cooling air duct over the engine.

dency to oil its plugs and backfire. The US market was starved of the T, E and S models in 1968, with only the emissions-compliant 'Normal' and L models being offered.

In August 1968, with the B-programme models, Bosch mechanical fuel injection was fitted to the 'Normal' and S models. This injection system, well-proven by Porsche since it was first tried on the 1966 Carrera 6 racing cars, employed a six-plunger metering unit (using variable stroke pistons) pumping fuel through six equal-length pipes to injectors inserted directly into the inlet ports. The metering unit was controlled by a 'space' cam, a three-dimensional position controller that governed the amount of fuel sprayed into each cylinder according to throttle position and engine revolutions. The amount of fuel injected was also controlled by a thermostat (permitting a richened mixture when the engine was not at normal working temperature), a barometric compensator, a cold-start enrichment solenoid and an over-run fuel cut-off. The pump was driven from the nose of the left-hand camshaft by a small toothed belt. The adoption of this injection system also forced the replacement of the original Bendix fuel pump with a higher pressure roller-type unit. Overall, the new injection added about 10bhp to the maximum output of those engines it was fitted to. Interestingly, Paul Frère noted that the injected cars seemed to be more fuel efficient at higher revolutions than the Weber-equipped models of the same basic engine.

The S also used the new Capacitative Discharge Ignition (CDI) system, which helped to keep the engine from oiling its plugs in traffic. CDI gave a fatter spark, but still used low tension contact breaker points. The S was also fitted with a second oil cooler mounted in front of the right-hand front wheel.

The new E model replaced the mid-range 'Normal' and L 911s. The E reverted to the valve timing of the 901/05 engine and a compression ratio of 9.1:1. It too had the new mechanical fuel injection in place of the Webers. The S now had 170bhp at 6800rpm and the E had 140bhp at 6600rpm.

The last major improvement introduced with all the B-programme models was that the crankcase halves were cast from magnesium rather than aluminium. This saved about 10kg (22lb).

The engine number for the classic 911s can be found stamped on the crankcase to the right of the cooling fan. Incidentally, you can tell a T, E or S just by looking at the colour of the cooling fan shroud in the engine compartment: the T was black or yellow, the E was green, and the S was red.

TRANSMISSION

The 911 was offered with a brand new five-speed gearbox (called the Type 901), driven from the front of the engine through a single diaphragm clutch. The gearbox, therefore, is sited under the central tunnel formed between the rear seats.

The new 911 gearbox was designed for the higher torque of the six-cylinder engine, but retained Porsche's unique and effective synchronising system developed through the life of the 356. This system, using a split ring and cone arrangement for each forward ratio, was further enhanced so that a gear could not be engaged until full synchronisation had been achieved. The housing was a single cast aluminium unit, which included at its rear an integral bell-housing for the clutch and differential that attached directly to the front of the engine crankcase. With the left-hand drive shaft removed, a cover could be removed from the gearbox housing for access to the differential. The main gear set comprised two shafts, onto which the second to fifth gear clusters were mounted. The gear sets were inserted through the open front of the casing. Assembly was completed by fitting the end-cover (which carried first and reverse gears and the gear selector shaft) to the front of this casing. This layout gave a 'dog-leg' gear shift pattern, with first over to the left and back, with reverse opposite. It was a good pattern for racing, but hard work around town.

Ratios could be specified, but normally a standardised set was used except on cars destined for the US, where generally the ratios for fourth and fifth were shorter. From launch the standard set was termed 901/0, but was updated in 1966 to 901/02. Special option sets covered myriad competition uses.

The 902 transmission was originally developed as a four-speed unit for the 912 and is very similar to the 901, except that there is no forward gear in the end cover. It was used on the 'Normal' or L version of the car until the new T model arrived for the 1968 model year.

The 905 was the Sportomatic transmission, launched in August 1967. This was a semi-automatic four-speed, giving manual operation but clutchless gearchanging. The two-pedal cars had a hard time from those reared on the macho image of the sports car driver rowing up through the gears, but the cars proved popular, especially in the US where up to 25 per cent of 911s were Sportomatics. Developed with Fichtel & Sachs, the transmission comprised an hydraulic torque converter, a single vacuum-operated diaphragm clutch and a conventional four-speed gearbox. The system used a lower crown wheel and pinion ratio of 7:27, instead of 7:31. The automatic clutch was only used for changing ratios and not for starting or stopping, which were the function of the torque converter. Microswitches at the base of the gear lever actuated the clutch as soon as the lever was moved by the driver: the switches operated a solenoid controlling a vacuum servo (connected to a vacuum reservoir purged by the engine intake), which in turn actuated the clutch release mechanism. It was a relatively simple but novel form of gear selection, not a full automatic, and it could ease the fatigue of town driving.

From the start of production the 911 was fitted with Nadella drive couplings at the differential end of the drive shafts. These featured a hinged link allowing axial movement of the drive shaft and prevented the lock-up sometimes seen with the cross-type joint. Unfortunately the Nadella joints also suffered from vibration. The need for a constant velocity coupling was addressed on the 1967 911S with the introduction of Lobro shafts using Rzeppa constant velocity joints. In larger and larger form, these latter joints have been used ever since.

ELECTRICAL EQUIPMENT & LIGHTING

A single 45Ah 12-volt battery, mounted in front of the left wheelarch and beside the fuel tank, was used until 1968. A simple 360-watt generator provided electrical power on the prototypes, but production cars used a more powerful 490-watt/35Ah unit. With the start of the B-programme cars, two 36Ah batteries were used in parallel, mounted in front of each wheelarch and accessed from the luggage compartment – their position also helped the handling!

The development of the fuse board gives a good idea of the 911's electrical complexity during the early years. On the 1965-67 models there were just 12 fuses, mounted at the back of the luggage compartment's left side. In order, these covered: stop lights; indicators; tail lights; interior light, cigarette lighter, clock; petrol/electric heater (option); windshield wipers/washers; fog lamps; licence plate light; boot light; front side light (RH); front side light (LH); low beam (RH); low beam (LH); high beam (RH); high beam (LH). The number of fuses went up to a potential 21 in 1968 with added items such as electric windows, sliding roof, fresh air fan, starter solenoid, Sportomatic control and rear window demister.

Optional Hella spot lights could be specified and fitted through special horn grilles.

Bosch asymmetric headlights were fitted to most 911s from launch, in either left-hand or right-hand drive types. These each had a single bulb with dual filaments rated at 45 watts (main) and 40 watts (dipped). Bosch took a step forward with the lighting of European-specification models for the 1968 model year when it introduced H1 halogen bulbs, giving a 55-watt main beam which greatly improved night illumination. Yellow bulbs were used in France, while for the US Hella sealed beam units were required. The sealed beam lamp fitted to the first 911s was housed within a similar casing to the European (non-sealed beam) headlamps. These units were rated at 50 watts (main) and 40 watts (dipped). The external glass was separate from the sealed beam unit's front glass until 1968, when a new Hella sealed lamp gave American 911s a look all of their own, with a much more pronounced rim to the lamp. The H1 and later H4 European specification headlamps give much better illumination, and it is possible to upgrade from the sealed beam units.

The 911 did much to enhance its reputation as a top grand tourer by offering sophisticated accessories. Worthy of particular mention are the electric sunroof (available as an option from the 1965 cars), and the electrically heated coupé rear window and window lifters (available from the start of the B-programme in August 1968). The first optional air conditioners were fitted in 1967, but the B-programme models saw a better installation with a system designed by Behr. That same year, 1968, the alternator was enlarged to 770 watts because the increased number of accessories had added to the battery charging requirement and there was a higher capacity fuel pump for the new mechanical fuel injection.

SUSPENSION & STEERING

At the front, the arrangement used was a MacPherson strut design. On each side, a telescopic shock absorber was mounted to a lower wishbone, itself actuating the 19mm torsion bar. The torsion bar was mounted forwards and longitudinally on the car's axis, allowing the fuel tank and the steering rack to

The front suspension of this 1965 car shows the MacPherson strut and, behind it, the actuating lever for the 13mm anti-roll bar – an early attempt to stiffen the front and delay the onset of oversteer. Brake discs were solid and at the front used the M-type cast iron caliper.

The front suspension of an early 911S shows off a red Koni strut and ventilated disc with the M-type cast iron caliper. The A-programme S model received a dual-circuit braking system, a safety factor which helped to cure the earlier tendency for the car to pull to one side under braking, and the B-programme S was given light alloy S-type front calipers.

be positioned lower between the wheels, increasing front luggage compartment space. The ZF rack and pinion steering system, quite advanced for the early 1960s, used a 1:16.5 ratio and an hydraulic damper.

Early cars had rather heavy steering, caused by the ingenious – and safety-conscious – column which contained two universal couplings to reach the centrally located rack. To initiate understeer from a car whose weight was notably rear biased, a 13mm anti-roll bar was fitted to the early models, but by the start of the 1968 model year the early handling problems were much improved and the 911L used a softer 11mm bar, while the T had no bar at all.

With the B-programme, self-levelling hydro-pneumatic struts became standard on the E and optional on the T and the S, in conjunction with 14in wheels. These struts replaced the front torsion bars and since they had a rising rate, no front anti-roll bar was used. From 1969, however, the self-levelling struts were no longer available for the S, because of their softer ride and the 15in wheels fitted to this model. The cost of the ZF steering rack had also caught attention, so the Porsche-designed rack used on the 914 was transferred to the 911. This had a lighter casing than the ZF unit and a slightly increased ratio of 17.78:1.

Various rear suspension layouts were tested during the development of the prototypes, but production 911s used a novel trailing wishbone layout which comprised a spring arm connected directly to a transverse torsion bar and a tapered tube. This latter tube acted as a steady arm between the torsion bar housing and the wheel hubs. The geometry meant the rear wheels responded to bounce and rebound with minimal camber change. Open half shafts were used, with Nadella couplings accommodating the out-of-centre shaft movements, while a telescopic shock absorber damped out the suspension travel. The first 911s used the same 23mm rear torsion bar as the 356 Carrera 2. From 1967, a rear anti-roll bar was added and Koni shock absorbers were fitted to the S.

BRAKES

From the start of production, the 911 followed on from the 356C by using disc brakes all round. Porsche had earned a reputation for building cars that stopped exceedingly well, but early 911s only achieved average comments from road testers. Unless the single-circuit system was set up correctly, the cars would pull to one side or brake unevenly.

Early prototypes started with small 235mm (9.2in) front and 243mm (9.5in) rear discs, but for series production these were replaced by the larger Ate solid discs and cast iron calipers (made under licence from Lockheed) used on the 356C. The front discs of 282mm (11.1in) diameter used the M-

The 4.5J × 15 ventilated steel wheel (far left) was mandatory until the classic Fuchs forged alloy wheel arrived for the 1967 model year. In 1968 the width of the Fuchs wheel was increased to 5½J (left), giving the 911 a more purposeful look. The following year the rear wheelarches were flared very slightly to accommodate new 6in rims.

type caliper with a pad surface area of 52.5sq cm (8.14sq in), while the rear discs of 290mm (11.2in) diameter used the L-type caliper with a pad area of 40sq cm (6.20sq in). The handbrake, independent of the disc system, was a novel arrangement that used the inner face of each rear disc hub as a brake drum. The S, introduced during 1966, used thicker ventilated brake discs which increased the width of the track front and rear.

The A-programme cars introduced a twin-circuit braking system in August 1967 and the new 911L model received at front and rear the ventilated discs that had been fitted to the S; these were also used on the E from the start of the B-programme in 1968. The 1968 S used light alloy S-type Ate calipers, which had been derived from the cast iron M-type used on the front of all previous 911s. From 1968, the M-type calipers were fitted to the rear on all models as well, but with 38mm (1.48in) pistons rather than the 48mm (1.87in) used at the front.

The classic Fuchs forged alloy wheel was introduced on the 1967 model year 911S, but the narrow rim width of 4.5in dismayed Car & Driver magazine. Note the restrained use of black paint on these early wheels and the elegance of the non-spoilered front profile.

WHEELS & TYRES

There were quite a few complaints about the skinny 165HR tyres fitted to the 4.5J × 15 steel wheels of the original 911. And for 1967, the new S dismayed *Car & Driver* by still using 4.5in rims for its 'flashy new wheels', and the magazine was none too complimentary about the Dunlop SP tyres either. These new wheels, manufactured by the Fuchs company, were the first of the classic five-spoke forged alloy wheels that would become a Porsche trademark in later years. In 4.5in width, the alloys were 2.3kg (5.1lb) lighter than their steel equivalents, and roundness was easier to control than with a stamped wheel. Clearly, the weight advantage of alloys was to increase as wheel rim width grew. So strong was the obsession to reduce unsprung weight that even the wheel nuts were light alloy, and still are today.

It was not until August 1967 that 5.5in rims became available for the S, and the size grew again to 6in for the E and the S with the following year's B-programme. Where hydro-pneumatic suspension was fitted, the ride was further improved by 5½J × 14 Fuchs wheels, the 1in reduction in wheel diameter giving a deeper and more flexible tyre wall. Dunlop tyres were still the preferred fit for the T and E, the E with the new 185/70VR size. The S went one better and was offered with new Michelin XVRs, tyres that significantly improved the cornering ability of the firmly-sprung car.

Data Section

IDENTIFICATION

Model year	Model	Engine	Gearbox	Chassis numbers	Engine numbers
O-programme					
1964	901 Coupé	901/01	901	Prototypes	Prototypes
1965	911 Coupé	901/01	901/0	300001-303390	900001-903550
1966	911 Coupé	901/01	902/01	303391-305100	903551-907000
1967	911 Coupé[1]	901/05	901/01	305101-307350	907001-909000
	911 Coupé[2]	901/06	902/01	307351-308522	911001-911190
	911 Targa[3]	901/05	902/01	500001-500718	911191-912050
	911S Coupé[4]	901/02	901/02	305101S-308523S	960001-961178
	911S Targa	901/02	901/02	500001S-500718S	960001-961178
A-programme					
1968	911 Coupé	901/06	902/01	11830001-11830473	3280001-3281606
	911 Coupé[5]	901/14	902/0 USA	11830001-11830473	3280001-3281606
	911 Coupé[6]	901/06	902/01	11835001-11835742	3080001 onwards
	911 Targa	901/06	902/01	11880001-11880268	3180001 onwards
	911 Targa[5]	901/14	902/0 USA	11880001-11880268	3180001 onwards
	911 Coupé	901/07	Sporto	11880001-11880268	3380001 onwards
	911L Coupé	901/03	902/01	11810001-11810720	3880001 onwards
	911L Coupé[5]	901/14	902/01 USA	11815001-11815549	3280001-3281606
	911L Targa	901/03	902/01	11860001-11860307	3280001-3281606
	911L Targa[5]	901/14	902/01 USA	11865001-11865134	3380001-3380464
	911L[5]	901/17	Sporto USA	11865001-11865134	3380001-3380464
	911T	901/03	901/10	11820001-11820928	2080001 onwards
	911T[6]	901/03	901/10	11825001-11825683	2080001 onwards
	911T Targa	901/03	901/10	11870001-11870521	2080001 onwards
	911T	901/13	Sporto	11870001-11870521	2180001 onwards
	911S	901/02	901/02	11800001-11801267	4080001-4081549
	911S[6]	901/08	Sporto	11800001-11801267	4180001-4180227
	911S Targa	901/02	901/02	11850001-11850442	4080001-4081549
B-programme					
1969	911T Coupé	901/03	901/06	119000001-119000343	6190001-6192455
	911T Coupé[6]	901/03	901/06	119120001-119123561	6190001-6192455
	911T Targa	901/03	901/06	119110001-119111282	6190001-6192455
	911T Coupé	901/13	Sporto	119110001-119111282	6193001-6193297
	911T	901/16	901/12 USA	119110001-119111282	6195001-6197292
	911T Coupé	901/19	Sporto USA	119110001-119111282	6198001-6198184
	911E Coupé	901/09	901/07	119200001-119200954	6190001-6192455
	911E Coupé[6]	901/09	901/07	119220001-119221014	6190001-6192455
	911E Targa	901/09	901/07	119210001-119210858	6190001-6192455
	911E	901/11	Sporto	119210001-119210858	6298001-6298583
	911S Coupé	901/10	901/07	119300001-119301492	6390001-6392126
	911S Targa	901/10	901/07	119310001-119310614	6390001-6392126
	911S	901/10	901/13 USA	119310001-119310614	6390001-6392126

General notes

Chassis numbering The original six-digit numbering system used by Porsche since the 356 days lasted until 1967. The only distinction was between coupé (which started with 30-) and Targa (which started with 50-). The new S model was simply given an additional S to its chassis number. In 1968, the chassis numbers changed to an eight-digit system, which identified the model and build year, for instance 11830001. The first two digits referred to the model type (ie, 911). The third referred to the build year (eg, 1968). The fourth digit was used for the bodyshell type (eg, 5=Targa S, 6=Targa L, 7=Targa T, etc), but this description introduces conflict with some of the factory numbers given above and the reader should take this into account. The fifth digit was used to denote a Karmann bodyshell (by using a 5). The last three digits were the build serial number. In 1969, the chassis numbers gained a ninth digit to allow the build serial number to go to four figures. Business was good!

Prototypes Chassis numbers are as follows: numbers 1-10, 13321-30; number 11, 13352; numbers 12-13 300001-2 (Nov 1964). It is believed 235 cars were made after production began and before the end of 1964 (as 1965 models).

Gearboxes Generally 901 gearbox is five-speed, 902 is four-speed. These numbers derived from the original type designation for the 911 and four-cylinder 912. But to quote from Paul Frère's '911 Story', it was quite normal to find 902 transmissions on 911 models, particularly export models. And 1968 USA 911L models had five-speed 902 gearboxes! Manual gearboxes were fitted with different gear sets for Europe and Rest of the World (RoW), hence 901/01 and 901/06 are five-speed Europe, 901/0 and 901/12 are five-speed USA.

Sportomatic Chassis numbers are to be found from the same series as equivalent manual models. Four-speed Sportomatic gearbox desgnation was 905/00 for 1968 USA models, 905/1 for European models on S and T, and 905/13 from start of 1969 model year.

Numbered notes

[1] From Mar 1966, with Weber carburettors; [2] From Nov 1966; [3] From Dec 1966; [4] From Oct 1966; [5] With emissions control equipment (with air pump); [6] Body built by Karmann.

The chassis number on early models is found on the left-hand door pillar. Also shown on the plate is the paint code (Farbton) – 6401 indicates Slate Grey.

The earliest 911s had pencil-thin rubbing strips on the sills, and the circular cover that gives access to the rear torsion bar was completely exposed.

The sills of the 911S featured deeper aluminium trim extrusions and 'wide' rubber trim. Peeping out from behind the trim is the circular torsion bar cover. The short-wheelbase 911s, built to the end of the 1968 model year, are visually identified by the closeness of the cover to the wheelarch.

PRODUCTION DATA

Model year	Model	Power (bhp DIN@rpm)	Torque (Nm@rpm)	Compression ratio	Weight (kg)	Number built
1964	901/911	130@6200	162@4600	9.0:1	1000	13[1]
1965	911	130@6100	174@4200	9.0:1	1080	235
1966	911	130@6100	174@4200	9.0:1	1080	4864
1967	911	130@6100	174@4200	9.0:1	1030	3421
	911 Targa	130@6100	174@4200	9.0:1	1080	718
	911S	160@6600	179@5200	9.8:1	1030	3422
	911S Targa	160@6600	179@5200	9.8:1	1080	718
1968	911	130@6100	176@4200	9.0:1	1075	473
	911[2]	130@6100	176@4200	9.0:1	1075	742
	911 Targa	130@6100	176@4200	9.0:1	1125	268
	911L	130@6100	176@4200	9.0:1	1075	720
	911L Targa	130@6100	176@4200	9.0:1	1125	307
	911L US	130@6100	176@4200	9.0:1	1075	449
	911 Targa US	130@6100	176@4200	9.0:1	1125	134
	911T	110@5800	156@4200	8.6:1	1075	928
	911T[2]	110@5800	156@4200	8.6:1	1075	683
	911T Targa	110@5800	156@4200	8.6:1	1125	521
	911S	160@6600	180@5200	9.8:1	1075	1267
	911S Targa	160@6600	180@5200	9.8:1	1125	442
1969	911T	110@5800	156@4200	8.6:1	1020	343
	911T[2]	110@5800	156@4200	8.6:1	1020	3561
	911T Targa	110@5800	156@4200	8.6:1	1070	1282
	911E	140@6500	175@4500	9.1:1	1020	954
	911E[2]	140@6500	175@4500	9.1:1	1020	1014
	911E Targa	140@6500	175@4500	9.1:1	1070	858
	911S	170@6800	183@5500	9.9:1	995	1492
	911S Targa	170@6800	183@5500	9.9:1	1045	614

General notes
All cars have a capacity of 1991cc, with a bore/stroke of 80mm/66mm. An assumption has been made here that Targas were approximately 50kg heavier than coupés.

Numbered notes
[1] 1964 models include the two four-cylinder 901 prototypes built; [2] Body built by Karmann.

PRODUCTION CHANGES

Sep 1963
901 shown at Frankfurt Motor Show.

Aug 1964 (START OF 0-PROGRAMME)
Start of pilot production; short wheelbase (torsion bar cover next to rear wheelarch); 4.5in steel wheels; cone-shaped external mirror (early model Durant) with no flange; intake/exhaust valves are 39mm/35mm respectively; exposed push buttons on exterior door handles; chromed-only bumper overriders standard on US models; opening front quarter windows; grab handle on passenger door; narrow vinyl-faced trim strip on sills under doors; single 12-volt battery; Eberspächer fuel heater for rapid interior heat/demist standard; single fuse panel at rear of luggage compartment; woven three-piece luggage compartment carpets; linked 'short' (gold anodised) Porsche script on engine cover, angled 911 logo; engine grille with narrow wire horizontals. The five-speed gearbox ratios at the start of production were as follows: first, 12/34; second, 18/32; third, 23/28; fourth, 26/25; fifth, 28/23; final drive, 7:31.

Oct 1964
Type number changed to 911.

Feb 1965
First models reach USA (price $6500).

May 1965
First RHD UK model (price £3438).

Late 1965
From engine 903070, cam lubrication now by spray bar.

Mar 1966
Weber 40 IDAs replace original Solex overflow carburettors.

Aug 1966
911 script moved to below engine grille. Gearbox ratios changed to: first, 11/34; second, 18/34; third, 22/29; fourth 25/26; fifth, 28/24.

Oct 1966
911S (for Super) production started (announced Jul 1966); red engine cooling duct cover instead of black (with 5mm smaller diameter fan); Weber 40 IDS carburettors; intake/exhaust valves increased to 42mm/38mm; forged pistons and new three-into-one exhaust/heat exchangers; 4.5J×15in five-spoke forged aluminium alloy wheels by Fuchs; thicker rubber strip on bumpers and side strips; ventilated disc brakes; front anti-roll bar increased from 13mm to 15mm; 16mm rear anti-roll bar introduced; Koni shock absorbers fitted; leather rim steering wheel; basket-weave lower dash replaces wood trim. On all models, forged valve rockers replaced with cast iron versions. Gear ratios were: first, 0.324; second, 0.529; third, 0.759; fourth, 0.962; fifth, 1.261.

Dec 1966
Start of Targa production (without vents in side of roll hoop and with zip-out soft rear window).

Aug 1967 (START OF A-PROGRAMME)
Black wipers; recessed push buttons on door handles; larger dual-circuit brake system; 5.5in wheel rims on 911S; all-plastic timing chain guides replace aluminium-backed early type; sealed unit chain tensioners replace open reservoir versions; engine weight of base model is approx 182kg; brushed aluminium dash trim for 911; bright anodised aluminium replaces chromed brass for window frames; engine grille has thicker top and bottom horizontals; S gets bright trim on doors; three-piece felt (Perlon) carpet in front compartment; spaced-out (gold anodised) Porsche script on engine cover; front anti-roll bar reduced to 11mm. 911L replaces basic 911 model. 911T (for Touring) introduced, replacing four-cylinder 912: four-speed manual gearbox; bright anodised script on engine cover; no anti-roll bar; Weber 40 IDT carburettors; same valve sizes as S, but small ports and less overlap on cam timing. US models, only 911 and 911L (for Lux) with Weber 40 IDAP carburettors and air pump; reflectors added to sides of body; five-speed gearbox; ventilated disc brakes; vinyl-trimmed overriders.

Aug 1968 (START OF B-PROGRAMME)
First major model upgrade for 911; extended wheelbase (torsion bar covers now set in from wheelarch); die-cast magnesium castings replace sand castings for crankcase, chain housings and valve covers; 911S model uses Bosch mechanical fuel injection, intake/exhaust valves increased to 45mm/39mm, plus 6in wheels; S engine weight is approx 196kg; 911E (for Einspritzung or injected) replaces 911 with same injection as S, initially with 5.5J×14in Fuchs wheels and Boge hydropneumatic gas/oil struts; E could be specified with conventional struts and 6in Fuchs wheels; E has green shroud on engine (generally!); E has same valve sizes as previous year's S and T, timing as 911/911L; leather steering wheels for S and E; T gets double valve springs of E and S and 5.5J×15in wheels. Gear ratios for all models – four-speed 902: first, 0.323; second, 0.613; third, 0.962; fourth, 1.261 – five-speed 901: first, 0.324; second, 0.529; third, 0.759; fourth, 0.962; fifth, 1.261. E and S use new Bosch CD ignition; S gets external radiator-type oil cooler in front right fender; 770W alternator on all models; in USA, T, E and S replace 911 and 911L and air pump removed; slightly flared rear wheelarches; larger, flanged external door mirror (late model Durant); narrow horn grilles and wider indicator lenses; engine lid grille changes to thin chromed extrusions for horizontals, with three verticals; rear reflectors next to overriders; two 12-volt batteries; reshaped spare wheel recess in fuel tank; vertical fuse panels on left front wall of luggage compartment; four-piece felt (Perlon) front compartment carpet; opening front quarter windows deleted on coupé and heater outlets moved from front of door sills to a mixer unit under the dash; new internal ventilation system with three-speed fan, controls in left-centre of dash (old position of ashtray, which moves below centre dash); internal mirror now mounted to windshield; instrument lettering changed from green to white, basket-weave dash trim standard on all models, with rubber knobs; hand throttle and heater control either side of handbrake lever; coat hooks change from beige 356 type to black; heated rear window on coupé; doors get separate storage compartments (not pockets) under arm rest; gate pattern shown on top of gear lever; green tinted glass becomes standard; vents added to rear sides of Targa hoop.

DIMENSIONS

Wheelbase
Prototypes, 2204mm; O- and A-programme, 2211mm; B-programme and subsequent models, 2271mm

Track (front/rear)
Prototypes, 1332mm/1312mm; O-programme, 1337mm/1317mm; A-programme, 1353mm/1321mm; B-programme, 1360mm/1342mm; B-programme with 14in wheels, 1362mm/1344mm

Length
Prototypes, 4135mm; subsequent production, 4163mm

Width
1610mm

OPTIONS

Factory list (1965)
9101 hub cap with coloured emblem (901 361 031 00); 9107 Phoenix 165HR15 tyres; 9108 Dunlop SP 165HR15 tyres; 9118 chrome-plated wheels (901 361 013 22); 9127 external mirror, left (901 731 111 00); 9128 external mirror, right (901 731 111 00); 9131 external mirror, Talbot, left (644 731 111 00); 9132 external mirror, Talbot, right (644 731 111 00); 9189 sisal floor mats (901 551 102 15); 9198 Velouran floor mats in carpet colour (901 551 101 15); 9200/9201 lap belt, left and right (644 803 901 01); 9204/9205 lap and diagonal belt, left and right (644 803

An electrically-operated sunroof was an option from the start of production. The small wind deflector at the leading edge popped up as the roof was opened, inhibiting wind buffeting. The interior mirror was initially attached to the roof by three screws, but for 1968 the mounting became a 'breakaway' design attached to the windshield.

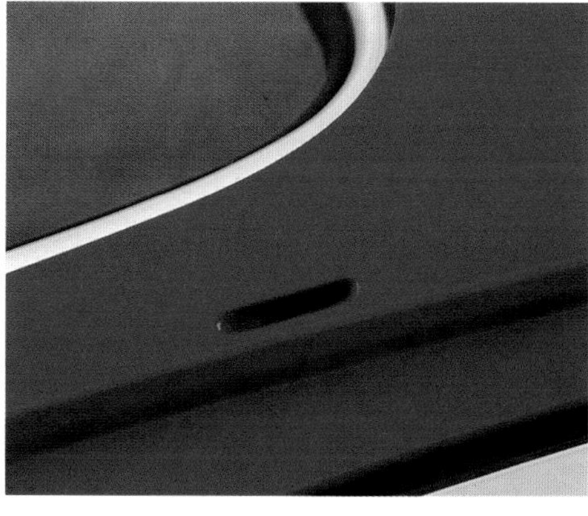

A feature of O- and A-programme models with a sunroof fitted at the factory were drain slots in the roof adjacent to the rear window.

901 03 or 06); 9208 US approved lap belt; 9217 travelling kit; 9220/9221 bumper horns with rubber pads (front left 901 505 031 21, front right 901 505 032 21, rear 901 505 033 21); 9224 four Koni shock absorbers (front 901 341 067 05, rear 901 333 051 12); 9229 gas heater (901 572 051 30); 9230 supplementary electric blower; 9237/9238/9248 black leather suitcases (small, medium and large); 9248 canvas suitcase in red/ black tartan; 9261 canvas bag in red/black tartan; 9264 suitcase SKAI-Dur in black; 9265 wooden (300mm) steering wheel (901 347 082 01); 9266 horn button, black (901 347 802 00); 9267 raised steering wheel hub (901 347 082 11); 9290 rear wiper; 9293 fog lights, pair (644 631 912 03); 9400 special paint, non-metallic; 9403 special paint, metallic; 9425 leather interior; 9427 seats raised by 20mm; 9428 leather seats only (left 901 521 001 50, right 901 521 002 50); 9442/9443 fittings for head rest (644 521 087 05); 9444/9445 fittings for leather head rest (644 521 085 13); 9446/9447 fittings for leatherette head rest (644 521 085 07); 9474 Golde electric sunroof (901 564 003 65); 9481 Catacolor tinted glass (all); 9482 Catacolor tinted windshield; 9483 Catacolor tinted rear window; 9505 roof rack (901 801 010 00); 9506 leather straps for roof rack (901 801 953 00); 9507 roof ski rack with eight leather straps (901 801 015 20); the radio options were the contemporary Blaupunkt Bremen, Frankfurt, Frankfurt-US, Köln and New Yorker, plus the Becker Monte Carlo, Europa and Mexico.

Factory list (1969 additions)
9107 Phoenix 165VR15 tyres; 9108 Dunlop SP 165VR15 tyres; 9120 light alloy wheels, forged; 9121 chrome-plated wheels; 9168/9169 outside thermometer; 9186 chrome-plated flap light in engine compartment; 9189/9190 Velouran floor mats for Sportomatic; 9198/9199 Velouran floor mats for manual shift; 9216 travelling kit, 911S; 9218 travelling kit, 911T; 9219 travelling kit, 911 USA/911L/911L USA; 9222 bumper guards with rubber pads; 9232 air conditioner; 9239 two leather straps to fasten suitcases on rear seats; 9240 travelling bag, leatherette; 9241 travelling bag, leather; 9249 leather suitcase to fit on top of rear seats; 9250 leather shirt case to fit on top of rear seats; 9263 leather shirt case, rear seats; 9268 leather steering wheel; 9273 iodine headlamps; 9278 US safety equipment; 9283 emergency flash light; 9291 iodine fog lamps, yellow lenses; 9292 iodine fog lamps, white lenses; 9294 fog lamps, white lenses; 9297 electrically operated antenna; 9298 suppression of radio interference; 9303 antenna; 9305 suppression of radio interference; 9307 loudspeaker; 9320 Blaupunkt Bremen radio; 9322 Blaupunkt Frankfurt radio; 9323 Blaupunkt Frankfurt USA radio; 9325 Blaupunkt Köln radio; 9326 Blaupunkt New Yorker USA radio; 9327 Blaupunkt Boston USA radio; 9340 Becker Monte Carlo radio; 9341 Becker Europa radio; 9342 Becker Europa USA radio; 9349 Becker Grand Prix radio; 9350 Becker Grand Prix USA radio; 9356 tonneau for Targa; 9388/9389 Recaro sports seats; 9400 special paint, according to special colour book; 9403 special paint, outside special colour book and silver metallic; 9420 long-range iodine lamps above bumper; 9421 iodine fog lamps, yellow lenses, above bumper; 9428 leather seats with dog-tooth inlay; 9437 headrest, wrap dog-tooth fabric; 9438 headrest, wrap corduroy; 9439 headrest, leather; 9440 headrest, leatherette; 9480 tinted glass all round for Targa; 9481 tinted glass all round for coupé; 9482 tinted windshield; 9483 tinted rear window (coupé only); 9484 electrically heated rear window for coupé; 9485 electrically heated, tinted rear window for coupé; 9499 special fuel tank, 26 US gallons; 9503 roof luggage rack with fittings for skis and straps; 9508 roof rack with eight leather straps for Targa; 9512 electrically heated fixed tinted rear window for Targa; 9520 stainless steel muffler skirt; 9521 towing hook, rear; 9574 limited slip differential; 9581 Sportomatic transmission; 9590 five-speed transmission.

Note The four-digit option numbers were replaced by numbers prefixed by an 'M' for 1970 onwards. It is not possible to reproduce options for every year because some lists are very long and some information was unavailable from the factory at the time of publication.

COLOUR SCHEMES

Colour names in English-speaking markets could vary. In other markets, alternative names were sometimes used. For example, the British colours of Lemon Yellow and Bush Green were respectively called Canary Yellow and Leaf Green in the US. The alternative names have been given where variations occur.

Early colour codings had the year of manufacture as the first two digits. From 1968, the paint type and manufacturer was noted in a two-digit prefix number and a single suffix letter (eg, 97 6802 L, where 97 refers to the paint type and L refers to Lesonal, the manufacturer). Other paint suppliers were Glasurit (G), Herberts (H) and Herbol (HL). The prefix R indicates that a colour could be obtained from all the manufacturers. The year indicator on the code appears to have been dropped after 1969.

1964/65
Standard body colours
Slate Grey (6401), Ruby Red (6402), Enamel Blue (6403), Light Ivory (6404), Champagne Yellow (6405), Irish Green (6406), Signal Red (6407).
Special order body colours
Dolphin Grey (6410), Togo Brown (6411), Bali Blue (6412), Black (6413).
Interior
Leatherette (vinyl) in red, black, brown or beige (leather optional at extra cost). Seat inlays in basket-weave leatherette or dog-tooth check (black with red or white, black with white, black with brown or white). The 912 interior was the same, except that seat inlays were in corduroy (red, black, cognac or stone grey). For 911S, interior leatherette was ST grained in the same colours. Carpets were in black velour (square-weave) except on the 912, which used black bouclé.

1966/67 (charts dated May 65 and Mar 67)
Standard body colours
Slate Grey (6601), Polo Red (6602), Gulf Blue (6603), Light Ivory (6604), Bahama Yellow (6605), Irish Green (6606), Sand Beige (6607), Aga Blue (6608), Black (6609).
Special order body colours
Burgundy Red (30868), Maroon (30736), Tangerine (P2002), Metallic Dark Red (30847), Champagne Yellow (16153), Signal Yellow (R1007), Lemon (Canary) Yellow (R1012), Medium Ivory (17657), Lido Gold (17656), Golden Green (62165), Signal Green (R6001), Bush (Leaf) Green (62163), Metallic Dark Green (62109), Turkey Green (R6016), Velvet Green (62162), Sea Green (62164), Crystal Blue (52254), Pastel Blue (R5012), Prussian Blue (R5009), Metallic Blue (52300), Ultra Blue (R5013), Olive (62166), Sepia Brown (R8007), Coffee Brown (80342), Stone Grey (75741), Light Grey (75742), Cloudy Grey (R7030), Beige Grey (70192), Black (95043), Silver Metallic (96024).
Interior
As for 1964/65.

1968 (chart dated May 67)
Standard body colours
Slate grey (6601), Polo Red (6602), Gulf Blue (6603), Light Ivory (6604), Bahama Yellow (6605), Irish Green (6606), Sand Beige (6607), Aga Blue (6608), Black (6609).
Special order colours
Burgundy Red (6808), Maroon (30736), Tangerine (6809/P2002), Metallic Dark Red (6854/30847), Champagne Yellow (6822/16153), Signal Yellow (6823/R1007), Lemon (Canary) Yellow (6824/R1012), Medium Ivory (6821/17657), Lido Gold (17656), Golden Green (6828/62165), Signal Green (6829/R6001), Bush Green (6830/62163), Metallic Dark Green (6852/62109), Turkey (Turquoise) Green (6831/R6016), Velvet (Irish) Green (6806/6216Z), Sea Green (62164), Crystal Blue (6825/52254), Pastel Blue (6826/R5012), Prussian (Ossi) Blue (6803/R5009), Metallic Blue (6853/52300), Ultra Blue (6827/R5013), Olive (6835/62166), Sepia Brown (6836/R8007), Coffee Brown (6837/80342), Stone Grey (75741), Light Grey (6832/75742), Cloudy Grey (6833/R7030), Beige Grey (6834/70192), Black (6838/95043), Silver Metallic (6851/96024).
Interior
For 911T and 912, basket-weave leatherette in red, black, brown or beige. Optional corduroy (in same colours) or dog-tooth check (in same colours as 1966/67). For 911L and 911S, ST grained leatherette in red, black, brown or beige, with option of dog-tooth check and corduroy. Optional at cost was leather seating (with basket-weave inlay on T, ST grain inlay on L and S) in the same four colours above. Carpet matched interior colours, with 911T in Perlon 'special', 911S in velour.

1969 (chart dated Oct 68)
Standard body colours
Slate Grey (6801), Polo Red (6802), Ossie Blue (6803), Light Ivory (6804), Bahama Yellow (6805), Irish Green (6806), Sand Beige (6807), Burgundy Red (6808), Tangerine (6809).
Special order colours
Medium Ivory (17657), Champagne Yellow (16153), Signal Yellow (R1007), Lemon (Canary) Yellow (R1012), Dark Red Metallic (30847), Crystal Blue (52254), Pastel Blue (R5012), Ultra Blue (R5013), Metallic Blue (52300), Lime Green (62165), Signal Green (R6001), Bush Green (62163) Dark Green Metallic (62109), Turkey Green (R6016), Grey White (75742), Fortuna Grey (R7030), Beige Grey (70192), Olive (62166), Sepia Brown (R8007), Coffee Brown (80342), Black (95043), Silver Metallic (96024).
Interior
As for 1968, but carpet on 911E in velour (and on T with 'comfort' option).

THE 2.2-LITRE 911 (1970-71)

By the time we get to the 911s of the early 1970s we are into the stuff of romance. The previous decade had been a time of transition for Porsche on the international racing scene, the time when it made the move from being class winners to contending for outright wins. When the 917 was revealed to the public in March 1969, Porsche entered the big league. The following years were sports car racing's best: a period that was marked by ultra-competitive endurance racing between Porsche and Ferrari; the time of Siffert, Rodriguez, Ickx and Andretti.

EVOLUTION OUTLINE

Aug 1969	911T, E and S now standardised as main production models, nominally with 2.2-litre engine; T (125bhp) has Zenith carburettors, E (155bhp) and S (180bhp) have mechanical fuel injection; T has CD ignition; Sportomatic deleted as an option on S.
Aug 1970	Selective hot zinc dip to exposed underbody sections.

To have a Porsche 911 as a road car made a statement – you knew about the best things in life. And do you remember Steve McQueen, his steely eyes twitching as he viewed the repaired crash barrier at the start of that cult racing movie, *Le Mans*? He was leaning on a 911. It was silver, of course, and it was a 2.2S. And how could we tell it was a 2.2S? By the glorious sound of its flat-six and virtually open fuel injection intakes!

The 2-litre engines of the early 911s were notable for lots of revs and power that tended to come in a rush towards the red line. In the mid-1960s, the chassis engineers had worked wonders on the handling and braking, and had made great progress with the refinement of the original design. The engine designers, meanwhile, had worked at reducing weight, reducing the effect of the engine overhang and improving the road manners of the six-cylinder engine. Improved carburation and, by 1969, the CD ignition system ensured that that year's 911s had had most of the bugs ironed out of the engine. The engineers then turned their attentions to improving the torque. In August 1969, the 911 received an engine with a capacity of 2195cc. It gave the unit more flexibility, flattening the torque curve, and the change was most noticeable at lower revs on the T and E.

The S, however, was no less effort to drive. The maximum power had been edged up to 180bhp from 170bhp, but you had to keep the revs above 5500rpm to enjoy it. It meant the five-speed 'box

Patrick Amos's concours-winning 1971 911T at Silverstone. This car has a high specification, including 5.5in Fuchs wheels, tinted glass and overriders.

A very clean 1971 2.2 Targa (above). Ventilation on the Targa had been improved for the 1969 model year by the addition of vertical cabin air outlets at the sides of the roll-over hoop. Although deleted from the coupé, the opening front quarterlights were retained on the Targa until 1977. Not often seen today is the 'Weltmeister 1969/70' decal in the left lower area of the windshield, celebrating the factory's consecutive World Championship of Makes racing titles.

A 2.2 911S owned by Mark Waring (below) and finished in the unusual colour of Olive. These cars make a quite glorious sound on hard acceleration, thanks to their largely unsilenced intake manifolding and pre-emissions control exhaust.

earned its keep, and drivers got used to sweating as well as having silly grins on their faces. This inflexibility was expected on a racing car, but could be a pain in normal town driving, especially in speed-restricted countries like the US. *Road & Track* magazine even advised that the T was a better car: 'The 911T is a bit stronger this year – we recommend it for all-round use.'

There was a secondary motive in increasing the engine capacity. It moved the 911 out of the up to 2000cc class in international GT racing and into the 2001cc to 2500cc class. This offered scope for the racing department to explore further increases in capacity and power. In time, it would establish the 911 on the international racing scene as *the* competitive customer racing car.

BODYSHELL

The 2.2-litre 911s are the C-and D-programme cars. Weight reduction was still a major effort, especially at the extremities of the car.

For the C-programme (August 1969) both the engine cover and the central part of the E and S bumpers were aluminium. All models received a flexible pvc underseal: this anti-corrosion treatment was a move towards extending the life of the 911, but

The interior of a 2.2 911 was now far removed from the early models. For the 1969 model year the lower dash had been revised to include more effective heating and ventilation controls. The ash-tray was moved to the central area, the glovebox lid was further revised and the speaker grille was now removable. From 1969, too, the seats could be tilted forward by operating a lever at the top of the seat back support, instead of down at the hinge point.

it would prove to be a bane for restorers in later years. The undercoat has a habit of peeling away in highly stressed areas and forming a perfect rust trap. What might look like a small tear in the coating would, when picked back with a screwdriver, reveal an expanse of orange rust. The thought was there – and if the coating had not been applied far fewer cars would be on the roads today.

For the D-programme (August 1970), limited zinc coating of the exposed underbody parts was introduced. This in itself did not prevent the dreaded worm gorging itself, but it was the start of a strategically very beneficial move by the factory. The progressive improvement in anti-corrosion treatment – Porsche was an industry leader in this – gives credibility to the claim that some 80-85 per cent of Porsches ever made are still on the roads.

The Targa roof section was improved, recognising that the open model was now becoming very popular – by 1970 the Targa was accounting for 31 per cent of all 911s produced. The revisions affected the way the roof sealed to the windshield, side windows and roll-over hoop. The method by which the roof section of the Targa collapsed down into a storable size was unaffected.

Racing was never far from the thoughts of Porsche engineers. An abortive effort had been made by racing manager Rico Steinemann to get the 911S accepted into the Touring Car category but the 1970 production cars were affected by the paperwork tactic used to qualify a competitive car for the special GT class. The 1970 S was listed in the catalogue in very basic form, suitable for competition only, and weighed a remarkable 838kg (1848lb). This car was stripped of all luxury items, it used aluminium for the bumpers and engine lid, lightweight seats were fitted, and pull straps replaced the door handles. A larger fuel tank of 110 litres (24.20 Imperial gallons, 29.06 US gallons) and a space saver tyre were the standard fit. However, most Ss were built with the M470 option package that made the car suitable for road customers, bringing the car up to the full luxury specification of that year's E.

BODY TRIM & FITTINGS

The most noticeable external change for the 1970 model year was new door handles with the opening trigger behind the handle. This offered a safer handle as well as being easier to use. Into 1971, this was the last year the pretty, round Durant external mirror was fitted as standard to cars for all markets. The following year legal requirements in the US and Germany for a larger glass area forced the introduction of a rectangular type, but several markets (including the UK) retained the round Durant mirror for some years.

From August 1966, the 911 logo on the engine lid had been presented in block letters (rather than the original italic) and positioned centrally below the grille. By 1970, the three six-cylinder models were labelled accordingly, but it is worth pointing out that the 911T logo was normally in aluminium, with the other two in a gold anodised finish (although the gold finish was a T option). The 2.2 cars also had a unique decal – an outline drawing of the flat-six engine with large '2.2' numbers on it – applied to the centre of the rear window. What better way to let your neighbour know you had the latest model! The 1971 models also carried a small decal on the

This 1971 S has the correct non-frosted top edge to its Bosch H1 headlamp glass. From 1973 the top edge was frosted and many owners retro-fitted the simpler single-bulb H4 unit.

Recaro sports seats, as in this 1971 S, offered excellent sideways and thigh support. These seats have 'crackle' finish back supports, which became standard across the range the following year.

The instrument panel on a 1971 T, showing only detail changes: the hazard warning flasher button, introduced in 1970, is on the left-hand lower dash, and there are improved switches with large rubber surrounds. The labelling behind the steering wheel indicates headlamp flash and turn signal operation, but is completely obscured from the driver!

New door trims were introduced for the 2.2 models. Their features were rigid storage pockets (the rear one hinged outwards) and a recessed door handle lever – much safer than the previous push-button release.

driver's side rear side window proclaiming victory in the 1969 and 1970 World Championship of Makes.

Interior Trim

The efforts being made to make the 911 more practical and more attractive to new buyers included improving the door trim and in particular the door pockets. The 1969 cars had featured a small locker in the door and this was now replaced with a larger opening compartment below the door handle. On the safety side, the interior door handle was now a recessed pull-type lever rather than an exposed button. The forward part of the compartment was open, with the area below the arm rest having an opening locker. The 1970 cars also offered electrically operated windows as an option.

DASHBOARD & INSTRUMENTS

Ergonomics were improved with a revised stalk arrangement that improved accessory operation without the driver having to take his or her hands off the steering wheel. The left-hand stalk (a new four-way design) worked the indicators, headlight flash and main/dipped control, and the right-hand stalk the windshield wipe/wash function.

From the 1970 model year, the main dials were each located by a neoprene ring around the circumference and inserted from the front, rather than being located by a rear bracket as previously. The instrument rims had lost their decorative 1960s chromed look from 1968 in favour of a more functional black look. The option of a steering lock had been introduced in 1969 and this went further on US cars when a buzzer was introduced in 1970. This irritating device let you know when you had both the keys in the ignition and the door open – very useful! Incidentally, the 1970 cars were the first with a plastic handle to the ignition key.

The heavy basket-weave finish to the dash was retained and the radio controls could be integrated into this finish, rather than being a more theft-prone separate unit. The 1970 model year was the last in which the model designation was shown on the glove compartment door.

LUGGAGE COMPARTMENT

The higher specification 911s had been fitted with two luggage compartment lights, but 1971 was the last year this luxury was available. Subsequently the E and S models copied the previous T in having a single light on the left-hand side (looking from the front). Fuel tank capacity remained at 62 litres (13.64 Imperial gallons, 16.38 US gallons), but 110 litres (24.20 Imperial gallons, 29.06 US gallons) was optional for the S.

ENGINE

Of all the changes, those to the engine were the most obvious. The capacity was now 2195cc (133.90cu in), found by increasing the bore from 80mm (3.12in) to 84mm (3.28in). In a pre-fuel crisis world, the increased fuel consumption was not regarded as a problem. While the E and the S needed 98 RON fuel, the T could use 96 RON.

The hinged panel behind the fuel tank covered the steering joints and the location for the optional petrol heater. The brake master cylinder was moved out of this compartment and up onto the left wing wall for the 1968 model year, when dual-circuit braking was introduced. The fuse box, larger than before, has been moved to just behind the left-hand battery.

Engine type numbers also changed, receiving a 911 prefix instead of the old 901 designation. Only the T had a special US version. The engine team, under the guidance of Paul Hensler, evolved a common cylinder head for the 2.2 models with 46mm (1.79in) inlet and 40mm (1.56in) exhaust valves, although the port sizes were different. The Helicoil insert in the spark plug hole was also discarded. Bruce Anderson notes that the factory had felt the Helicoils caused 'inconsistent effective spark plug heat ranges'. A new cylinder head gasket, comprising a thin metal C-shaped ring trapping a continuous spring, replaced the earlier more conventional gasket. The barrels were designed to allow the racers to increase engine capacity still further, and the number of cooling fins was increased. Since the stronger con rods used longer big end bolts, the ends of the barrels were modified to clear the sweep of the longer bolts. A shell bearing was added to the internal end of the intermediate shaft as the new magnesium crankcases (introduced for the 1969 model year) had a tendency to wear faster than the original aluminium.

The T changed to the cheaper Zenith 40 TIN triple-choke carburettors, in place of Webers, and benefited from the CD ignition system. Some 1971 Ts used Webers, however, for reasons unknown. The T was becoming a very desirable and practical sports car. The E, meanwhile, was softened to improve its desirability to mainstream buyers, its engine receiving the cams (with less overlap) from the 1968 911 engine (the 901/06).

For 1970, all USA models received a new fuel evaporative control system to prevent the release of vapour into the atmosphere. The system passed vapour through an expansion tank and over an activated charcoal filter. Vapour was piped back into the air cleaner housing and drawn into the engine.

For the 1971 model year, the undersides of the pistons on all models were cooled by oil squirters. A feature that had been extensively tested in racing, this had the effect of dramatically reducing piston crown temperatures. On the 1971 models, the fuel pump was moved from the front suspension cross member to a new position next to the left-hand rear suspension arm.

TRANSMISSION

With progressively increasing engine power, the clutch reached the point where it had to be improved. For 1970, the Fichtel & Sachs item was increased in diameter by 10mm (0.39in) to 225mm (8.86in) and included a redesigned diaphragm action to make pedal effort a little less tiring.

Like the engine, the gearbox was given a new prefix, being termed 911 rather than 901. The gearbox internals were largely unchanged and the five-speed 'box still offered a dog-leg first gear arrangement – with first over to the left and back and reverse opposite – as on the 2-litre cars. The T retained the four-speed 'box as standard, with a five-speed as an option.

Recognising that automatics, even semi-automatics, do not go well with the image of an out-an-out sports car, Porsche deleted the Sportomatic as an option for the S. Of interest to seriously sporty customers, however, was a new limited slip differential option. The ZF unit was offered with a locking factor of either 40 per cent or 80 per cent.

This decal appeared in the rear window of all 2.2 models. The simple chromed engine lid grille has a black-painted mesh beneath to stop objects falling into the engine compartment.

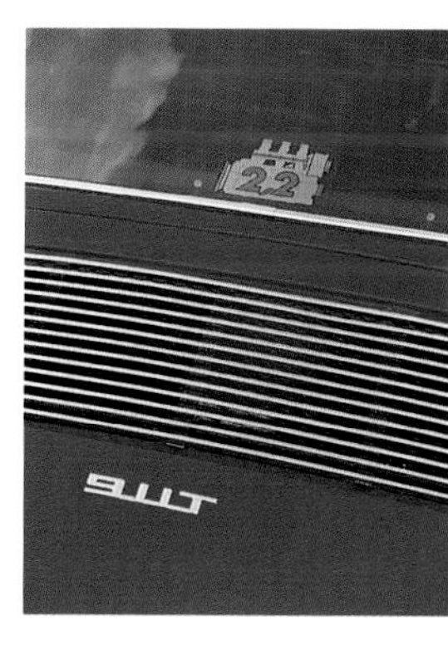

ELECTRICAL EQUIPMENT & LIGHTING

Another luxury feature introduced in mid-1969 was electrically operated side windows. These could be specified in place of the manual winders and had the added benefit that the driver could close the passenger window from the switches on the driver's door. All models retained a 770-watt alternator and two 36Ah batteries. There were other detail improvements, too, like a small light for the ashtray mounted in the centre of the knee-board under the dash. The ignition switch was now a four-position unit, with positions for accessory/off/run/start.

The Bosch H1 headlight continued for the majority of markets, with American 911s retaining Hella sealed beam 50/40-watt units as standard.

SUSPENSION & STEERING

The anchorage points of the front suspension struts moved forward by 14mm to reduce front wheel castor, making the steering lighter at lower speeds and reducing the amount of road vibration fed back to the steering wheel. A steering lock made its first appearance in 1970. On the T and S, the front torsion bars were made easier to adjust – the E kept the hydro-pneumatic struts.

BRAKES

The 911T received the ventilated disc brakes that were standard fit on the E and S. The disc sizes were 282mm (11.0in) front and 290mm (11.3in) rear. The only other change was that the light alloy front calipers, previously only fitted to the S, were added to the E.

WHEELS & TYRES

The 6J × 15 Fuchs wheel became the usual fit across the range of models, not only because these wheels had become synonymous with Porsche and its success, but also because the other size that was available as an option – a 14in rim – was generally unpopular. The smaller wheel was produced to allow fitment of 85-series tyres, which had more flexible sidewalls than the 70-series. The 14in rim was fitted to Sportomatics to start with, but many customers wanted to stay with the 15in wheels – and the firmer ride that went with them. The 14in wheels were options on the T through 1970 and 1971, and were then deleted. On the T in many markets, the 5.5J × 15 steel wheel was still the standard offering, but few customers wanted these old-fashioned wheels.

The standard tyre for the T was the 165HR15, but the 185/70VR15 option was much more popular – the 185HR14 was also available.

Data Section

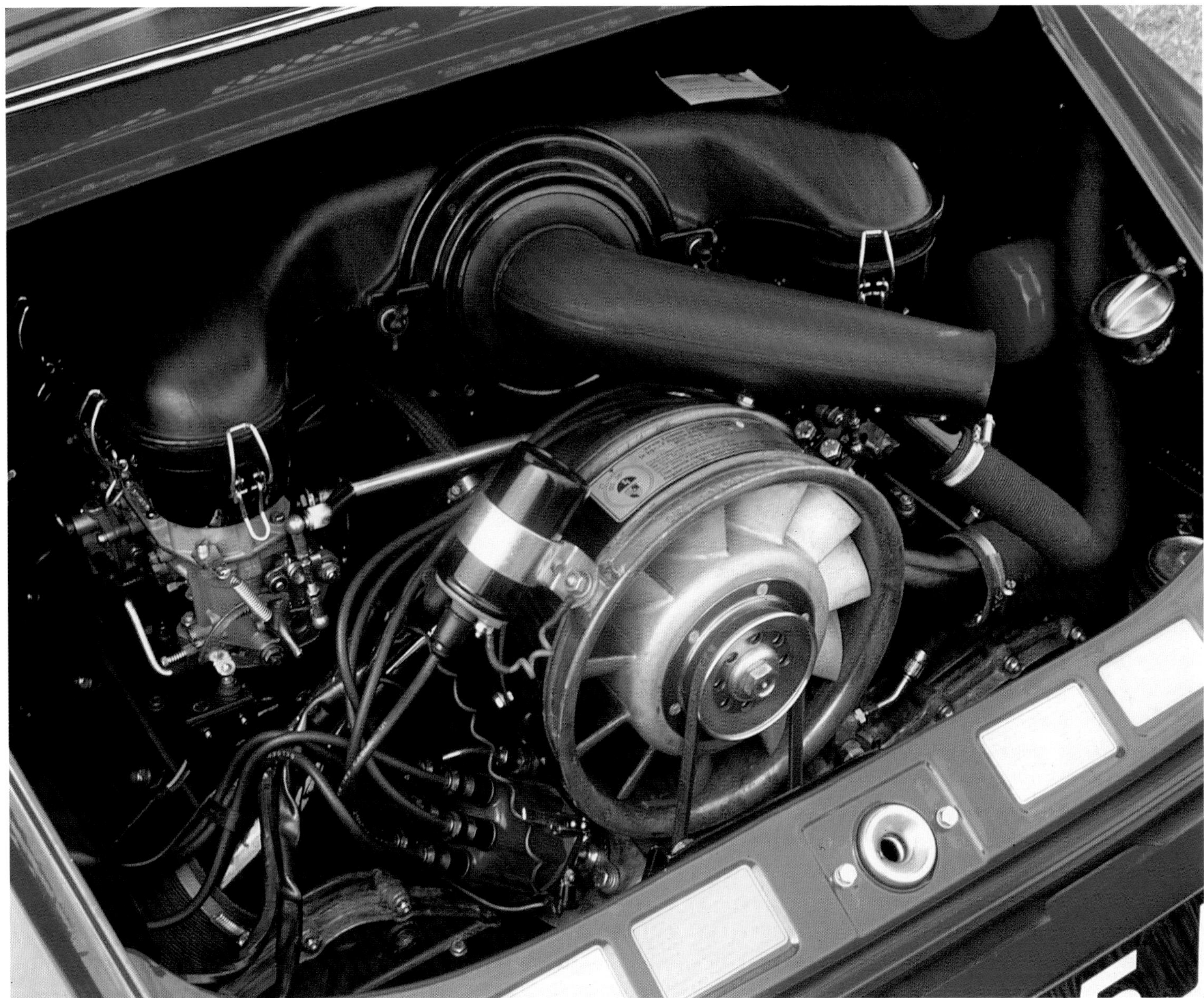

The European 2.2T used two triple-choke Zenith TIN 40 carburettors. The oil filler neck is on the right-hand side with the oil filter just behind.

PRODUCTION CHANGES

Aug 1969 (START OF C-PROGRAMME)
Engine cover and central part of the E and S bumpers made from aluminium; all models receive a flexible pvc undercoat; chromed engine lid grille has five verticals under the horizontal; sealing around Targa roof section improved; new door handles with the opening trigger behind the handle; door trim has larger opening compartment; steering column stalks revised; main dials located by neoprene ring; T gets two luggage compartment lights (like E and S); Bosch H1 headlight improved; engine capacity increased to 2195cc; engine and gearboxes get 911 designations; helicoil spark plug insert deleted; thin metal C-shaped head gasket replaces original type; more fins on barrels, longer big end bolts; shell bearing added to internal end of intermediate shaft; T uses Zenith 40 TIN triple-choke carburettors, plus CD ignition; E gets earlier softer cams; USA models have fuel tank vent kit; clutch size increased to 225mm diameter with redesigned diaphragm and action; gear ratios for four-speed gearbox: first, 0.324; second, 0.613; third, 0.962, fourth, 1.318. For five-speed gearbox (all markets): first, 0.324; second 0.563; third, 0.821: fourth, 1.080; fifth, 1.318; reverse, 0.688; final drive, 0.226. Sportomatic (all markets) gearbox final drive is 0.259 with ratios 0.417, 0.645, 0.889, 1.167. Sportomatic was no longer available as an option for the S; anchorage points of front suspension struts moved forward by 14mm to reduce front wheel castor; front torsion bar adjustment improved; T gets ventilated disc brakes; light alloy front calipers fitted to the E; 6J×15 Fuchs wheel becomes standard fit on all models; intermittent wipe facility.

Aug 1970 (START OF D-PROGRAMME)
Selective hot dip zinc coating to exposed underbody sections; fuel pump moved from front suspension cross member to adjacent to the left-hand rear suspension arm; crankcase squirters introduced to improve piston cooling; new sealed-type chain tensioner universally introduced; fuel evaporative control system fitted to US models; glovebox top handle deleted, lock (at left of centre) moved to middle of compartment lid, with integrated knob with twist and pull operation.

DIMENSIONS

Wheelbase
2268mm

Track (front/rear)
T, 1362mm/1343mm; E and S, 1372mm/1354mm

Length
4163mm

Width
1610mm

OPTIONS

1970 (popular new options)
Electric window lifters, ZF limited slip differential with either a 40% or 80% locking factor, 5.5J × 15 cast magnesium (Mahle) wheels for T (alongside the 5.5J × 14 Fuchs wheel or chromed 5.5J × 15 steel wheel).

1971 (popular new options)
Heated front windshield, H3 equipped fog and spot lights in US, convex lens for Durant mirror.

COLOUR SCHEMES

For 1970, the three-digit number given here is the code as it appears on the paint identification plate, attached to the left-

For 1970 there was another revised exterior door handle with the introduction of the definitive hidden trigger-release. Door operation now had to be a deliberate activity with no possibility of accidental opening. The keyhole was given a hinged cover, which reduced the possibility of the lock freezing up.

hand front door pillar. For 1971, the four-digit number shown is the factory paint code as identified in the model colour charts. On Targa models, the last two digits of the paint code are replaced by 10 (eg, Olive is 3939 on a coupé, 3910 on a Targa). Beginning with the 1970 models, all metallic finishes were applied with a two-coat wet-on-wet process.

1970 (chart dated Aug 69)

Standard body colours

Burgundy Red (017), Tangerine (018), Bahia Red (022), Signal Orange (116), Light Ivory (131), Medium Ivory (132), Irish Green (213), Turquoise Green (220), Conda Green (222), Pastel Blue (321), Albert Blue (325).

Optional body colours

Metallic Green (221), Metallic Blue (324), Metallic Red (021), Black (700), Silver Metallic (924, 925)

Special order body colours

Crystal Blue (320), Glacier Blue (326), Turquoise (340), Signal Yellow (114), Olive (414), Light Yellow (117), Light Red (023), Signal Green (217), Leaf Green (218), Sepia Brown (415), Grey White (620), Beige Grey (622).

Interior

Leatherette was standard in black, brown or beige. Leather was an extra cost option in the same colours. Seat inlays were basket-weave leatherette in black/brown/beige, or leather with basket-weave finish. Fabrics were corduroy in black/brown/beige and dog-tooth check in black/white or black/brown/white. Carpets were black or brown, in special Perlon on the T and in velour on the E and S.

1971 (chart dated Aug 70)

Standard body colours

Light Ivory (1111), Bahia Red (1313), Signal Orange (1414), Irish Green (1515), Albert Blue (1818), Pastel Blue (2020), Tangerine (2323), Burgundy (2424), Conda Green (2626).

Optional body colours

Silver Metallic (8080), Green Metallic (8383), Blue Metallic (8484), Gemini Blue Metallic (8484), Gold Metallic (8888).

Special order body colours

Olive (3939), Ivory (4646), Light Yellow (6262), Turquoise (6464), Green Turquoise (6565), Glacier Blue (6666), Signal Yellow (7272), Crystal Blue (7373), Sepia Brown (7474), Beige Grey (7575), White Grey (7676), Leaf Green (7777), Signal Green (7878), Light Red (7979), Black (1010).

Interior

All unchanged from 1970.

IDENTIFICATION

Model year	Model	Engine	Gearbox	Chassis numbers	Engine numbers
C-programme					
1970	911T	911/03	911/00	9110100001-9110102418	6100001 onwards
	911T[1]	911/03	911/00	9110120001-9110124126	6100001 onwards
	911T Targa	911/03	911/00	9110110001-9110112545	6100001 onwards
	911T Sporto	911/06	905/20	9110110001-9110112545	6103001 onwards
	911T US	911/07	911/00	9110110001-9110112545	6103501 onwards
	911T Targa US	911/07	911/00	9110110001-9110112545	6103501 onwards
	911T Sporto US	911/08	905/20	9110110001-9110112545	6105001 onwards
	911E	911/01	911/01	9110200001-9110201304	6200001 onwards
	911E[1]	911/01	911/01	9110220001-9110220667	6200001 onwards
	911E Targa	911/01	911/01	9110210001-9110210933	6200001 onwards
	911E Sporto	911/04	905/20	9110210001-9110210933	6208001 onwards
	911S	911/02	911/01	9110300001-9110301744	6300001 onwards
	911S Targa	911/02	911/01	9110310001-9110310729	6300001 onwards
D-programme					
1971	911T	911/03	911/00	9111100001-9111110583	6110001 onwards
	911T[1]	911/07	911/00	9111120001-9111121934	6110001 onwards
	911T Targa	911/06	911/00	9111110001-9111113476	6110001 onwards
	911T US	911/07	911/00	9111110001-9111113476	6114001 onwards
	911T Targa US	911/07	911/00	9111110001-9111113476	6114001 onwards
	911T Sporto	911/06	905/20	9111110001-9111113476	6119501 onwards
	911T Sporto US	911/08	905/20	9111110001-9111113476	6119501 onwards
	911E	911/01	911/01	9111200001-9111201088	6210001 onwards
	911E Targa	911/01	911/01	9111210001-9111210935	6210001 onwards
	911E Sporto	911/04	905/20	9111210001-9111210935	6218001 onwards
	911S	911/02	911/01	9111300001-9111301430	6310001 onwards
	911S Targa	911/02	911/01	9111310001-9111310788	6310001 onwards

General notes

Chassis numbering In 1970 the chassis numbering system changed to a ten-digit method, for instance 9110120001. The first three digits referred to the model, the fourth to the model year (0 for 1970), the fifth to the engine type (1=RoW 2.2 litre T, etc), the sixth to the body type (0=coupé, 1=Targa, 2=Karmann-manufactured coupé), and the last four digits to the build serial number. This numbering method continued until 1979.

Engines E and S engines were the same for Europe and the Rest of the World, including the US.

Gearboxes 911/00 is four-speed gearbox for 911T, 911/01 is five-speed, 905/20 is Sportomatic.

Numbered note

[1] Body built by Karmann.

PRODUCTION DATA

Model year	Model	Power (bhp DIN@rpm)	Torque (Nm@rpm)	Compression ratio	Weight (kg)	Number built
1970	911T	125@5800	177@4200	8.6:1	1020	2418
	911T[1]	125@5800	177@4200	8.6:1	1020	4126
	911T Targa	125@5800	177@4200	8.6:1	1070	2545
	911E	155@6200	191@4500	9.1:1	1020	1304
	911E[1]	155@6200	191@4500	9.1:1	1020	667
	911E Targa	155@6200	191@4500	9.1:1	1070	933
	911S	180@6500	199@5200	9.8:1	1020	1744
	911S Targa	180@6500	199@5200	9.8:1	1070	729
1971	911T	125@5800	177@4200	8.6:1	1020	583
	911T[1]	125@5800	177@4200	8.6:1	1020	1934
	911T Targa	125@5800	177@4200	8.6:1	1070	3476
	911E	155@6200	191@4500	9.1:1	1020	1088
	911E Targa	155@6200	191@4500	9.1:1	1070	935
	911S	180@6500	199@5200	9.8:1	1020	1430
	911S Targa	180@6500	199@5200	9.8:1	1070	788

Numbered note

[1] Body built by Karmann.

THE 2.4-LITRE 911 (1972-73)

Ah – the 2.4s! In these cars we see the fruits of all the development effort to produce an unmatched high performance sports car. *The* classic mainstream production 911 is a 2.4, and depending on how far your pocket can stretch, the choice is between three outstanding examples of the automobile engineer's art – the T, E or S. It has been said that the 911 is a triumph of development over design and nowhere is it more apparent than on a 2.4. Even the T, supposedly the base model in the range, had so much appeal.

In mechanical terms, the 2.4s were a major upgrade. It was the factory's general intention to try to restrict major changes to every two years, but this policy became a little clouded through the 1960s as the engineers worked flat out to develop the 911. Things looked as though they were settling down after the announcement of the much-improved 1969 models, but the then-new 2-litre fuel-injected engine lasted only a year before being enlarged to 2.2 litres. Factory discipline more or less reigned after that and the next big changes arrived in August 1971. These included not only the extra cubic capacity, new camshafts and improved breathing, but also the introduction of the 915 gearbox and improved high-speed handling.

There was more overall performance than previous models and, to the credit of the engineers, it was more manageable too. The new E was almost as quick as the 2.2S and would pull in fifth from as little as 2500rpm. But fuel consumption was at an all-time low – 14mpg would be typical for a hard-driven S. And it was just a year before the first major world fuel crisis...

We look back on the cars and tend to ignore the lifestyles of the time. This was the age of the beautiful people, long hair and flared pants. But, as in any time, success was what every Porsche buyer craved. And to be associated with Porsche was to be associated with winning. Sales of 911s continued to improve through the late 1960s and early 1970s, as

EVOLUTION OUTLINE

Aug 1971	Engine size increased to 2341cc (2.4-litres); oil filler flap external in rear right wing; black anodised lettering replaces gold on engine cover; cookie-cutter wheels on E; S is fitted with front lip spoiler.
Aug 1972	Horn grilles change to black; front spoiler standard on E; Targa available in right-hand drive for first time.
Jan 1973	Fuel-injected T models (US) change to Bosch K-Jetronic.

By 1973 the performance of the production 911 had reached a peak. This German-registered 2.4T shows off the lip spoiler introduced with the previous year's S model, and optional for the T and E. For 1973 models the finish for the horn grilles and the trim around the driving lights changed from bright plated to black.

Dave Gray's 1973 2.4E is a high-specification UK model. Note the Durant mirror, which in most other markets was superseded by a much plainer rectangular mirror, in order to give a larger glass area.

the production volume data shows. This was in no small part due to the effectiveness of Porsche's main marketing tool – motor racing. In 1970 and '71, the Wyer Engineering/Gulf 917s absolutely dominated endurance racing, driven by some of the world's top Grand Prix drivers. In 1972 the big sports car would be banned and Porsche simply transferred the effort over to the American CanAm Challenge and the European Interserie. It was a good time on the track and, if you cared what others thought about you, a good time to be seen driving a Porsche.

As well as producing some legendary prototype racing cars, the factory continued to develop the 911 for racing and rallying. The 1971 Le Mans 24 Hours saw a number of 911Ss with engines bored out to around 2.4-litres and one, driven by factory man Jurgen Barth, used an experimental engine of 2410cc, with a longer-throw crank. This engine pointed the way to a reliable increase in capacity for the road cars, but in fact the Barth Le Mans 2.4 had little in common with the new production 2.4 introduced in August of the same year. But the on-track variety was part of the learning experience and was typical of the meticulous way Porsche went about its development.

The main reason for achieving the capacity increase by lengthening the stroke was to comply with California's new air pollution laws – taking out the bores would not have met this requirement. With a move in the US towards 91 RON lead-free fuel, compression ratios also had to be lower than previously. In a speed-restricted US, the T tended to be seen as the most practical 911: complete with an S option kit (spoiler, alloy wheels, etc) it provided the looks of the higher powered models without the temperament.

The 1972 models witnessed the first substantial increase in weight for the 911. Over the previous ten years the engineers had managed to trim the weight of the basic car from the original 1080kg (2381lb) to a best, in 1969, of just 995kg (2194lb). The objective had been to improve the handling, for instance by reducing the overhung weight of the engine and gearbox at the rear. But the progressive increase in power from 1970 meant components in the engine had to be strengthened, and the introduction of the higher-torque 915 transmission in 1972 added some 9kg (19.8lb) over the earlier 901 unit. The brakes and suspension had been improved too, but with some weight penalty. Crash resistance, and with it chassis weight, was improved in response to changes in legislation across the world in the early 1970s. By 1972, the basic weight of the S was back up to around 1075kg (2370lb), depending on fittings. But a comparison of the power to weight ratios shows the overall improvement.

A 1964 2-litre car had 0.120bhp/kg compared to the 1972 figure of 0.176bhp/kg, but if we want an early 'hot ship' then we need look no further than the 1969 S with its 0.171bhp/kg. And the figures do not convey the 1969 car's almost kart-like lightweight feel. Of course, this is a discussion only to be found among classic Porsche enthusiasts. All the 1973 and earlier 911s feel wonderfully light and responsive compared with their later, more luxurious offspring.

The increases in capacity had originally been intended to improve the opportunity for success in GT racing. It worked. In 1972, bored-out 2.5-litre 911s with the new 915 gearboxes won the European GT Championship (John Fitzpatrick) and the US IMSA GT Championship (Hurley Haywood). With some justification, some observers were saying the 911 was at its peak. They were asking how it could be improved further. There were rumours of a new 911 replacement in development at the brand new research facility at Weissach...

As a tailpiece to the general comments on the 2.4-litre 911, these models marked the peak of Ferdinand Piech's influence over the 911, as development chief. A big shake-out in the company's senior management came in 1972, when members of the Porsche and Piech families voluntarily stepped out of the day to day running of the business. Dr Ferry Porsche was concerned that internal family politics were affecting the performance of the business. It meant that Piech, whose track record in the development engineering side of Porsche had been outstanding, joined Audi-NSU, where he would excel and later rise to head the giant VW-Audi empire. At the end of 1972, the Porsche company changed from being a limited partnership (Porsche KG) to a partly shareholder-owned Porsche AG. It was a massive change in the way the company was run, allowing the management team to be selected on the basis of merit rather than background. That said, the implications of the loss of Piech, especially, were perhaps not fully realised at the time.

Piech's replacement was Ernst Fuhrmann, father of the four-cam racing engine of the 1950s and a firm believer that Porsche's racing cars should be developed from its road cars. That was very good news for the 911. The first result of Fuhrmann's direction was the appearance of the Carrera RS at the October 1972 Paris Salon. It was Fuhrmann's decision to go for the RS in place of the proposed 2.7-litre 911S for 1973, a decision prompted by the change in international racing regulations in May 1972 that allowed stripped-out homologation specials to be built in series of at least 500. The concept of the racing department modifying the heavier production 2.7S was dropped, even though preparations for the 2.7S had gone as far as preparing all the marketing brochures, and photographs were taken of a number of prototypes. Instead we had the 2.4S for 1973, and the limited edition RS would act as a springboard to much greater things for Porsche in competition.

BODYSHELL

The 1972 models were classified internally at Porsche as the E-programme, and the 1973 models as the F-programme.

The no-expense-spared development effort to improve the handling of the 911 reached a peak with the E-programme. The most obvious recognition feature of these models is the oil tank filler just behind the right-hand door, with its flap opened from a button in the adjacent door pillar. The two-gallon oil tank, larger and made of stainless steel, was moved from behind the right-hand rear wheel (where it had been filled from within the engine compartment) to a new position in front of the wheel. This, the engineers said, reduced the polar moment of inertia and improved the predictability of the handling. It was also claimed that oil surge was minimised in hard cornering (this had been proved in racing with the 911R), and on a purely practical level the new location took the oil tank out of the firing line of stones thrown up by the rear wheel. This detail was typical of the time, showing how much control the engineers had over the specification of the cars. The new oil system also included a remote oil filter housing so that the engine, complete with oil system, could be easily fitted to Porsche specials. Now, how many people would need that facility?

The trouble was that the new oil tank arrangement also had an unforseen snag, and the following year the tank moved back to where it had been on the 2.2s. Too many filling station attendants put fuel in the oil tank...

The other main feature to change on the E-programme was the adoption of a front air dam on the S as a result of intensive wind tunnel testing. The testing, on an earlier 2-litre car, had shown that aerodynamic lift was present over the front axle at high speed, but that the lift was greater over the rear axle – and in side winds the lift appeared to increase. This confirmed the reports received from the racers that high-speed stability was not all it should have been. The engineers proposed a small spoiler at the front and this was included on the S for 1972, as well as being optional on the E and T. It proved to be so popular that on the F-programme it was standard across the range. By later standards, the air dam was merely a small lip on the bottom of the existing front valence, but it made a difference to stability (a claimed 40 per cent reduction in front-end lift at high speed) and, probably more important for most customers, it looked great.

Tests also showed that the rear-end lift problem had not been addressed and subsequent testing led to a proposal for a rear spoiler mounted on the engine lid, the whole unit being made from glass-reinforced plastic. This was considered impractical for road use

A 1972 model 2.4 can be identified by the oil filler flap on the right-hand rear wing – where it remained for only one year. Placing the oil tank within the wheelbase helped the handling, but this arrangement proved to be impractical because filling station attendants sometimes put petrol in the oil tank...

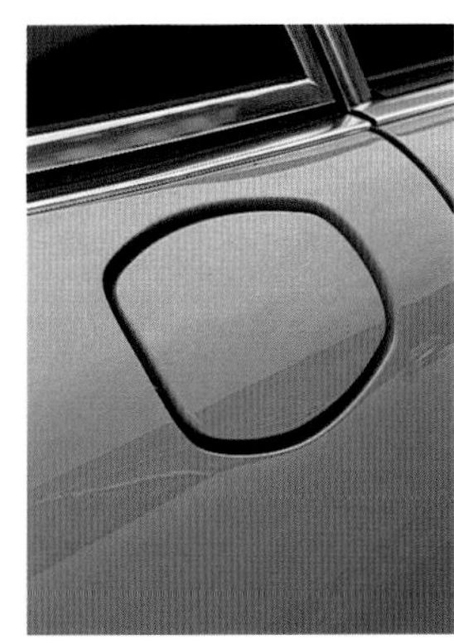

The interior of the 2.4E reflects a fashion in the 1970s for minimal chromework. An interesting point is the blank cover plate on the central tunnel. On early models (to 1967) a petrol heater was standard, but then became an option on left-hand drive cars until 1973. Intake air for this device would have been drawn through an open grille mounted in this position.

as well as likely to upset the authorities in several countries because of its hard, upturned edge. But the 'ducktail' spoiler, as it became known, was very effective at curing high-speed oversteer and was adopted on the limited edition Carrera RS.

From 1972, US models had the chassis number stamped onto a plate riveted to the windshield pillar, in accordance with new federal legislation.

Last, but by no means least, the London Motor Show in the autumn of 1972 saw the announcement of the Targa in right-hand drive form. Deliveries of the T, E or S in Targa form were promised in Britain from February 1973.

This T has the more pronounced chromed headlamp flange that goes with the sealed beam units fitted to US cars. These headlamps were unpopular, as shown by this car having the more powerful Lucas H4 units retro-fitted. Also visible is the large elastomer overrider used only in 1973.

Body Trim & Fittings

The details which identify a 1972 model from earlier years are many. Look for the black engine lid grille with a '2.4' logo on the right-hand side. The 'Porsche' and '911' lettering on the engine lid changed from the gold anodised finish to a dark grey (or gunmetal) colour. It is also quite easy to tell 1972 cars from 1973 cars. The most obvious trim differences are that the rims of the side-light and tail-light lenses changed from chrome to black, as did the horn grilles.

The European S, with its new front spoiler, now came without the standard overriders of the earlier cars, although they were listed as an option and remained standard, in bright and dark chrome finish, on US cars. In 1973, US cars could be delivered with large foam rubber 'bumper guards' that went some way to offering low-speed impact protection, but looked awful. These would be replaced with a completely redesigned – and elegant – bumper the following year. The E became more frugal in that the standard external bumper and sill trim matched that of the T rather than the S, but the trim specification could be taken up to the S level at extra cost.

A change to the rules concerning rearwards visibility meant American models had a larger, rectangular driver's door mirror. Getting into magnifying glass detail, the label on the engine fan housing and the chassis plate changed at the start of 1973 to acknowledge the fact that Porsche KG had become Porsche AG.

Interior Trim

The most noticeable difference in a period when interior changes were few was to the seats. These now had a black crackle finish to the back recliners and featured a new seat-locking mechanism for fore/aft adjustment. On the 1972 models the lock lever moved to the inside of the slider, and buzzers were fitted to the seat belt mechanisms on US cars. The seat coverings could be in standard vinyl or optional leather.

DASHBOARD & INSTRUMENTS

The centre section of the dash was standardised in black, irrespective of the interior colour, and covered in matching material. The basket-weave vinyl that had covered the lower dash area of the earlier cars was replaced in 1972 by a leather-look finish that matched the door and upholstery trim. The 911 logo on the passenger side glove compartment lid was deleted. The familiar four-spoke design of the 400mm (15.6in) steering wheel was largely unchanged, a leather-covered version being standard on the E and S, the T making do with an alternative hard rubber version.

LUGGAGE COMPARTMENT

A new option was an 85-litre fuel tank (18.70 Imperial gallons, 22.46 US gallons), a consequence of the thirstier engine now being used. This new tank was shaped to accept the new, more compact Goodrich Space-Saver spare tyre, which came with a small compressor that could be powered from the cigarette lighter inside the car. The crossply construction of the Space-Saver made mixing this with the 911's standard radials illegal in the UK. The T had a standard 62-litre tank (13.64 Imperial gallons, 16.38 US gallons), with the S still being offered with the optional 110 litres (24.20 Imperial gallons, 29.06 US gallons). With this latter tank, there was little room for anything else in the front compartment. The luggage compartment was now lit by just one lamp on the right-hand side of the car.

ENGINE

The obvious difference was that the engine was enlarged to 2341cc (142.8cu in). This was closer to 2.3-litres, but it suited Porsche's marketing people to label the car '2.4' because this seemed a more attractive increase in size. Whereas the previous capacity increase had been achieved by enlarging the bore, this time it was the stroke that was increased, going from 66mm (2.57in) to 70.4mm (2.75in). A lower compression ratio, achieved by lowering the height of the piston crowns, enabled low-octane (91 RON) fuel to be used.

The stroke increase was obtained by reducing the diameter of the big end journals, so that the rod cen-

Nancy MacLean's smart 1973 Sportomatic has a two-pedal arrangement (above) and a conventional-looking gear lever (below). Porsche's automatic was quite different from any other manufacturer's. There was no clutch, but the driver still changed gear by moving the lever through a conventional gate. Sportomatic's popularity waned through the 1970s.

For the 2.4 models the engine air intake ducting was revised to incorporate a cold-start flap, with the opening moved from the right-hand to the left-hand side of the engine compartment. When the engine was cold, the flap prevented ambient air entering the intake ducting and warm air was drawn from around the left-hand heat exchanger.

US specification 911T models changed from carburettors to the Bosch K-Jetronic continuous fuel injection system in January 1973. This gave American Ts a boost in performance and significantly changed the look of the engine compartment.

tre could be moved further from the crank centre. The con rods were shortened by 2.2mm (.09in) and the big ends increased in width. The architecture and strength of these improved and lightened rods had been fully proven in the flat-12 engine of the 917 sports racing car.

These modifications were achieved while keeping within the envelope of the previous 2.2 crankcase (but with additional strengthening webs) and using the same crankshaft blank. The non-counter-weighted cast crankshaft previously used on the T was deleted in favour of a common forged crankshaft across the range. On the 1973 models, airflow to the engine oil cooler was improved by modifying the air baffles.

In the US all models used Bosch mechanical fuel injection, with closer tolerances on the injection pump and different set-ups for the fuel distributor for the T, E and S models. Although the valve sizes stayed the same for all models, the size of the ports and the plastic intake trumpets increased with each more powerful model. For all other markets the T was fitted with Zenith 40 TIN triple-choke carburettors which dropped power output to 130bhp compared with the 140bhp of the fuel-injected

American T. Power outputs for the E and S were 165bhp and 190bhp.

From January 1973, the fuel injection system on the US 911T changed to the new Bosch K-Jetronic Continuous Injection System (CIS). Although this sounds like an electronic system, it was another type of mechanical injection but using electrically operated sensors. The air sucked into the engine was measured by the displacement of a disc placed in an intake pipe shaped like a wine glass. The degree of displacement of the disc controlled the amount of fuel distributed to the cylinders. The US 911T with this K-Jetronic injection also had new camshafts with reduced valve opening timing (overlap).

For 1972, the S came with a second oil cooler (a matrix-type) fitted in the right-hand front wing. Many cars were later converted to the labyrinth-type tubular system introduced in 1973.

TRANSMISSION

The gearbox was new for the 2.4s. Known as the 915, it was derived from the transaxle developed for the 1968-69 908 sports racing car and was designed for both four-speed and five-speed gear clusters. The gear cluster was contained in a magnesium casting separate from the aluminium differential housing. The fifth speed was housed with reverse in the end cover, while on the four-speed alternative the fifth gear wheel was simply deleted from the end of the gear set.

The principal benefit of the new gearbox was greater torque capacity, but the gears were also easier to use. The T and E came with the four-speed version as standard in most markets, including the US, but most customers chose the five-speed option – and the S was always five-speed. Gone was the race-bred 'dog-leg' first gear that was rather inconvenient for town use: the new five-speed gearbox had a 'street' pattern gate, with first to fourth in the conventional 'H' with fifth over to the right and forward.

The popularity of the Sportomatic was dwindling and it was now only available to special order.

ELECTRICAL EQUIPMENT & LIGHTING

The new Bosch H4 single-bulb headlight was standardised in all markets except the US (which kept Hella sealed beam units) and France (where the yellow H1 was still used). The H4 was rated at 60-watt (main) and 55-watt (dipped), compared with the 50/40-watt equivalent of the Hella sealed beam unit. The H4's external glass looked slightly different from that of the H1, in that the ribbing inside the glass had a dipped beam sector and the face was slightly more vertical. Only two adjustment screws were used as opposed to four.

Another detail is that the frosted finish around the top of the rim of the H4 glass was a later addition – the glass was clear on the 2.4 models. That said, these H4 glasses have a reputation for cracking or chipping very easily and many cars received later glasses after stocks of the originals became exhausted. The later glasses also have a larger 'H4' moulded into the centre of the lens.

SUSPENSION & STEERING

The no-expense-spared development effort to improve the handling of the 911 reached a peak with the E-programme, all the 2.4 cars having a detail change to the rear suspension geometry. The shock absorber strut had previously angled back from the mounting on the swing arm (when viewed from the side), resulting in a slight compound movement of the strut as the wheel moved up and down. The new arrangement changed the location of the top and bottom shock absorber strut mountings and eliminated that rearwards tilt. In addition, a sharply inward angled mounting of the top of the strut (when viewed from the front) improved the response to wheel movement. It also improved the travel of the shock absorber and thus gave a more comfortable ride over rough surfaces.

On the 911E, the Boge hydro-pneumatic front suspension struts were relegated to the option list, so this mid-range model acquired the more popular torsion bar and MacPherson strut arrangement of the T and S. The T and E used Boge shock absorbers while the S continued with Konis.

WHEELS & TYRES

The standard factory fitting on the T for the 1972 and 1973 model years was the 5.5J × 15 non-chromed steel wheel with Dunlop CB57 165/70HR tyres. The E used 6J × 15 steel wheels as standard in some markets with Dunlop CB57 185/70VR tyres, while the S continued to use the (five times) more expensive 6J × 15 Fuchs forged alloy wheels (an option for the other models) with Michelin XVR 185/70VR tyres. In several markets, the forged alloy wheels were fitted to the T and E as standard.

Earlier experiments with the Stuttgart-based Mahle company into magnesium casting had led directly to the development of a cast aluminium alloy wheel. It was cheaper to make than the forged alloy wheel, although it was not as strong. This new 6J × 15 wheel, made by the German company ATS and known as the 'cookie-cutter' because of its appearance, was standard on the 1973 model year E, and would remain in use until 1983.

The new five-speed 915 gearbox for the 2.4 models had a conventional gearchange pattern, with fifth to the right and forwards. The larger gear lever boot seen here arrived for the 1973 model year.

CARRERA RS

The RS was a unique limited edition model that has become, perhaps, the most important of all 911 models. The term Carrera was first used by Porsche in 1955 to celebrate a class victory in the 1953 Carrera Panamericana road race. Carrera means 'race' in Spanish and until 1974 was only given to Porsche's most sporting models. Much to the dismay of some enthusiasts, from this date Porsche began to use the title to adorn its regular production models – but that is another discussion!

The origins of the 1972-73 RS (RennSport) lay in the racing department's desire to widen the scope for the 911 in Group 4 Special GT racing. The RS was developed from the F-programme and applied the lessons learned from earlier stripped-out rally and customer race cars. The RS could be specified by the customer in one of four forms.

The RSH (for Homologation) was the very basic model that was taken to the Stuttgart city scales for weight certification – it weighed just 960kg (2117lb). Only 17 cars were actually delivered to customers in this specification. From the RSH, two more practical models were offered for road use.

The RS Sport (the M471 option) was one stage up from the homologation cars and weighed around 975kg (2150lb). The M471 was still very basic, with minimal undercoating and sound-proofing, elementary door trim with manual windows, and simple interior upholstery with felt carpets and rubber footwell mats. There were lightweight Recaro bucket seats for the driver and passenger, but the rear seats were deleted. There was no clock, no passenger sunvisor and a black headlining.

The RS Touring (the M472 option) was trimmed like the contemporary S although a 380mm (14.8in) steering wheel was fitted, and it weighed some 100kg (220lb) more than the RS Sport. Nearly 200 RSH and RS Sport models were delivered, the remainder of the 1580 RS Carreras produced to the end of July 1973 being RS Touring versions.

The fourth model was the racing version, the 2.8-litre RSR (the M491 option). This model (55 were built) will not be discussed here.

The RS offered improved performance over the S, its 2.7-litre engine producing 210bhp at 6300rpm, with maximum torque of 255Nm at 5100rpm. This was achieved principally through an increase in bore size to 90mm (3.51in), using Nikasil-coated aluminium cylinders – Nikasil was a trade name for the nickel-silicon carbide coating deposited to a few hundredths of a millimetre on the bores. This technique had been developed on the 917 racers and allowed the increased bore to be adopted without causing cylinder strength problems. The new coating also offered reduced sliding friction, leading to an increased power output over previous equivalent bores of the same dimensions. The increased bore resulted in an engine capacity of 2687cc (163.9cu in). Apart from the bore sizing and the material, the 911/83 engine was the same as the 2.4S. A heavier clutch spring was required to cope with the additional torque but the 915 gearbox had sufficient

Mark Waring's Carrera RS, painted Jade Green, is an M472 Touring model. Many RSs were delivered in the production colours available for the 1973 model year.

The evocative message on the tail of what is, for some, the most desirable 911 of all.

capacity for the 2.7 engine, although fourth (27/25) and fifth (29/21) gears were taller than on the S.

The suspension was improved by fitting gas-filled Bilsteins (lighter and stiffer than the Konis used on the S), 18mm front and 19mm rear anti-roll bars, and a light alloy front suspension support. The suspension mountings front and rear were strengthened, but the production brakes were unchanged from the S – the RS prototype's cross-drilled discs were not used for the series build cars.

In terms of running gear and bodywork, an early production RS differs considerably in detail from a 2.4S – and this is where the casual observer steps into a minefield of conflicting information! Because the model was planned as an homologation special, only 500 were initially scheduled for production, starting in November 1972. Lightness was a major goal for the engineers, so a uniquely lightened bodyshell with thinner gauge steel was used for its unstressed body panels, which included the roof, wings (with the rears flared by 50mm each side for wider wheels) and bonnet. These bodyshell differences were common to all versions. On the M471, glass-reinforced plastic was used for both bumpers and the rear engine cover, which had an aluminium support frame. On the M472, the bumper trim, rear bumper and centre panel came from the 2.4S. On later Sport models the steel bumpers of the Touring models were used with plain chromed overriders and an aluminium centre panel. This was partly to do with restrictive regulations imposed by certain European countries. The windshield and rear side window glass were made from thinner safety glass (and was subsequently less robust), manufactured by the Belgian company Glaverbel. The remainder of the glass was made by Sekurit, the regular suppliers of glass to Porsche. To the long-term detriment (from rust) of the early lightweight cars, the heavy pvc underseal was applied only around the wheelarch areas.

Just over half of the 109 3-litre Carrera RS models built were roadgoing variants (top). This version used the heavier production bodyshell and featured a new 'whaletail' rear spoiler. The M471 Sport model (above) is notable for its elementary equipment specification in the pursuit of performance.

Interestingly, one story says that only factory competition and preferred customers received true lightweight RSs that had a complete complement of thin-gauge panels. But this has been disputed by the legendary Porsche development engineer Peter Falk, who has said that there was no conscious effort to make 'lighter' lightweights. If some cars had a larger number of thinner panels or lighter plastic parts, it was simply due to the inconsistency of the manufac-

The interior of the M472 was equipped to the level of the production S model. Note the sports seats and the large gear lever boot – a new feature for 1973.

turing processes. There are those who would also argue that there is no conclusive evidence that the first 500 or 1000 used up all the lightweight panels, and that the remainder of the RS line used body parts from the heavier 2.4 production model, as has been generally thought to have been the case.

Externally, the RS can be identified by its ducktail spoiler (although it was an option and some cars may not have this fitted) and the larger rear wheel-arch flares that accommodate the 7in Fuchs alloys used for the rear wheels. The RS was fitted with Pirelli CN36 tyres of different sizes front and rear (185/70VR15 on 6J front wheels, 215/VR15 on 7J rear wheels), although Dunlops were used later in the production run. The most popular colour was light yellow, while Grand Prix White was a special colour for the RS. Many were delivered in the production colours available in the 1973 model year. Special side stripes were an option, derived from the Carrera logo first seen on the 356 four-cam model. These could be specified in blue, red, green or black with matching colour coding to the wheel centres. The RSH models were set apart by their black-only script. A 'positive' decal was used for the two cars in the original sales brochure, but the series cars used a 'negative' rendering.

Once the RS was in the showrooms, demand exceeded the Marketing Department's dreams – the first 500 sold out immediately and production was extended to 1000 in order to homologate the car in the Group 3 production GT racing class. These cars were still taken to the Stuttgart city scales and a certificate produced noting their lightweight specification compared to the mainstream production cars. But the demand still continued beyond 1000 and subsequent RS bodyshells were manufactured on the main Zuffenhausen production line. Chassis numbers for the RS run from 11 to 1590.

Supplies of the lightweight components started to become short with the later models from late April 1973 (from around chassis 1230). Progressively, these later cars used more of the same heavier shell, panels, glass and components of the regular production models (although they still retained the prestigious ducktail engine lid) and by this time full underseal was being applied to the cars. Late model original RSs, therefore, are quite likely to have opening rear quarter windows and steel front support bars, among many other detail changes (and improvements) from the earlier RSs. These improvements make the later cars just as interesting, in that development was moving towards the 3-litre version. By the end of the series, the RS had the later Silumin alloy crankcase in place of the previous magnesium item and revised mounting points for the rear trailing arms.

To complete the RS roadgoing story, we will make very brief mention of the car that followed the 2.7RS in late 1973. Just 109 3-litre RS models were built. Because all the lightweight bodyshell parts of the original RS series had run out earlier in 1973, these cars used regular 'heavy' bodyshells. The extra weight explains why the 3-litre RS is not much quicker than a 2.7 model. Just over half (59) were road models, and only six right-hand drive models were made (one for Australia, five for the UK). The 3-litre RS was fitted with 8in front and 9in rear wheels wearing 215/60 and 235/60 Pirelli CN36 tyres respectively. Power was 230bhp at 6200rpm.

Rear ends of an M472 RS Touring (right) and an early M471 RS Sport (far right). The Touring has steel bumpers, a nudge bar, a chromed silencer skirt and a moulded badge under the 'ducktail'. The Sport has a one-piece glass-fibre 'bumper', the engine lid is secured with racing-style elastic toggles, and the badges are colour-coded decals.

Data Section

Pointing to the 911's aerodynamic future, the Carrera RS was the first model to sprout a rear spoiler, although the 'ducktail' was actually an option.

PRODUCTION CHANGES

Aug 1971 (START OF E-PROGRAMME)

Oil filler flap now just behind right-hand door; S gets front spoiler lip, optional on E and T; black engine lid grille with 2.4 logo on right-hand side; lettering on engine lid changed from gold anodised to dark metallised grey; seat metalwork now black crinkle finish instead of chromed; H4 headlamp standard except in US; 911 logo on passenger-side dash deleted; leather-look finish on middle dash replaces previous basket-weave; inertia reel seat belts and buzzers on US models; larger rectangular external driver's mirror; door sill kick plates standard on S, optional on E and T; E interior now based on T rather than S; front overriders now optional; one lamp only for luggage compartment; rear suspension struts aligned vertically when viewed from side; rear swing arms revised to allow removal without removing the engine; Boge hydro-pneumatic front struts now only an option; ATS 'cookie-cutter' wheels standard on E; chromed steel wheels deleted; door handles common on both sides; S has 15mm anti-roll bars front and rear; wheelbase extended by 3mm; engine enlarged to 2341cc, stroke increased to 70.4mm by 2.2mm shorter steel rods, on S these were Tenifer-treated instead of soft-nitrided as on 2.2S; lower compression ratio (see production data table) from reduced-height piston crowns, which are cooled by individual oil jet sprays; larger big ends and full crankshaft counter-balancing; crankcase stiffened around main bearings; valves unchanged but porting improved; camshafts same for S but on E and T timing retarded by 1 degree (T) and 2 degrees (E); US T gets six-plunger mechanical injection (and 140bhp) to meet emissions laws (this version also sold to Australia, Japan and Canada); new remote oil filter housing including thermostat and by-pass valve; new 915 gearbox with 'street' pattern gate; 915 features torque capacity of 245Nm, three-piece transmission housing and fifth gear next to reverse at back of gear cluster; four-speed is standard in most markets, but for UK E and S have five-speed as standard; four-speed ratios are: first, 11:35; second, 18:32; third, 24:27; fourth, 28:23; reverse, 12:21; final drive, 7:31; five-speed ratios are: first, 11:35 (11:36 in US); second, 18:35; third, 23:29; fourth, 26:25; fifth, 29:22; reverse, 12:21; final drive, 7:31; 925 Sportomatic introduced to cope with greater torque of E and S models (905 retained for T); torque capacity increased to 230Nm, using larger diameter torque converter and clutch, a larger crown wheel and pinion and a stronger differential; 925 transmission housing reinforced with extra ribbing; 925/00 (for E) and 925/01 (for S) are last of the four-speed Sportomatics.

Mechanical fuel injection manifolding on a European 1973 911E, with the correct green-finished cooling duct. The metal fuel injection pipes enter the cylinder heads at the base of the intake trumpets.

Aug 1972 (START OF F-PROGRAMME)

Oil tank and filler moved back inside engine bay, now made from copper-coated steel; front lip spoiler and ATS cast wheels standard on E; rear wiper standard (except Carrera RS); rims of front driving light and rear tail-light lens changed from chromed to black; front horn grilles changed to black; US cars had large elastomer overriders front and rear; interior upholstery more fire-resistant and seat anchorages strengthened; door beams for increased side-impact resistance; RHD offered for Targa for the first time; improved cast gear lever support mechanism and larger protective boot; S and Carrera RS models change to labyrinth (tube-type) secondary oil cooler in front of right-front wheel.

Jan 1973

Fuel-injected T models change from mechanical to CIS (Bosch K-Jetronic).

DIMENSIONS

Wheelbase
2271mm

Track (front/rear)
T, 1360mm/1342mm; E, S and Sportomatic, 1372mm/1354mm; Carrera RS, 1372mm/1394mm

Length
T, E and S, 4127mm; Carrera RS, 4147mm

Width
1610mm

OPTIONS

Factory list (dated Sep 1971)

M400 light metal wheels 6J×15 with 185/70VR tyres; M444 steel wheels 6J×15 with 185/70VR tyres; M485 pressure cast wheels 5.5J×15 with 165HR tyres; M976

The 915 five-speed gearbox (to the right) and the exhaust pipes leading forward into the heat exchanger boxes (to the left). Air is circulated around the exhaust pipes and taken forward to warm the cabin.

chromed wheels with crest 5.5J×15 with 165HR tyres; M470 comfort kit; M429 fog light, white Halogen H3, under bumper; M430 fog light, yellow Halogen H3, under bumper; M433 fog light, white Halogen H3, above bumper; M434 fog light, yellow Halogen H3, above bumper; M432 spot light, white Halogen H3, above bumper; M571 fog light, rear; M425 rear window wiper; M650 electric sunroof (coupé only, including RS); M258 seat head restraints, left and right; M409 sports seats, left and right; M410 sports seat, driver only; M419 automatic seat belts, left and right; M549 three-point seat belts, left and right. Other options not numbered: separately listed radios; special paints and fabrics; leather unholstery; leather seats; custom interiors; leather steering wheel on the T; five-speed gearbox; Sportomatic; limited slip differential; electric window lifters; air conditioning; 85-litre fuel tank with space-saver tyre; S spoiler for T and E (1973 only, standard in some markets).

COLOUR SCHEMES

1972 (chart dated Jul 71)

Standard body colours
Tangerine (018), Bahia Red (022), Aubergine (025), Signal Yellow (114), Light Yellow (117), Light Ivory (131), Emerald Green (225), Albert Blue (325), Sepia Brown (415).

Special order body colours
Gulf Orange (019), Rose Red (024), Signal Orange (116), Ivory (132), Irish Green (213), Leaf Green (218), Lime Green (226), Jade Green (227), Glacier Blue (326), Gulf Blue (328), Oxford Blue (329), Royal Purple (341), Olive (414), Beige Grey (622), Black (700), Gold Metallic (133), Metallic Green (224), Metallic Blue (324), Gemini (blue/grey) Metallic (330), Silver Metallic (925).

Fabrics
Standard trim: leatherette (999.551.001.40) in brown (406), tan (502), red (003), blue (301) or black (708). Option at extra cost: leather (999.551.071.40) in brown (404), tan (503) or black (700). No cost option on seats: corduroy fabric (999.551.032.40) in brown (400), tan (500) or black (700); dog-tooth check fabric (000.551.531.00) in brown/white/black (430) or black/white (730); tartan 'Madras' fabric (999.551.031.40) in reds (43), blues (41) or browns (42), optional with matching leather (or leatherette) and carpet. Seat fabric combinations: brown leatherette (406), tan leatherette (502) or black (708); leatherette or leather and cord in brown (487), tan (578) or black (779); leatherette and dog-tooth check in brown (486), tan (577) or black (778); leatherette and 'Madras' tartan in reds (079), blues (374) or browns (488).

Carpets
Pile carpet (000.551.570.00) in dark grey (401) or black (700); needle loom carpet (front compartment) in brown (401) or black (700); nylon velour carpet (999.551.052.40) in maroon (001), blue/green (301) or dark tan (402).

1973 (charts 1000.14 and 1001.14)

Standard body colours
Bahia Red (022), Emerald (Viper) Green (225), Sepia Brown (415), Light Ivory (131), Aubergine (025), Light Yellow (117), Tangerine (018), Signal Yellow (114).

Special order body colours
Gulf Orange (019), Rose Red (024), Signal Orange (116), Ivory (132), Irish Green (213), Leaf Green (218), Lime Green (226), Jade Green (227), Glacier Blue (326), Gulf Blue (328), Oxford Blue (329), Royal Purple (341), Olive (414), Beige Grey (622), Black (700), Gold Metallic (144), Metallic Green (230), Metallic Blue (334), Gemini (blue/grey) Metallic (335), Silver Metallic (936). Note: RS Carrera body colours included alternative special order colours (eg, Grand Prix White).

Fabrics
Generally as 1972. Leatherette (standard) in black, brown or beige; leather optional at extra cost; seats were leatherette in black, brown or beige with inlays in corduroy or dog-tooth check (black/white or black/brown/white).

Carpets
The T had 'special' nylon, the E and S had velour pile in black or brown.

Note
Custom external colours and interiors were available to special order.

IDENTIFICATION

Model year	Model	Engine	Gearbox	Chassis numbers	Engine numbers
E-programme 1972	911T	911/57	915/12	9112500001-9112501963	6520001-6523284
	911T Targa	911/57	915/12	9112510001-9112511523	6520001-6523284
	911T Sporto	911/67	905/21	9112510001-9112511523	6529001-6529224
	911T US	911/51	915/12	9112100001-9112102931	6120001-6124478
	911T US Targa	911/51	915/12	9112110001-9112111821	6120001-6124478
	911T US Sporto	911/61	925/00	9112110001-9112111821	6129001-6129293
	911E	911/52	915/12	9112200001-9112201124	6220001-6221765
	911E Targa	911/52	915/12	9112210001-9112210861	6220001-6221765
	911E Sporto	911/62	925/00	9112210001-9112210861	6229001-6229248
	911S	911/53	915/12	9112300001-9112301750	6320001-6322586
	911S Targa	911/53	915/12	9112310001-9112310989	6320001-6322586
	911S Sporto	911/63	925/01	9112310001-9112310989	6329001 6329147
F-programme 1973	911T	911/57	915/12	9113500001-9113501875	6530001-6533239
	911T Targa	911/57	915/12	9113510001-9113511541	6530001-6533239
	911T Sporto	911/67	905/21	9113510001-9113511541	6539001-6539197
	911T US	911/51	915/12	9113100001-9113101252	6130001-6131926
	911T US Targa	911/51	915/12	9113110001-9113110781	6130001-6131926
	911T US Sporto	911/61	925/00	9113110001-9113110781	6139001-6139149
	911T US[1]	911/91	915/12	9113101501-9113103444	6133001-6136092
	911T US Targa[1]	911/91	915/12	9113110001-9113112302	6133001-6136092
	911T US Sporto[1]	911/96	925/00	9113110001-9113112302	6139301-6139502
	911E	911/52	915/12	9113200001-9113201366	6230001-6232125
	911E Targa	911/52	915/12	9113210001-9113211055	6230001-6232125
	911E Sporto	911/62	925/00	9113210001-9113211055	6239001-6239319
	911S	911/53	915/12	9113300001-9113301430	6330001-6332231
	911S Targa	911/53	915/12	9113310001-9113310925	6330001-6332231
	911S Sporto	911/63	925/01	9113310001-9113310925	6339001-6339136
	911 RS Carrera	911/83	915/08	9113600011-9113601590	6630001-6631549

General notes

Gearboxes The four-speed 915 was given the designation 915/12 and the five-speed version was 915/02. The four-speed Sportomatic was now designated 925/21 for Europe and 925/00 for the US and the Rest of the World, but the 911S Sportomatic was 925/01.

Numbered note

[1] US 911T with new fuel injection (Bosch K-Jetronic, Continuous Injection System) from Jan 1973.

PRODUCTION DATA

Model year	Model	Power (bhp DIN@rpm)	Torque (Nm@rpm)	Compression ratio	Weight (kg)	Number built
1972	911T	130@5600	196@4000	7.5:1	1050	1963
	911T Targa	130@5600	196@4000	7.5:1	1100	1523
	911T US	140@5600	200@4000	7.5:1	1050	2931
	911T US Targa	140@5600	200@4000	7.5:1	1100	1821
	911E	165@6200	206@4500	8.0:1	1050	1124
	911E Targa	165@6200	206@4500	8.0:1	1100	861
	911S	190@6500	216@5200	8.5:1	1050	1750
	911S Targa	190@6500	216@5200	8.5:1	1100	989
1973	911T	130@5600	196@4000	7.5:1	1050	1875
	911T Targa	130@5600	196@4000	7.5:1	1100	1541
	911T US	140@5600	200@4000	7.5:1	1050	1252
	911T US Targa	140@5600	200@4000	7.5:1	1100	751
	911T US[1]	140@5700	201@4000	8.0:1	1050	1944
	911T Targa US[1]	140@5700	201@4000	8.0:1	1100	1302
	911E	165@6200	206@4500	8.0:1	1050	1366
	911E Targa	165@6200	206@4500	8.0:1	1100	1055
	911S	190@6500	216@5200	8.5:1	1050	1430
	911S Targa	190@6500	216@5200	8.5:1	1100	925
	911 RS Carrera	210@6300	255@5100	8.5:1	975	1580

Numbered note

[1] US 911T with new fuel injection (Bosch K-Jetronic, Continuous Injection System) from Jan 1973.

THE 2.7-LITRE 911 (1974-77)

The first major fuel crisis hit the world in 1973. The effect on Porsche sales was dramatic, with volumes falling some 25 per cent. Fuel was no longer cheap and customers were looking for more efficient use of this now-valuable commodity. It was not acceptable that a hard-driven 911S would only cover 12 or 15 miles to the imperial gallon. And what was suddenly a very difficult time for Porsche was compounded by two other external influences, both initiated in the US, that would also force changes to the 911.

In a series of new laws that aimed to institutionalise the motor car into a more environmentally friendly armoured vehicle, the US federal government and in particular the state of California gave notice of a significant tightening-up of exhaust emissions and crash resistance. It seemed to outsiders that American legislators wanted to wipe out the sports car completely.

The two-year cycle of 911 upgrades was now well-known in the industry and many observers were suggesting that in fact the 911, now ten years old, would be replaced by a new model in 1974. There were rumours of a new four-seater project (the 928), so the observers had some credibility. But there was never really any doubt within Porsche about the continuation of the 911. Certainly it would have to grow up, become a bit more serious and maybe more concerned with the world around it. But there was life in the old dog yet. The new Research & Development Centre at Weissach, west of Stuttgart, had recently opened and in the new environment the engineers and stylists would have to innovate their way out of the problems.

Exciting new 911 types were appearing in racing in 1974, like the 3.0-litre RSR for customers and the 2.8-litre Turbo Carrera – a 911 like no other. These were cars that would point the way to new chapters in the history of Porsche in racing and of the 911. The production 911 was on the verge of a new lease of life and would find a new maturity in the changed economic climate of the 1970s.

The 1973 model 911T for the US had been the first Porsche to use the cleaner-running Bosch K-Jetronic injection, and this ingenious and effective system appeared on the new 2.7-litre 911 and 911S lines in 1974. Extra engine capacity combined with more fuel-efficient injection to give the 911 more flexibility, with better power delivery at low revs. This allowed the 911 to meet the new American legislation for exhaust emissions.

The other change that had to be made for the 1974 models was the introduction of energy-absorbing bumpers to improve low-speed crash resistance. Other manufacturers, such as MG, had made beautiful cars look awful with the addition of ugly black deformable bumpers, but the Porsche stylists (notably Wolfgang Möbius) introduced impact bumpers and by a clever mix of design and function actually managed to lift the image of the 911. The transformation was complete. Sales steadied and then started to rise through the mid-1970s. The new 911 had defied its critics.

In 1974, the model line changed from the familiar T/E/S format to a more marketable 911, 911S and 911 Carrera. It was, frankly, a cheapening of the Carrera name to use it on the top-of-the-range production model. The models sold to the US became

EVOLUTION OUTLINE

Aug 1973	911 (150bhp), 911S (175bhp) and 911 Carrera (210bhp) replace previous T, E, S and RS models; new cars all have 2.7-litre engines and impact-absorbing bumpers; side window demist vents on dash; start of models with significant emissions control devices for American and certain other markets (with even tighter specifications for California).
Aug 1974	New 'whaletail' spoiler for US Carreras.
Aug 1975	Introduction of Carrera 3.0 in non-US markets; all models receive hot dip zinc galvanising over whole bodyshell; Sportomatic goes from four speeds to three; electric external door mirror introduced; Silver Anniversary model.
Aug 1976	Central face level vents in dash introduced.
Aug 1977	Dilavar cylinder head studs; Targas get black roll-over hoop.

The 'ducktail' rear spoiler was offered as an option in most markets for 1974. It was banned in Germany, however, because the authorities judged that there was too great a risk of pedestrian injury from its hard edges.

Joe Hartman's superb 1974 2.7 Carrera illustrates the changing shape of the 911 in the 1970s. The new bumpers and revised side trims gave the car a lower look.

The late Tony Knapp's 911 is a superb example of a European-specification 1975 2.7 Carrera. Note that this British car still has the round Durant external mirror, an item deleted in many other markets in 1973 because the glass area did not meet local regulations.

a little more complex, and this is explained further in the 'Engine' section (pages 60-62).

The regular 911 was a better car than the previous T, its 150bhp up 10bhp on the old fuel-injected version and 20bhp on the carburettor type. The 1974 S gained 10bhp (to 175bhp) over the previous year's E model, against which it must be compared. Because it was fitted with the new fuel injection, the S engine had a more flexible torque curve, peaking at 235Nm at 4000rpm (compared with 206Nm at 4500rpm for the old 2.4E). You did not have to stir the gearbox so much and on the world's progressively more congested roads this made for a more manageable car. Fuel consumption did indeed reduce, and on the regular 911 over 20mpg (8km/litre) was now possible. Refinement was further enhanced by 12,000-mile (or 20,000km) service intervals, quite something for a high performance sports car in the mid-1970s, as it is today.

The 1974 European Carrera shared the 210bhp of

The Targa took on a new maturity with the elimination of chrome from its exterior. This 1975 German model is typical of many 911s in not having an external passenger door mirror – oddly this feature was an extra-cost option until the late 1980s.

the previous year's RS, but there the comparison blurs. It should not be confused with the 1973 RS and probably aligns more with the 1973 911S model. The 1974 Carrera retained the mechanical fuel injection and the ducktail was an option for those who had missed out on the RS. The engine was identical to the RS's unit and this endowed the 1974 Carrera with excellent performance – certainly better than the previous year's S. The Carrera was only available with full equipment, to a similar specification to the end-of-line RSs. The ducktail, however, had run into controversy in its home market concerning its safety and had been outlawed there.

In the US, however, the 1974 picture was not so good for those with a thirst was for power. The regular 911 delivered 150bhp, but the bad news was that the Carrera shared the S's 175bhp engine. In 1975 the standard 911 was dropped altogether and two versions of the S engine were now required, with different levels of emissions equipment. The first was termed a '49-state' engine with 165bhp, while California's ever-stricter legislation resulted in its own 160bhp variant, complete with air pump, thermal reactors and exhaust gas recirculation. Both these engines were detuned versions of the 175bhp engine in the 2.7 911S sold to the rest of the world. The Californian engine did find another 5bhp to reach 165bhp in 1976, but the 2.7 Carrera model, unsurprisingly, was deleted after 1975.

In 1974, the factory celebrated 25 years of the Porsche sports car and this was marked with a special run of Silver Anniversary 911s, using the new 1975 model year 911 as a base. Each was painted in what was termed Diamond Silver Metallic. The cars featured a special silver and black tweed interior and had a numbered plaque attached to the passenger side of the dash. Another special was sold in 1976, called the Signature 911S. This version was fitted with the Carrera's three-spoke steering wheel with an embossed Ferry Porsche signature. It had the 'black-look' and beige tweed upholstery, and was painted in metallic platinum with colour-coded wheels. Porsche was getting the hang of profitable special edition models...

But American enthusiasts, offered only the 911S alongside the new Turbo in 1976, had to look in

This 1976 UK-specification 2.7 911 shows off the ATS 'cookie-cutter' wheels that had first appeared on the 1973 911E. The electrically-operated driver's door mirror was new for the 1976 model year.

The Carrera 3.0 revitalised the image of the 911 in Europe for the 1976 model year. There were many improvements that year, but surely the most far-reaching was the introduction of hot-dipped zinc coating for the entire bodyshell, a process applied across the 911 range. This UK-specification Sport version is owned by Peter Hatfield.

envy at the new 911 model that was not available to them, but was on sale to the rest of the world. The Carrera 3.0, as it was known, replaced the 2.7 Carrera and received what was effectively a 930 engine without the turbocharger, with an output of 200bhp. Given that the 2.7 engine was recognised as being at the end of a long development cycle, the adoption of the large redesigned turbo engine was a smart move.

The 911 was moving towards a new type of buyer, one who did not look for the last fraction of performance but who demanded comfort, smoothness and easier driving. By 1977, the transition of the 911 into a thoroughly refined automobile was nearly complete.

BODYSHELL

The 1974 model year cars were termed the G-programme models and were instantly recognisable by their new bumpers.

The bumpers were designed to absorb impacts up to 5mph and then recover their original position. Unlike other manufacturers' efforts, the Porsche bumpers absorbed impacts by moving backwards in their entirety (rather than deforming) up to a maximum of 50mm, either against collapsible steel tubes (Europe) or hydraulic shock absorbers (US). The hydraulic rams resulted in the American cars having bumpers which projected further than their European counterparts, although hydraulic rams could be fitted as an option to a car destined for any market.

The new bumpers required changes to the front and rear wings and the front bonnet (hood) to accommodate the higher bumper line. The potential movement meant that between bumper and body was a gap, which was filled by flexible concertina-type bellows that were integrated into the body shape with an additional side panel at the front and a shaped lower panel at the rear. At the back of the car, the central panel over the silencer disappeared (it did anyway after a few years, thanks to rust!) and was replaced with a one piece wrap-around bumper formed from a complex aluminium extrusion. Two large flexible overriders carried the number plate lights and the gap between engine lid and bumper line was filled by a reflective band – a much-copied Porsche styling innovation. As a footnote to the introduction of the new bumpers, the overall dry weight only increased by 25kg, demonstrating some very careful design work.

The side sills were extended so that the jacking points came through the panel rather than being sited below them. Some road testers felt that the slightly increased length of the 911, with its new bumpers, improved the response to side winds. On Targas, the fold-away roof was replaced by a fixed panel, which could be stowed in the front luggage compartment. The folding roof now became an option for cars with air conditioning. The 1973 RS could not be ordered in Targa form, but the 1974

Carrera could – and came in the 'black-look'. Standard Targas would not be delivered in standard form in the 'black-look' until the 1977 model year, although it was an option from 1976.

The H-programme cars (1975 model year) had extra sound insulation as an added refinement, but otherwise there were no changes.

The I-programme cars (1976 model year) brought one of the most far-reaching improvements to the 911 line with the introduction of Thyssen zinc-coated steel. A hot dip process was applied to both sides of the steel and was used for all chassis and bodywork parts. This was a significant improvement on the previous level of zinc-coating, applied to the underside only of cars after August 1970, and new cars were immediately offered in most markets with a six year anti-corrosion warranty. It was the final effort in the continuing battle against rust, which unfortunately could affect the earlier models quite badly, sometimes after only two or three years in a poor winter climate. It also ensured that in later years those enthusiasts who could not afford the new cars would be able to buy near showroom condition models, even when five or more years old. It was an astute business move by the factory because it underwrote a good resale price for their customers and contributed much to the 'hewn from stone' image of quality that the 911 was gaining.

Body Trim & Fittings

A neoprene rubbing strip on the impact bumpers allowed touch parking without risk of damage to paintwork. At the front, the side lights and indicators were integrated into the bumper. Fitted to the top of the front bumper were optional (but standard in some markets) high-pressure headlamp washers. These were fed from an 8.5-litre reservoir mounted in the wing behind the left-hand headlight. This was to meet a new Swedish law, but Porsche adopted the washers across the product range. The front spoiler was not so pronounced as on earlier models. It was the elegant integration of all these features that made the change to the impact bumpers so visually successful on the 911.

Black trim had been used earlier for details like wipers (from the 1968 models), badging (from the first 2.4 models) and the horn grilles (from the 1973 models), but on the 1974 Carrera the fashion could be extended to all 'brightwork', including the window trim and door handles. When a car was finished in this way, no chrome was visible on the exterior.

The 'ducktail' rear spoiler was only available as an option outside Germany (where it was criticised by the authorities for being dangerous to pedestrians in the event of an accident), but 1975 saw a 'safer' rear spoiler emerge in the form of the 'whaletail' that could be specified for the Carrera. To balance the

By a superbly clever mix of design and function, Porsche's stylists turned a potentially disfiguring legal requirement for energy-absorbing bumpers into an image-enhancing feature. Just visible here is the flexible lip extension to the new front spoiler, an important detail that improved the aerodynamic balance of the car when the rear 'ducktail' was fitted.

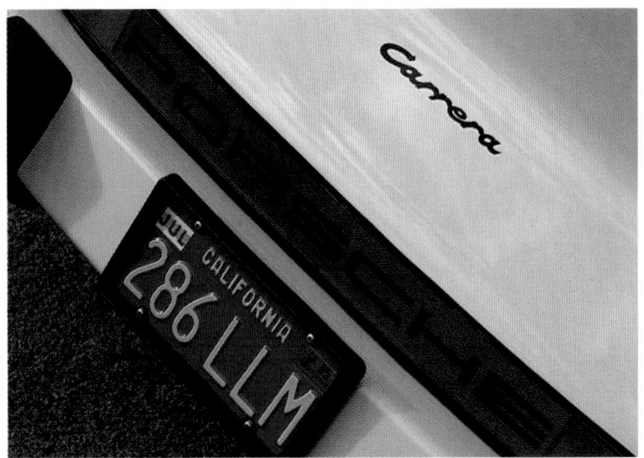

The new bumpers were neat one-piece aluminium extrusions front and rear. The rear aspect of the 911 was further changed by the addition of a full-width reflector strip between the light clusters. Possibly too flashy on some cars, it worked well on the 911. The Carrera logo had always been reserved for limited-edition high-performance models.

Keeping the 911 stable at speed had become a priority in the early 1970s. Following the introduction of the 'ducktail', this 'whaletail' arrived in 1975 to satisfy German legal requirements. This was a productionised version of the rear spoiler first seen on the 3-litre Carrera RS.

The wipers on the 911 had changed for 1968 so that they always parked in front of the driver, whether the car was left-hand or right-hand drive. Since then the 911 designers have not been able to change the wiper arrangement significantly through the entire life of the model because of the cost of retooling.

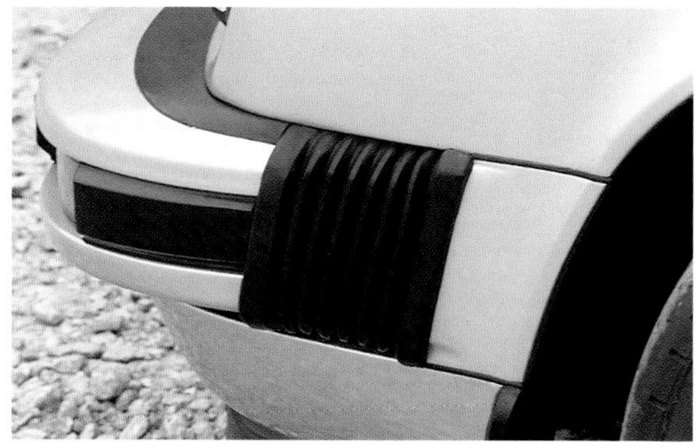
The design of the impact bumpers allowed them to move backwards in a low-speed collision. Movement was resisted either by two shock absorber units or collapsible tubes fitted between the bumper and the front part of the wing inner walls. The external bellows at the sides of the bumpers were a tidy method of accommodating this potential for movement.

The 1974 model year saw the introduction of high-pressure headlamp washers as an option in most markets (and standard in some). The new Carrera 3.0 had them as standard, as well as colour-coded headlamp surrounds.

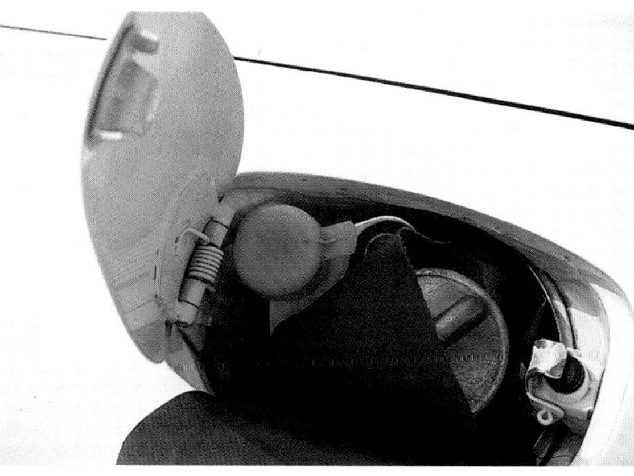
The fuel filler flap has hardly changed throughout the life of the 911. The canvas flap shields the paintwork from drips, while the washer bottle filler is to the left.

Large exterior mirrors were introduced in 1976. The body of the mirror was colour-coded, while the mirror itself was electrically adjustable and heated.

increased aerodynamic forces of the larger rear spoilers, a mandatory elastomer 'chin' extension was now specified for the front spoiler. The 'whaletail' was formed mainly from flexible elastomer and addressed the earlier arguments against the 'ducktail' in Germany. The 'whaletail' was derived from the spoiler first seen in 1973 on the 3-litre RSR and then on the new production 930 Turbo model. Unlike the 'ducktail', the 'whaletail' could be specified in conjunction with a rear wiper. Other details to distinguish these 1975 Carreras from the 1974 models were colour-coded headlamp surrounds, new wheelarch protection mouldings, and anti-stone chip steel under-door sill covers.

The badges on the engine lid changed to a simple '911' for the base model, with a chromed '2.7' on the right-hand side of the grille. There was no 'Porsche' script at the lower edge of the lid, this being embossed in red on the full-width reflector strip that bridged the gap between the lid and the rear bumper.

The 1976 model year saw the debut of another Porsche feature that would become an old friend to enthusiasts – the 'elephant's ear' door mirror. This unit was electrically adjusted and heated, and was sprayed in the body colour. The way it protruded brought a new thrill to driving past oncoming traffic in narrow country lanes.

In 1976, the new European Carrera 3.0 could be distinguished from the other models by the 'black-look' introduced for the 1974 Carreras and wider flares for the rear wheels.

INTERIOR TRIM

A glance at this chapter's data section (page 64) shows the incredible selection of interiors available to 911 buyers. Exclusivity has always been a major selling feature of Porsche and customers could choose from a wide range of materials and colours, within the bounds of the model. Alternatively, they could decide to use their own fabrics and colours and create a completely customised interior. This area of special orders would grow for Porsche as more customers sought to make unique statements about their lifestyles.

New seats with better lateral and thigh support, achieved by lengthening the front of the seats, were found on the 2.7s. These had integral head restraints in the seat backs. Repa inertia reel seat belts were now standard in all markets. Opening rear quarter windows were standard on the Carrera but optional on the 911 and S. Carpets were now all velour pile, with the earlier – and cheaper – 'special' nylons of the 911T being discontinued. The door trim was redesigned to provide a more accessible storage bin, with a lid that opened from the top and doubled as an armrest.

There were new seats for 1974, featuring more thigh support and integral head restraints. Although rear passengers found it more difficult to see ahead, getting in the back was easier because the releases on the seat backs were more accessible. When air conditioning was fitted, as here, the outlets ran across the lower dash area, integrating well with the existing design but reducing knee-room.

The heater had always been an area for criticism on the 911 because deriving warmth from the exhaust heat was not easy. The design of the heating system had basically changed little since the car's launch ten years previously. Heat exchangers wrapped around the exhaust manifolds on each side of the engine, fresh air was warmed by passing it over the hot exhaust pipes contained within these heat exchangers, and the amount of warmed air admitted to the cabin was controlled by a single lever next to the handbrake. This lever opened or closed butterfly valves mounted just downstream of each heat exchanger. If no heat was required in the cabin, then the butterfly valves exhausted the warmed air to the atmosphere. If the valves were closed then all the warmed air was ducted through the sills and into the cabin. In theory heat control was performed by mixing this warm air with fresh cool air from the inlet ahead of the windshield, but the reality was that the supply of warmed air was fairly unpredictable. If the engine ran fast you had a lot of heat, but around town, with a slow-running engine, heat tended to come in bursts. It would be a while before 911s had heating and ventilation that was effective, but the engineers were working on it...

For 1974, side window demisting vents were fitted into each end of the dash – at last the side windows could be demisted on wet days! Then, in 1975, an additional electrical fan boosted the heater output (but not on European Carreras because of their

The door trim on the 1974 models received another revision. The rear compartment was now deeper and had a conventionally-hinged top lid to replace the elastic bungee sprung 'clamshell' of the previous design.

The door trim changed again in 1976, in response to the growing problem of car theft. Instead of the mushroom-shaped lock pull (which a thief could easily 'hook' open) at the top of the door trim, this knob had to be turned to lock or unlock the car from the inside.

The 1974 Carrera retained the 380mm steering wheel of the RS. The new side vent in the lower dash greatly improved side window demisting. The red line on the rev counter starts at 6300rpm and shows that this model was no RS – the latter was red-lined at 7200rpm.

A new option for 1976, and standard on the 3-litre Carrera, was automatic regulation of cabin temperature. A controller was fitted between the seats and monitored inputs from sensors. The controller drove a servo motor that opened or closed butterfly valves on the heat exchangers.

mechanical fuel injection) at low engine speeds and there were left and right side heat controls. The interior sound insulation was improved too. But a new option (standard on the new 3-litre Carrera and Turbo) offered in 1976 went a long way to providing regulated hands-off control of the interior heat. A thermostat was fitted into the heat exchanger and another into the cabin between the sun visors, and there was a third manual selector switch. Between the seats a control unit monitored the inputs from these three sensors and drove a servo motor remotely attached to the butterfly mechanism on the exchangers. It was a complex system and over the years it proved to be fragile, but it was a significant improvement for new car buyers. In some markets this automatic system was termed 'dial-a-heat'.

Not until the 1977 model year did the occupants finally have the luxury of face-level ventilation, with the introduction of two adjustable vents in the middle of the dash. These also doubled as air conditioning outlets when this was fitted.

Improved door locks for 1976 reflected growing concern about theft. This was followed in 1977 by an arrangement which allowed the interior push buttons to disappear into the top of the doors when they were locked. A recessed knob in the door trim was turned to raise the button and unlock the door. At the same time the opening quarter windows on the Targa were deleted altogether – they were largely redundant now that there was adequate face-level ventilation inside the cabin.

The 1977 models were more lavishly trimmed than ever, with improved carpeting and rear bulkhead sound insulation, together with a new pinstripe fabric for the Carrera 3.0. The doors now had their lower edge carpeted and sported a smart slanted pleat pattern.

DASHBOARD & INSTRUMENTS

A new 400mm (15.6in) steering wheel was to be found on the 911 and 911S. Derived from the horizontal 'X' pattern of previous models, the new wheel obscured the lower dash in front of the driver completely since most of the 'X' was filled with padding. It was said the new wheel would be the basis for a future air-bag system. The Carrera, however, used a 380mm (14.8in) three-spoke design with a thick leather-trimmed rim.

The main instruments were changed slightly, using new colours and regrouped warning lights. The most obvious change was the elimination of the central chromed disc on each of the instruments. A new electronic rev counter and a quartz clock were fitted. Chrome was eliminated from the dash and the doors generally, while new soft knobs had clear symbols indicating their function.

The 1976 model year saw the introduction of the first cruise control for a Porsche, termed 'Tempostat' in Europe and Automatic Speed Control in the US. In 1977 the heater controls on the dash were revised so that there were individual controls for fan and heater delivery.

Luggage Compartment

G-programme cars used a new steel 80-litre (17.60 Imperial gallons, 21.14 US gallons) fuel tank, complete with a recess for the Goodrich Space-Saver tyre. On European cars this was pumped up from a storage bottle, whereas a small electric compressor did the job more effectively in the US.

The new fixed panel Targa top would not fit into the front luggage area on 1974 cars when air conditioning was specified, so in this case the old folding top had to be used. The 8.5-litre (1.87 Imperial gallons, 2.25 US gallons) water reservoir for the headlamp and windshield washer system was sited ahead of the left front wheel inside the luggage compartment. The system was replenished from a supplementary filler neck next to the fuel filler.

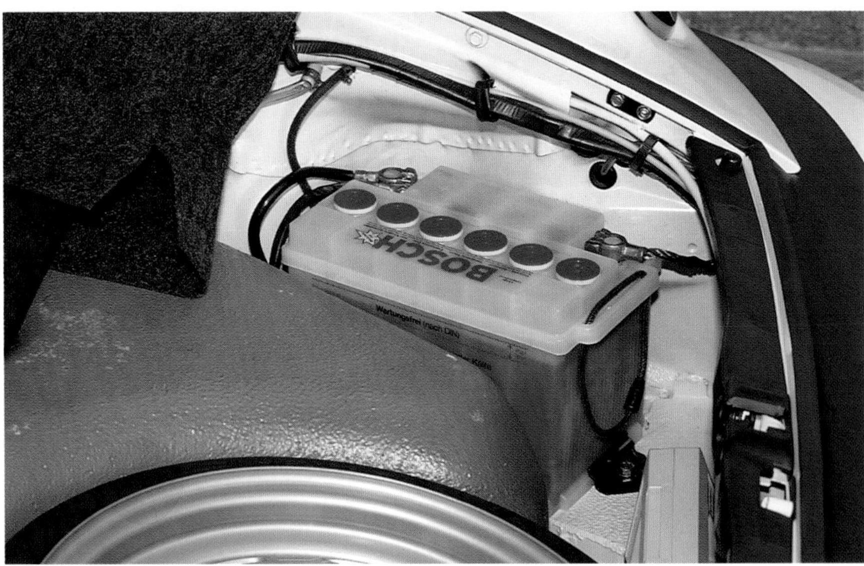

The 1974 cars had a new 80-litre fuel tank (top) with a spare wheel recess reshaped for a Goodrich Space-Saver tyre. With the introduction of impact bumpers, the chassis plate moved to the right-hand wall of the luggage compartment, adjacent to the spare wheel. The two batteries of the previous models (above) were replaced by a single unit for 1974. The 66Ah battery was now charged by a 770-watt alternator. In front of the Space-Saver spare wheel can be seen the air compressor, used for inflating the tyre.

Engine

By now there were significant differences between US engines and those available to the rest of the world. Before we get into this, the engine type numbers given here refer only to manual transmission versions: Sportomatics would have a different number (see page 62).

For 1974, the standard 'rest-of-the-world' range was the 2.7-litre 911 (engine type 911/92), 911S (engine type 911/93) and Carrera (engine type 911/83, still with mechanical injection). In the US the model offering shared the same titles, but the 911/93 engine was found in 175bhp form (with retarded cams) in both the S and the Carrera. The 1974 2.7-litre engines entered production with the Nikasil barrels that had been used on the Carrera RS, but these were soon changed to a new material called Alusil. This new alloy of aluminium and silicon was formed as a die-casting and used no cylinder liner. The piston skirts were plated with cast iron to prevent pick-up between the piston and the bore. The use of aluminium improved heat transfer away from the cylinders as well as enabling the larger 90mm (3.5in) bore, without a liner, required for the 2687cc (163.9cu in) engine.

During 1974, work progressed on improving the exhaust system in response to the higher temperatures that were now being generated, partly as a result of the lower exhaust emissions. It is worth mentioning, too, that noise was becoming an issue, especially in Switzerland. Until then, European 911s had used an efficient three-into-one manifold system sheathed by the heat exchanger jacket. A new system was developed which used an aluminium coating on the heat exchangers and a double stainless steel skin design for the silencer. The new system, which was further developed in 1975, was quieter, but some power was again lost in the process of making the 911 a more refined sports car. The oil tank was now

While European 1974 Carreras used the engine of the previous year's RS, US models adopted that market's S engine and Bosch K-Jetronic injection. With just 175bhp, the US Carreras were at a significant power disadvantage against the 210bhp Carreras offered in most other markets.

This underside view shows the forged semi-trailing arms (with embossed build date) that replaced the more flexible fabricated steel units in 1974. Other points of interest are the glimpse of the green Bilstein gas shock absorber, the fuel pump tucked away behind and above it, and the delicate mounting for the anti-roll bar.

also made from stainless steel and was enlarged, permitting an increase from the previous 6000-mile (100,000km) service intervals to 12,000 miles (20,000km).

The 1975 model offering in the US was driven by ever stricter exhaust emissions policy. Only the 2.7-litre S engine (911/43) was used, with K-Jetronic injection and an air pump (injecting clean air downstream of the exhaust valves) for what were termed the '49-state' cars. For California, where the exhaust laws were even more difficult to meet, separate models were offered with engine type 911/44. These had the unloved thermal reactors and exhaust gas recirculation. The California 911S managed just 160bhp at a time when the 911S in Europe delivered 175bhp, which itself was nothing to write home about. The 1975 models used 6mm thick sound absorbing material on the lower (exhaust) valve covers in an effort to reduce exterior noise levels. That year also saw an updated, but not fundamentally changed, chain tensioner – a small step forward in improving the reliability of this suspect item – that was accompanied by new harder wearing but noisier chain guide ramps in brown plastic.

In Europe, things started to happen in the autumn of 1975 with the introduction of the new 3-litre Carrera, which replaced the 2.7 Carrera. The S was also dropped for the 1976 model year. The new 3-litre engine, type 930/02, was derived from the Turbo unit. It used the same 95mm (3.70in) bore and 70.4mm (2.75in) stroke as the Turbo, but the compression ratio was increased to 8.5:1 by using higher domed pistons. Valve size was unchanged at 49mm (1.91in) for the inlets and 41.5mm (1.62in) for the exhausts, and these sizes would remain the same for all later 930-based engines (SC, Turbo and the later 3.2 Carreras to 1989). The Carrera 3.0 used the aluminium die-cast crankcase, Nikasil cylinders and Bosch K-Jetronic injection from the 930. The output for the 930/02 was 200bhp at 6000rpm on 91 RON fuel.

In markets where it was available, the 911 Lux adopted the old S engine (911/81) and went from 150bhp to 165bhp for the 1976 model year. It used the four journal camshaft housings from the 930 engine. Most noticeable on the 1976 cars was the five-blade cooling fan, which had the same 245mm (9.6in) diameter as the earlier 11-blade unit but ran at a higher speed (1.8:1 instead of 1.3:1) to improve alternator output. Inside the engine, the oil pump was revised to improve oil circulation in the hotter-running engines.

In the US, the range for the 1976 model year was simpler but the engines were not. There were still separate engines for '49-state' cars and for California, but things were simplified for the factory in 1977 when all cars destined for the US could at least use

The 1974-75 European Carreras still used the 911/83 engine from the RS. Combined with the same overall weight, these cars were almost as desirable as the preceding limited edition. This car is fitted with air conditioning: the compressor is on the right, driven from the crankshaft pulley, and the condensor is mounted on the engine lid.

the same emissions equipment – air pump, twin thermal reactors and exhaust gas re-circulation. These 2.7-litre 911s were also sold to Canada and Japan. That year also, the K-Jetronic was improved with more stainless steel components and finer fuel filters, and a return circuit was provided around the fuel accumulator to cope with higher fuel delivery pressure.

TRANSMISSION

The fact that the 2.7-litre engines were more flexible and produced their torque at lower revolutions allowed longer ratios to be used in both the 1974 and 1975 models, as the improvements were introduced. In America four speeds were the standard offering on the 915 gearbox across the range, with the fifth speed being an option. On manual cars, except the European Carrera, the clutch pedal was 30 per cent lighter to operate owing to a new centre plate, cable and throw-out mechanism. The S had new ratios in the gearbox and the crown wheel and pinion, to maximise the benefits of its greater engine torque.

In 1977 the 915 gearbox was improved by machining first gear to prevent accidental engagement at speed – an alarming possibility. The first and second gear arm of the 'H' pattern was fitted with detentes for the same reason.

As torque levels rose, the Sportomatic transmission reached the limit of its torque capacity for a second time, so it had to be uprated in 1976. This time it was reduced to three speeds and became the 925/09 unit. It was said at the time that three speeds were sufficient for the broader torque curve of the new 2.7 engines, but the fact was that the Sportomatic's popularity declined even further, despite now being a no-cost option.

The 1976 Carrera 3.0 used the same 915 gearbox as specified for that year's 2.7 911 and American S.

The 3-litre Carrera's engine was derived from the Turbo's, its designation changing from 911 to 930. The faster-running five-blade cooling fan is the most obvious distinguishing feature of these cars.

ELECTRICAL EQUIPMENT & LIGHTING

Because of the location of the new bumpers, a single 66Ah battery replaced the twin batteries of previous models. This was located in the front left-hand side of the luggage compartment, ahead of the front wheel. The alternator changed to a 55A/770-watt unit. The new impact bumpers also meant revisions to the sidelights, indicators, rear tail lights and number plate lights. Electric windows were listed as a factory option, but several markets (including the UK) specified them as standard.

In 1975 the alternator was upgraded to 70A/980 watt to handle the increasing amount of electrical equipment – especially the new constant-running heater system fan.

SUSPENSION & STEERING

On the 911 and 911S, a 16mm front anti-roll bar was standard and made to a simpler design than before; the Carrera front anti-roll bar was stiffer at 20mm. When the Carrera's 18mm rear anti-roll bar was fitted as an option to the 911 or 911S instead of the standard 16mm item, the front bar was also uprated to 20mm on these more basic models to maintain an understeering tendency. The Carrera was fitted with Bilstein gas-filled shock absorbers all round.

The main change at the rear was the move to forged aluminium alloy semi-trailing arms. These new 'bananas' were 3.5kg (7.7lb) lighter than the original fabricated steel items and were also considerably stiffer. At the same time a stronger rear wheel bearing was incorporated into the arm design.

In 1976 the standard 911 front struts were angled inwards slightly more to improve camber adjustment. In 1977 the sheet steel rear spring plates were made in two pieces, clamped together by eccentric bolts to allow easier – but not easy! – adjustment of the rear ride height. The new Carrera 3.0 suspension used the same anti-roll bar sizes as the outgoing 2.7 Carrera, but the torsion bar diameter increased to 19mm at the front and 23mm at the rear. Among the options available for the 3-litre Carrera (but standard in the UK's Sport package) were Bilstein shock absorbers to give a firmer ride.

BRAKES

There were no significant changes to the brakes for the 1974 or 1975 model years, except that the pedal was made slightly longer to reduce effort. The standard 911 and 911S used the M-type caliper front and rear (of 52.5sq cm swept area), whereas the Carrera used S-type aluminium calipers on the front (of 78sq cm swept area). In 1976, the standard 911 received cast iron A-type calipers (also of 78sq cm swept area). The A-type caliper, derived from the earlier S-type, was stronger and narrower in section than the previous M-type, and earned its designation because it had been developed under contract for Alfa Romeo.

The 1977 model year saw the introduction of a brake servo on the Sportomatic 911. This was a major improvement in driveability and made the car more attractive to those who were not endowed like Tarzan, but much of the feel provided by the original heavy pedal was lost.

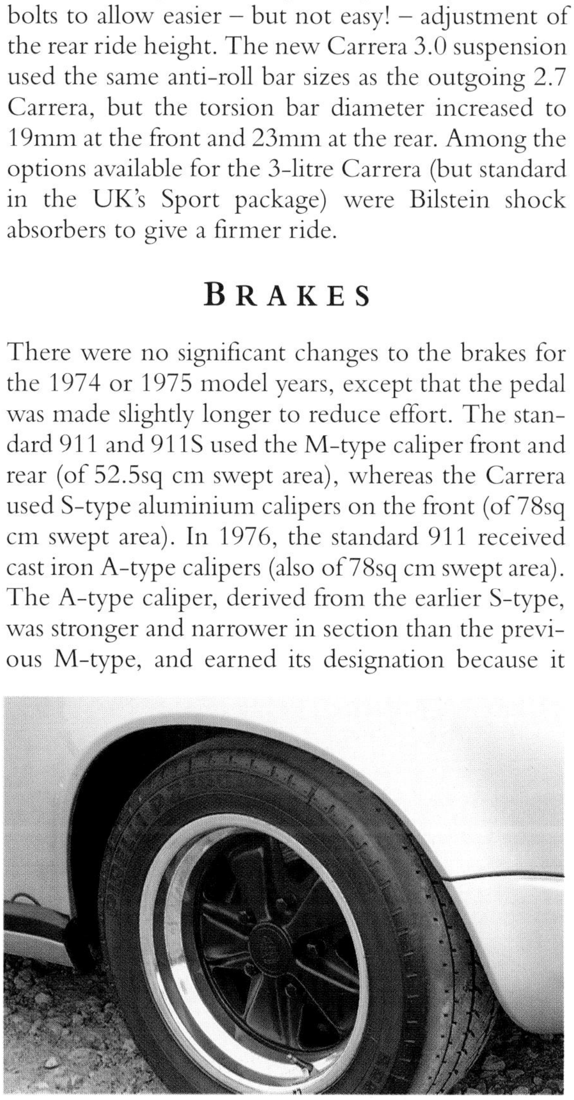

By 1975, the Fuchs forged alloy wheel had become the required fitting. From the early narrow examples, changes had centred on increasing the wheel width and improving the finish of the rim. The RS had introduced different front/rear wheel sizes, and this practice was carried over to the later 2.7 Carreras. This is a rear 7J x 15 wheel with a non-standard 225/50 tyre.

WHEELS & TYRES

For 1974 in the US, the standard wheels for the 911 were still in steel, size 5.5J × 15 with 165/70HR tyres. For most other markets the cast alloy ATS 'cookie-cutter' wheels were specified. The S used the 6J × 15 ATS wheels with 185/70VR tyres while the Carrera sported the now-classic Fuchs five-spoke alloy wheels of 6J × 15 at the front (with 185/70VR tyres) and 7J × 15 (with 215/60VR tyres) at the rear. The spare for all models (except the UK) was the Goodrich Space-Saver. This was naturally much narrower than the tyres on the car and its use was limited to low-speed 'get-you-home-only' mode – and if the car was full of luggage there was nowhere to put a dirty flat tyre.

New bumper height rules in the US prevented the use of 50-series tyres on the new 911s, although these were an option on the 1976 Carrera 3.0 in Europe. A 1977 option list defined a comfort pack for that year's 911s. This included softer Bilstein shock absorbers (Boges were standard) and 14in Fuchs forged alloy wheels with Uniroyal 185HR Rallye tyres. Curiously, these tyres were not rated for speeds above 130mph so the engine was governed to that maximum. In the US the comfort pack came with cruise control and electric windows.

SILVER ANNIVERSARY MODEL

A total of 1063 silver anniversary 911s were made in coupé and Targa form during the 1975 model year to celebrate 25 years of Porsche sports car manufacture. Production was split as follows: 154 'Rest of the World' coupés, 150 'Rest of the World' Targas, 510 US coupés and 249 US Targas. The anniversary models were customised 911 and 911S models.

Grouped as the option M426, the following individual options enhanced the standard car's specification: two-stage heated rear window (M102), headlamp washers (M288), Blaupunkt Bamberg radio (M422), electric antenna (M461), pressure cast 6in wheels (M458), 18mm rear anti-roll bar (M404), 'black-look' trim (M496), 380mm diameter sports steering wheel (M565) and a five-speed gearbox (M481). The cars were finished in a special diamond silver metallic paint finish. Each car carried a '*25 Jahre Fahren in seiner schönsten Form*' plaque on the dash.

Data Section

PRODUCTION CHANGES

Aug 1973 (START OF G-PROGRAMME)
Impact bumpers front and rear with integrated sidelights and indicators, new fenders, new reflective strip under engine lid; 'Porsche' logo moved from rear lid to reflector strip; side sills extended; black-look trim for Carrera (with ducktail and lettering in US); Carrera available in coupé or Targa form; wide rubbing strips face bumpers front and rear with two large elastomer overriders at rear (including number plate lamps); new seats with integral head restraints, side window demist vents on dash and inertia reel seat belts standard in all markets; top entry storage bins in doors; new 400mm four-spoke steering wheel; chrome disc removed from centre of restyled instruments; restyled indicator stalk; electronic rev counter and quartz clock fitted; soft knobs on centre dash; 80-litre steel fuel tank (although some markets used the plastic version) and Goodrich Space-Saver tyre; new hard Targa top (for cars without air conditioning) with third locating peg on windshield; single 66Ah battery replaces previous twin arrangement; batteries now charged by a 55A/770w alternator; engine size increased to 2687cc with Bosch K-Jetronic injection for standard 911 and 911S, and cast (not forged) pistons (see text for US model differences); transition to Alusil barrels (from Nikasil); new heat exchanger design; 13-litre engine oil capacity (Sporto is 15-litre); valve overlap retarded relative to 1973 2.7 engine and port size on both models reduced; new silencer to fit new bumper design, new heat exchanger design; larger (stainless steel) oil tank allows 12,000-mile service intervals to be introduced; longer ratios (fourth, 0.926; fifth, 0.724) in top two gears for 915 gearbox; new over-centre mechanism for clutch pedal; brake pedal lengthened from 232mm to 250mm to enable lighter action; one-piece front anti-roll bar; towing eye welded to right-hand side wishbone mount; standard 911 and 911S use cast-iron M-type front calipers; 16mm front/rear anti-roll bar on 911 and 911S, 20mm front and 18mm rear on Carrera; forged alloy semi-trailing arms at rear (with larger wheel bearing); standard 911 and 911S use ATS 'cookie-cutter' wheels.

Aug 1974 (START OF H-PROGRAMME)
Extra sound insulation; colour-coded headlamp surrounds for Carreras; new whaletail rear spoiler and front chin spoiler for US Carreras; additional electric fan for heating system with left and right side heater control; noise insulation on engine cam covers; alternator increased to 70A/980w; US 49-state models receive exhaust air pump, California cars have this plus thermal reactors and exhaust gas recirculation (EGR); in US Carrera uses S engine, but S gets tinted glass, five-speed gearbox, intermittent front wipe and heated rear window as standard; steel wheels deleted; high-pressure headlamp washers with 8.5-litre water reservoir introduced for specific markets as an option.

Aug 1975 (START OF I-PROGRAMME)
In Europe, all models receive hot dipped zinc coated steel for all bodyshell parts; Carrera 3.0 introduced with 2994cc Turbo-based 930 engine (weight is 184kg); standard 911 uses previous year's S engine (165bhp) with larger capacity oil pump (weight is 175kg, with magnesium crankcase); five-blade, faster turning (1.8:1) cooling fan; K-Jetronic has automatic cold start enrichment; lower valve covers changed to die-cast aluminium (not magnesium), for better sealing; fuel pump moved to front of car; Sportomatic gearbox drops from four speeds to three; clutch cable strengthened and mounting improved; standard 911 (911 Lux in UK) gets larger (A-type) cast iron calipers; inward angle of front struts increased; cast front suspension cross-member introduced (first seen on RS Carrera and Turbo in 1975); improved door locks; one-piece interior carpet; new door trims; Targa has improved front three-quarter window locking; driver's door mirror now colour-coded, electrically adjustable and heated; more sound insulation; 80-litre fuel

Comparison views of a 1975 2.7 Carrera with body trim in the normal chrome (above) and a 1977 Carrera 3.0 Sport with the 'black-look' and side decals (below).

IDENTIFICATION

Model year	Model	Engine	Gearbox	Chassis numbers	Engine numbers
G-programme					
1974	911	911/92	915/16	9114100001-9114104014	6140001-6146625
	911 Targa	911/92	915/16	9114110001-9114113110	6140001-6146625
	911 Sporto	911/97	925/02	9114110001-9114113110	6149001-6149517
	911S	911/93	915/16	9114300001-9114301359	6340001-6342804
	911S Targa	911/93	915/16	9114310001-9114310898	6340001-6342804
	911S Sporto	911/98	925/02	9114310001-9114310898	6349001-6349236
	Carrera	911/83	915/16	9114600001-9114601036	6640001-6641456
	Carrera Targa	911/83	915/16	9114610001-9114610433	6640001-6641456
	Carrera US	911/93	915/16	9114400001-9114400528	6340001-6342804
	Carrera US Targa	911/93	915/16	9114410001-9114410246	6340001-6342804
	Carrera RS 3.0	911/77	915/08	9114609001-9114609109	6640001-6640200
H-programme					
1975	911	911/41	915/48	9115100001-9115101238	6150001-6152007
	911 Targa	911/41	915/48	9115110001-9115110998	6150001-6152007
	911 Sporto	911/46	925/04	9115110001-9115110998	6159001-6159252
	911S	911/42	915/45	9115300001-9115300385	6350001-6350567
	911S Targa	911/42	915/45	9115310001-9115310266	6350001-6350567
	911S Sporto	911/47	925/04	9115310001-9115310266	6359001-6359105
	911S US49	911/43	915/45	9115200001-9115202310	6450001-6452440
	911S US49 Targa	911/43	915/45	9115210001-9115211517	6450001-6452440
	911S US49 Sporto	911/48	925/04	9115210001-9115211517	6459001-6459135
	911S Cal	911/44	915/45	9115210001-9115211517	6459001-6459135
	911S Cal Targa	911/44	915/45	9115210001-9115211517	6459001-6459135
	911S Cal Sporto	911/49	925/04	9115210001-9115211517	6459001-6459135
	Carrera	911/83	915/16	9115600001-9115600518	6650021-6650712
	Carrera Targa	911/83	915/16	9115610001-9115610197	6650021-6650712
	Carrera US	911/43	915/16	9115400001-9115400395	6450001-6452440
	Carrera US Sporto	911/48	925/04	9115400001-9115400395	6459001-6459135
	Carrera Cal	911/44	915/16	9115400001-9115400395	6450001-6452440
	Carrera Cal Sporto	911/49	925/04	9115400001-9115400395	6459001-6459135
I-programme					
1976	911	911/81	915/49	9116300001-9116301868	6360001-6363029
	911 Targa	911/81	915/49	9116310001-9116311576	6360001-6363029
	911 Sporto	911/86	925/09	9116310001-9116311576	6369001-6369435
	911S US49	911/82	915/44	9116200001-9116202079	6460001-6462305
	911S US49 Targa	911/82	915/44	9116210001-9116212175	6560001-6561837
	911S Cal	911/84	915/44	9116210001-9116212175	6560001-6561837
	911S US Sporto	911/89	925/12	9116210001-9116212175	6569001-6569160
	Carrera 3.0	930/02	915/44	9116600001-9116601093	6660001-6661385
	Carrera 3.0 Targa	930/02	915/44	9116610001-9116610479	6660001-6661385
	Carrera 3.0 Sporto	930/12	925/13	9116610001-9116610479	6669001-6669212
J-programme					
1977	911	911/81	915/60	9117300001-9117302449	6370001-6373531
	911 Targa	911/81	915/60	9117310001-9117311724	6370001-6373531
	911S US	911/85	915/61	9117200001-9117203388	6270001-6276041
	911S US Targa	911/85	915/61	9117210001-9117212747	6270001-6276041
	911S US Sporto	911/90	925/17	9117210001-9117212747	6279001-6279113
	Carrera 3.0	930/02	915/61	9117600001-9117601473	6670001-6671932
	Carrera 3.0 Targa	930/02	915/61	9117610001-9117600646	6670001-6671932
	Carrera 3.0 Sporto	930/12	925/16	9117610001-9117600646	6679001-6679215

General notes

US specification For 1975-76, American specification models are divided into '49-state' cars (US49 above) and California cars (Cal above). For 1977, US cars were all to the same specification. The above listing excludes models specific to the Japanese market, which were delivered with California specification emissions equipment on the 911/41 or 911/42 engines.

Gearboxes For 1974 the five-speed 915 gearbox was known as the 915/06 (with the four-speed being the 915/16). For 1975 the gearbox was variously defined as the 915/48 (four-speed for 911 RoW), 915/43 (five-speed for 911 RoW), 915/45 (four-speed for 911S RoW and US), 915/40 (five-speed for 911S RoW and US, and Carrera US), 915/16 (four-speed for Carrera RoW) or 915/06 (five-speed for Carrera RoW). For 1976 it was 915/44 (five-speed for 911 and 911S US) or 915/49 (four-speed 911 RoW). For 1977 it was 915/60 (five-speed for 911 RoW), 915/65 (four-speed for 911 RoW), 915/61 (four-speed 911S US) or 915/66 (911S for Japan).

tank lead-lined.

Aug 1976 (START OF J-PROGRAMME)

Reduced section middle air deflectors fitted below cylinders for improved cooling; Dilavar cylinder head studs introduced for lower line on late model Carreras and 2.7 engines; higher flow rate fuel pump and fine mesh fuel filters; upgraded K-Jetronic components; supplementary air slide (controlled by a bi-metallic spiral) on intake pipes for numbers 5 and 6 cylinders improves hot starting; first/second gear arm of selector gate baulked on 915 gearbox; booster spring to make clutch operation lighter; two-piece steel spring plates with ride height adjustment; Targas get black-look roll-over hoop; central face-level fresh air/heater vents in top of dash; improved heater controls; carpet on door storage boxes; Targa loses opening three-quarter windows; door buttons disappeared into door as locked, opened with knurled knob; 7in brake servo, auto heat control and pressure headlamp wash standard on Carrera 3.0; new option is Comfort kit which includes 185HR14 tyres on Fuchs wheels, automatic speed governor (to 130mph) and softer gas dampers (in US this included Automatic Speed Control and electric windows); brake servo on Sportomatic models; centre console ahead of gear lever (M590).

DIMENSIONS

Wheelbase
2271mm

Track (front/rear)
911 and 911S, 1360mm/1342mm; Carrera, 1372mm/1354mm

Length
4291mm

Width
911 and 911S, 1610mm; Carrera and Carrera 3, 1652mm

OPTIONS

Factory list dated Aug 1973

Metallic paint and custom colours to order; Sportomatic gearbox; leather upholstery; M058 impact-absorbing dampers for bumpers; M060 additional heater; M197 88Ah battery; M093 external manual passenger door mirror; M102 two-stage rear window heater; M220 limited slip differential (80%); M261 external electric passenger door mirror; M288 high-pressure headlamp washers with 8.5-litre water reservoir; M402 Koni dampers; M404 rear anti-roll bar, 18mm; M405 protective lacquer finish, orange; M406 protective lacquer finish, green; M407/8 front seats raised 26mm left/right; M409 Sports Recaro seats, both; M410 Sports Recaro seat, driver only; M412 front oil cooler; M414 oil pressure and oil level gauges (basic 911 only); M416 leather steering wheel with raised hub; M417 Porsche script on doors, orange; M419 Porsche script on doors, green; M422 Blaupunkt Bamberg stereo; M425 rear window wiper; M427 Carrera script on the doors, gold; M428 protective lacquer finish, gold; M429 fog light, H3 white, rectangular under bumper; M430 fog light, H3 yellow, rectangular under bumper; M432 protective lacquer finish, black; M436 Targa folding roof; M438 Porsche script on doors, gold; M439 Porsche script on doors, black; M440 mechanical antenna (left) with speakers and wiring; M441 electric antenna (right) with speakers and wiring; M443 tinted side/front glass, heated windshield and rear window; M446 chrome trim (Carrera only); M449 Blaupunkt Lübeck stereo; M450 light alloy wheels, black, 6J×15 with 185/70VR15 front tyres and 7J×15 with 215/60VR15 rear tyres (Carrera only); M451 as M450 but in comet diamant metallic; M452 Blaupunkt Frankfurt radio; M454 Blaupunkt Coburg radio; M458 6J×15 light alloy wheels in silver green diamant finish with 185/70VR15 tyres; M459 as M458 but comet diamant metallic; M460 as M458 but grey blue metallic; M461 electric antenna (right) with wiring; M462 Carrera script on doors, black; M468 air compressor for spare wheel; M469 black headlining; M474 Bilstein dampers; M477 6J×15 llight alloy wheels with 185/70VR15 tyres (standard on S); M477 6J×15 front, 7J×15 rear light alloy wheels with 185/70VR15 front, 215/60VR15 rear tyres (Carrera only); M481 five-speed gearbox; M482 engine compartment light; M485 5.5J×15 light alloy wheels with 165HR/15 tyres; M490 mechanical antenna (left) with wiring; M497 self starter; M498 engine lid without model designation;

M559 air conditioning; M567 graduated tint windshield; M568 tinted side and windshield glass for Targa or coupé; M571 rear fog light; M650 electric sliding sunroof; M651 electric window lifters; M652 intermittent windshield wipe; M659 as M429 with rear protection light; M565 sports steering wheel, 380mm.

Factory list dated Sep 1975 (where different from above)

M009 three-speed Sportomatic transmission; M220 limited slip differential (80% or 40%); M392 interior in Scottish tweed; M393/4 turbo decal in black (or white) for rear fender (Turbo only); M395 Pirelli P7 205/50VR15 (front) and 225/50VR15 (rear) tyres; M399 air conditioning; M400 forged alloy wheels, 6J×15 (front and rear) with 185/70VR15 tyres; M401 forged alloy wheels, 7J×15 (front) and 8J×15 (rear) with 185/70VR15 and 215/60VR15 tyres (Carrera only); M403 aluminium trim strip under door; M418 aluminium trim strip around wheelarches; M424 automatic heating control; M454 tempostat speed control; M494 two stereo loudspeakers on the rear shelf; M496 black-look trim with colour-coded headlamp surrounds (standard on Carrera).

COLOUR SCHEMES

1974 (chart 1030,31.14)

Standard body colours

Guards Red (Indischrot, 027), Peru Red (042), Signal Orange (116), Light Yellow (117), Lime Green (Gelbgrün, 137) Orange (156), Mexico Blue (336), Bitter Chocolate (Cockney, 408), Sahara Beige (516), Grand Prix White (908).

Special order body colours

Magenta (Karminrot, 009), Rose Red (Fraise, 024), Aubergine (025), Irish Green (213), Jade Green (Hellgrün, 227), Birch Green (Lichtgrün, 253), Gulf Blue (328), Royal Purple (Flieder, 341), Bahama Blue (Acid, 354), Olive (414), Black (700), Salmon Metallic (036), Emerald Green Metallic (Vipergrün, 249), Ice Green Metallic (Silbergrün Diamant, 250), Metallic Blue (334), Gemini Metallic (335), Gazelle Metallic (Comet Diamant, 406), Copper Brown Metallic (Braunkupferdiamant, 432), Steel Blue Metallic (Graublaudiamant, 631), Silver Metallic (936).

Fabrics

Leatherette light grain (000.551.615.11) in dark red (002), tan (503) or black (709); leatherette light basket weave (999.551.002.41) in dark red (002), tan (503) or black (709); leatherette Roy Flex heavy grain (999.551.001.40) in red (003), blue (301) or black (406); leather (999.551.071.41) in red (002), tan (504) or black (701). 'Madras' check fabrics (999.551.031.40) in reds (000), blues (300) or browns (400). Available as no-cost options were: Shetland seat centre panels (999.551.032.41) in dark red (000), tan (500) or black (700); Tweed seat centre panels (999.551.034.40) in red/white (000), black/white/turquoise (300) or tan (500); and Twill seat side panels (999.551.035.40) in dark red (000), tan (500) or black (700.

Carpets

Nylon velour 430 (999.551.052.40) in red (001), blue/green (301) or tan (402); nylon velour 626 (999.551.051.41) in red (001), tan (501) or black (701); special velour (999.551.061.41) in red (001), tan (501) or black (701).

1975 (chart 1050,51.14)

Standard body colours

Guards Red (Indischrot, 027), Peru Red (042), Light Yellow (117), Lime Green (Gelbgrün, 137), Orange (156), Mexico Blue (336), Bitter Chocolate (Cockney, 408), Sahara Beige (516), Grand Prix White (908).

Special order body colours

Magenta (Karminrot, 009), Rose Red (Fraise, 024), Aubergine (025), Signal Orange (116), Irish Green (213), Jade Green (Hellgrün, 227), Birch Green (Lichtgrün, 253), Gulf Blue (328), Royal Purple (Flieder, 341), Bahama Blue (Acid, 354), Olive (414), Black (700), Salmon Metallic (036), Emerald Green Metallic (249), Ice Green Metallic (250), Metallic Blue (334), Gemini Metallic (335), Gazelle Metallic (406), Copper Brown Metallic (432), Steel Blue Metallic (631, wheels for 25-year model), Silver Metallic (936).

Fabrics

No-grain leatherette (000.551.615.03) in black (713), tan (413) or ivory (513); basket-weave (pierced hole stitched appearance) leatherette (000.551.615.12) in black (713), tan (413) or ivory (513); light-grain leatherette (999.551.001.41) in dark red (002), tan (503) or black (709); leatherette light basket-weave as 1974; leatherette Roy Flex light-grain (999.551.021.40) in red (003), blue (301) or brown (406). Leather, 'Madras' check, twill, Shetland and Tweed as 1974.

Carpets

Perlon 999.551.051.41 (Needle velour 626) in red (001), tan (501) or black (701); nylon velour and special velour as 1974. Velour pile (Carrera only) 999.551.075.41 in yellow (1AG), dark green (2AG), burgundy (4AG), tan (5AG), dark blue/grey (7AG), jubilee car, dark red (8AG) or orange (8AP).

1976 (chart 1080,81.14)

Standard body colours

Guards Red (027), Talbot Yellow (106), Continental Orange (107), Light Yellow (117), Ascot Green (Speedway, 258), Arrow Blue (305), Bitter Chocolate (408), Black (700), Grand Prix White (908).

Special order body colours

Magenta (009), Peru Red (042), Lime Green (137), Irish Green (213), Apple Green (Daphne, 260), Ice Blue (Coppaflorio, 360), Sahara Beige (516), Emerald Green Metallic (264), Oak Green Metallic (265), Ice Green Metallic (Silver Green, 266), Minerva Blue (304), Copper Brown Metallic (443), Silver Metallic (936), Platinum Metallic (944), Sienna Metallic (436). Note: some colours have new codes because of finer bronze powder (eg, Ice Green Metallic changes from 250 to 266); an 'A' suffix to the paint code would indicate an acrylic paint.

Fabrics

Light grain and light basket-weave leatherettes as 1975; leather (999.551.073.40) in orange (1AG), brown (2AG), green (2AP), blue (3AG), dark brown (4AG), tan (5AG), black (7AG), mid brown (8AG), red (8AT) or white (9AG); Twill, Tweed and Shetland as 1974. Tartan dress tweeds (new no-cost option, 999.551.083.40) in red (8AB), green (2AC) or brown/beige (4AD).

Carpets

Velour pile as 1975 Carrera; special velour as 1974.

1977

Standard body colours

Guards Red (027), Talbot Yellow (106), Continental Orange (107), Light Yellow (117), Ascot Green (Speedway, 258), Arrow Blue (305), Bitter Chocolate (408), Black (700), Grand Prix White (908).

Special order body colours

Magenta (009), Peru Red (042), Lime Green (137), Irish Green (213), Apple Green (Daphne, 260), Ice Blue (Copaflorio, 360), Sahara Beige (516), Emerald Green Metallic (264), Oak Green Metallic (265), Ice Green Metallic (Silver Green, 266), Minerva Blue (304), Copper Brown Metallic (443), Silver Metallic (936), Platinum Metallic (944), Sienna Metallic (436).

Fabrics

Heavy-grain leatherette standard (999.551.012.40) in black (7AU), red (8AU) or tan (5AU); leatherette new light basket-weave (999.551.009.40) in black (7AT), lobster (8AT) or cork (5AT); leather (999.551.073.40) in gold/yellow (1AG), dark green (2AG), light green (2AP), blue (3AG), dark brown (4AG), cork (5AH), black (7AG), lobster (8AH), light red (8AT) or white (9AG); pin-stripe velour (999.551.039.40), no-cost option in black with white stripes (7AK), lobster with black stripes (8AK) or cork with black stripes (5AK); Tartan dress tweeds as 1976.

Carpets

Velours pile (999.551.092.40) in yellow (1AY), green (2AY), dark brown (4AY), cork (5AZ), black (7AZ), lobster (8AB) or light red (8AZ).

PRODUCTION DATA

Model year	Model	Power (bhp DIN@rpm)	Torque (Nm@rpm)	Compression ratio	Weight (kg)	Number built
1974	911	150@5700	235@3800	8.0:1	1075	4014
	911 Targa	150@5700	235@3800	8.0:1	1125	3110
	911S	175@5800	235@4000	8.5:1	1075	1359
	911S Targa	175@5800	235@4000	8.5:1	1125	898
	Carrera	210@6300	255@5100	8.5:1	1075	1036
	Carrera Targa	210@6300	255@5100	8.5:1	1125	433
	Carrera US	175@5800	235@4000	8.5:1	1075	528
	Carrera RS3.0	230@6200	275@5000	9.8:1	900	59
1975	911	150@5700	235@3800	8.0:1	1075	1238
	911 Targa	150@5700	235@3800	8.0:1	1125	998
	911S	175@5800	235@4000	8.5:1	1075	385
	911S Targa	175@5800	235@4000	8.5:1	1125	266
	911S US49	165@5800	225@4000	8.5:1	1100	2310
	911S US Targa	165@5800	225@4000	8.5:1	1150	1517
	Carrera	210@6300	255@5100	8.5:1	1120	518
	Carrera Targa	210@6300	255@5100	8.5:1	1170	197
	Carrera US	165@5800	225@4000	8.5:1	1100	395
1976	911	165@5800	235@4000	8.5:1	1120	1868
	911 Targa	165@5800	235@4000	8.5:1	1170	1576
	911S US	165@5800	235@4000	8.5:1	1145	2079
	911S US Targa	165@5800	235@4000	8.5:1	1195	2175
	911 Japan	165@5800	235@4000	8.5:1	1195	130
	Carrera 3.0	200@6000	255@4200	8.5:1	1120	1093
	Carrera 3.0 Targa	200@6000	255@4200	8.5:1	1170	479
1977	911	165@5800	235@4000	8.5:1	1075	2449
	911 Targa	165@5800	235@4000	8.5:1	1170	1724
	911S US	165@5800	235@4000	8.5:1	1145	3388
	911S US Targa	165@5800	235@4000	8.5:1	1195	2747
	911S Japan	165@5800	235@4000	8.5:1	1195	383
	Carrera 3.0	200@6000	255@4200	8.5:1	1120	1473
	Carrera 3.0 Targa	200@6000	255@4200	8.5:1	1170	646

THE 911SC (1978-83)

Thirteen years in production would be a significant achievement for any modern car, and by 1977 this was the point the 911 had reached. This was despite the hurdles imposed by the fuel crisis and new US legislation concerning emissions and impact resistance. Yet here was the 911 going from strength to strength. The change to impact bumpers had been a triumph for the stylists at Weissach and, combined with a deliberate move to make the 911 more attractive to the non-enthusiast, a transformation had occurred. The 911 was now a more subtle, refined grand tourer on which you could depend completely.

As the 1970s had progressed, Porsche had deliberately sought not just the enthusiast-drivers who until then had made up the core of its customers, but the company also went looking for a new type of owner. Market research had shown that the profile of the new owner might typically be a small business person, perhaps with a young family, who could justify the 911 as a business tool while enjoying its performance abilities. This new type of driver wanted easier driveability, better reliability and good value for money. The first two factors were achieved, but poor value for money was a recurring comment in contemporary road tests from around the world. The factory argued – and still does – that exclusivity had to be paid for...

As ever, the racing association was a vital selling ingredient. At the end of 1971 the mighty 917 sports racing cars that had duelled with Ferrari were banned. This had seemed a body blow to the racing department, but it soon picked itself up, dusted down the 917 and turbocharged it for the Can-Am, and set about turning the 911 racer into a world beater in Europe. By 1976, the prototype 936 had won Le Mans with an engine derived from the 911 and Porsche was back at the top of sports car racing. Once again, to buy a Porsche was to be associated with that success.

After the impact bumpers of 1974, there had been two more stepping stones to what might be termed the ubiquitous production 911 – the 1978 911SC. The first had been the adoption of a fully galvanised

EVOLUTION OUTLINE

Aug 1977	911SC (180bhp) replaces 911, 911S and Carrera (3.0) models; brake servo added; Martini stripes available for SC.
Aug 1979	50-state car introduced in US with three-way catalytic converter and Lambda sensor; power on Rest of World models raised to 188bhp; Sportomatic discontinued; special 'Weissach' model in US.
Aug 1980	Power on Rest of World models raised to 204bhp; small side repeaters on front wings.
Aug 1981	Options now listed on vehicle identification plate.
Mar 1982	Cabriolet launched at Geneva Motor Show.
Oct 1982	Cabriolet production starts (left-hand drive, Germany).

Sue Baker's black 1979 911SC Targa. The 'tea-tray' spoiler, first seen on the Turbo the previous year, was introduced on Targas before coupés, which at this time retained the 'whaletail' spoiler.

This 1980 911SC is the special edition 'Weissach' model sold only in the US, and has been owned from new by Brian Carleton.

bodyshell, an industry-leading development that at last offered longevity over years of exposure to salt-covered winter roads.

The second had been to seek complete reliability. The 2.7 unit had been good, with a broader torque curve than the peaky 2.4, but it had stretched the original design to its limits. Some parts had tended to wear at a higher rate than was expected in a Porsche and the engine ran hot in warmer climates. Although this engine was reliable compared with most others, it did not offer the bullet-proof reliability the engineers were seeking. The new Turbo's 3-litre engine, unblown, offered that potential.

While the Carrera 3.0 had combined power and reliability with improving refinement, the launch of the 911SC in August 1977 extended the refinement still further. The SC was now the only normally-aspirated 911 available, replacing the 911S in the US and the Carrera and the 2.7 in Rest of the World markets. For Americans the SC offered a useful extra 15bhp over the 911S, but for all other buyers power fell from the Carrera's healthy 200bhp to 180bhp. However, the engineers had worked to achieve a flatter torque curve, thus increasing the appeal of the car to that much-sought new type of customer. The new buyer probably would not have noticed new details like the brake servo (fitted for the first time across the range), which greatly improved driveability around town and reduced pedal effort when the brakes were cold.

The SC was Porsche's first attempt at a 'world' car, for an exhaust emission air pump was fitted even to European models. Hardened 911 enthusiasts, who also grumbled about the new 'soft' brakes having lost their feel, soon had these air pumps decorating their garage walls...

The SC used the same mechanical components as the Carrera 3.0 and kept the attractive flared rear wheelarches. Outright performance was not much changed by the loss of 20bhp, but the effect of advancing the timing of the same camshafts by just six degrees allowed the SC to pull confidently from surprisingly low revs – a feature of the 911 that has remained ever since. The problem for enthusiasts was that as the 911's appeal was broadened to a wider market, it was losing power (in Europe at least) *and* putting on weight. The SC's increase in kerb weight to 1160kg (2558lb) ensured that it was not the best performer among 911s. And with the addition of items like electric windows, an electric sunroof and, from 1980 especially, air conditioning in the US, weight continued to rise.

The 911 was due for replacement in the early 1980s, but demand continued strongly with the SC outselling its declared successor, the 928, by nearly 50 per cent. Power improvements hurriedly introduced in 1980 (not for the US) and 1981 (this time including the US) were intended to give the car new life in its twilight years by addressing criticisms that it was becoming middle-aged and, with all the weight, slower. To be fair, these power rises were accompanied by useful improvements in fuel consumption, even if the 1981 204bhp 'world' model reverted to using premium 97 RON fuel. By 1981, however, the factory had changed its mind over the future of the 911 and with this new direction the SC

Peter Foskett's 1982 911SC is a UK Sport model, recognisable by its front and rear spoilers and black-finished wheels. The flush-mounted headlamp washers were introduced for 1980, while the side repeaters are the mark of a post-1981 model.

The black-finished Targa hoop was attractively accented by gold 'Targa' script. Even the beading in the window trim was darkened.

began to re-discover some of the aggressiveness that had been lost with the Carrera 3.0.

The British weekly newspaper *Motoring News* tried one of the new 204bhp SCs in December 1980. Its comments are interesting and showed where the 911 was at the start of the decade: 'The 924 and 928 should have marked the death of this 15-year-old model. However, this 1960s design remains in production...I'm sure the 911 is still THE Porsche...as yet the 924 and 928 lack the charisma.'

Bodyshell

The 1978 models were known as the K-programme and bodily were largely unchanged from the previous year, except for colour variations. The SC kept the flared rear wheelarches from the Carrera, while the SC Targa lost the opening front quarter-lights that had been unique to this model.

The internal factory 'programme' designation changed for the 1980 model year. Since the original

O-programme cars of 1964 would be followed by another potential O-programme of the same car 16 years later, a change was necessary to prevent duplication and possible confusion. It coincided with the adoption of a new chassis numbering system, which came about as a result of new European Community and US legislation requiring that the chassis should be identifiable on a worldwide basis for a period of 30 years by a 17-digit number. Starting in 1980, a preliminary 10-digit system was used across all Porsche models, not just the 911. The following year the full international 17-digit Vehicle Identification Number (VIN) was used. For an explanation of the new numbers, see the data tables (page 77).

A concept car called the 'Studie' was revealed on the Porsche stand at the Frankfurt Motor Show in 1981. This was a four-wheel drive 911 with a cabriolet body. So strong was the reaction that by the following March's Geneva Motor Show a prototype 911SC Cabriolet was shown, with the press being allowed rides in pre-production cars through the summer of 1982. Production models started to be delivered in Germany in October 1982, with most other markets (including right-hand drive ones) receiving theirs from February 1983.

Surprisingly, the Cabrio required few structural stiffening changes to the basic building block – the Targa bodyshell. Stripped of the Targa's roll-over hoop, production Cabrios were claimed to equal the coupé's weight by being about 14kg (31lb) lighter than the Targa, but the reality was that both open models weighed about the same. Mounted on a light alloy hood frame, the hood material was a three-layer sandwich comprising a tough polyester/polyacrylic surface, a middle insulating layer and waterproof soft cotton lining. The hood had a detachable rear screen to allow covered but ventilated motoring, but an optional heated panel could replace the plastic screen. The hood was manually operated as standard (electric operation was a later option) and folded back into a space behind the rear seats; a roll-over bar was also an option.

The Cabrio's windshield was left at the existing model's rake angle in preference to the lower roof line of the Speedster model that the engineers also proposed at the time. The Cabrio's launch turned out to be the beginning of the end for the Targa model: in the early 1980s sales of Targas had virtually matched those of the coupé, especially in the US, but as Cabrio production increased so Targa production decreased. The Targa took a long time to die, however, finally being deleted in 1993.

BODY TRIM & FITTINGS

The SC came with chrome trim as standard, but the black look option (M496) first seen on the 2.7 Carrera was growing in popularity.

US models with impact bumpers had an extra indicator lens in each side of the front bumper moulding. This 'Weissach' model also shows off its additional driving lights below the bumper.

Unleaded fuel only for US 911s. Californian cars had their previous two-way catalytic converters replaced with more effective three-way systems in 1980.

The usual comprehensive range of other factory options was offered for the SC in all markets. In the larger markets, importers would often group a collection of options together to make life easier for their customers. Typical of these was the Sport package offered to UK customers. These models were identified by an all-elastomer whaletail, front spoiler chin extension, Bilstein gas dampers and forged alloy 16in wheels with Pirelli's new low-profile P7 tyres. Inside the driver and passenger were held firmly in place by sports seats and what the press handout called 'a high quality stereo cassette/radio player with electric aerial'.

The 1980 models had the black-look as standard on the coupé and the Targa (including the roll-over hoop). This also meant the headlamp surrounds were colour-coded to the body. The protruding headlamp washers were replaced with units that were flush-fitting to the top of the bumper surface. In 1981 side repeaters were fitted to the front wings – a good way of spotting the later 204bhp models.

In September 1981, a revised and more elegant form of rear spoiler structure was fitted to the SC, with a large flat central cooling grille as on the Turbo, but cut back on the underside.

On the new Cabrio, both driver and passenger door mirrors were standard. From the 1982 model year the options fitted to a particular model could now be found (by M code) on the vehicle identification plate.

First used in series production on the 1975 Carrera, the 'whaletail' spoiler changed in detail on the 911SC. At first the most noticeable difference was a deeper black flexible part of the assembly (right), but further revisions for 1982 meant that the centre section was built up on its top surface, like the Turbo version, and the underside was cut back (far right).

The seating of this 'Weissach' model is full leather in Doric Grey with Burgundy piping. The Burgundy theme extends to the door pockets and carpeting. Note the modest speedometer calibration – a new dial for US cars arrived for the 1980 model year and read to only 85mph!

INTERIOR TRIM

The smart interior choice of pinstripe as well as the popular tartan schemes were carried over from the Carrera 3.0, but into the 1980s Porsche became much more adventurous with its interior fabrics. For 1980 came a wavy check upholstery style called Pascha, probably one of the more controversial Porsche fabrics that had been first seen on the 928 – you either loved it or hated it. The following year the more conservative Berber fabric was introduced.

Until the 1980 model year the steering wheel diameter had been 400mm (15.6in) except for the 380mm (14.8in) wheel used on the 2.7 Carrera and the Turbo, but from August 1979 the 380mm three-spoke wheel was transferred to the SC. This attracted some criticism from road testers as it was now more difficult to read the speedometer – quite important in a 911!

For 1980, the folding rear seats were upholstered in the same cloth material as the front seats. A centre console, first seen on the Turbo, now kept cas-

Smart Berber upholstery was introduced for 1981. The plaque on the glove compartment lid indicates that this car has been a Porsche Club GB concours competitor.

settes and oddments tidy. For the 1982 models the heater control was revised to improve warmth at low engine speeds, and on 1983 models the over-ride lever for the heater (positioned between the seats) was deleted.

On the new 1983 Cabrio model the automatic heater control, standard on most 911s, was replaced by a manual system because the automatic system could become confused during open air motoring. The rear seat backs were reduced in height by 125mm (4.9in), and the Cabrio was unique in having leather seats as standard.

DASHBOARD & INSTRUMENTS

The introduction of an oxygen sensor in 1980 for US models resulted in an 'OXS' warning lamp appearing on the upper dash between the rev counter and the speedometer. This would light when sensor replacement was due at 30,000 miles. As with the Carrera 3.0 and the 2.7s, the SC was equipped with a 7000rpm rev counter.

LUGGAGE COMPARTMENT

The new brake servo and fluid reservoir fitted from 1978 reduced the space in the rear area of the front compartment. In 1981, the engine compartment received a light.

ENGINE

The SC used the Turbo-based 930 engine of 2994cc (182.63cu in) that had been developed for the European Carrera 3.0. The extra capacity was achieved by increasing the bore size from 90mm (3.5in) to 95mm (3.71in). Stroke remained at 70.4mm (2.75in) although a new crankshaft with larger main and con rod bearings was used. The crankcase was made from die-cast aluminium, whereas between 1968-77 it had been magnesium. The SC continued the use of Nikasil for the cylinder barrels. Milder camshafts pushed up the maximum torque and improved the engine's flexibility.

The cooling fan reverted to an 11-blade item that was smaller at 226mm (8.8in) than the previous five-blade fan, although it ran at the same 1.8:1 speed. A new capacitor discharge and contactless system was introduced for the ignition – this system can be recognised because the distributor rotor turns anti-clockwise. A dual vacuum advance and retard was standard on US cars from 1980.

Camshaft chain noise was reduced by fitting new, taller, black-coloured chain guides in five of the six positions, the previous brown guide still being used in the lower right-hand position. The reliability of the cam drive was improved again in 1980, when a new timing chain tensioner idler arm was introduced to ease the workload of the tensioner. Porsche studies had found that a proportion of the unexpected

The instrument panel of the SC was little changed from the European Carrera 3.0. Points to note are the 380mm steering wheel (which obscured important sections of the speedometer) and the rocker switch for the headlamp washers sited between the speedometer and the clock.

A busy engine compartment on this Californian-specification 1980 911SC, with the air conditioning compressor (and revised condensor coil) on the right. This was the first year the SC was not fitted with an air injection pump: this was replaced by a sensor that measured the oxygen in the exhaust and was linked to the fuel injection system.

'Rest of the World' models retained the air injection pump, seen here on the left of this 1982 engine compartment. The air filter for the pump can be seen behind it, with a red wing nut on top. After a brief period when a five-blade cooling fan had been used, the SC returned to an 11-blade version. This fan and many of the fittings around the engine have been highly polished, to good effect.

tensioner failures had been due to idler arms seizing on their shafts, so the arm was modified to include a wider double bush. The modified arm needed more space to operate in, so the tensioner body itself was slimmed down (but the internal mechanics remained the same). This improved timing chain tensioner reliability, but the engineers still had not eliminated this notorious problem. A once-and-for-all solution was still a few years away...

The front wing oil cooler was revised for most markets in 1980 with the use of a finned brass tube unit that improved heat dissipation. US models retained the older coiled pipe type of cooler until the 1983 models.

The first SCs were fitted with an air injection pump, which did nothing for access to the left-hand spark plugs. The pump was driven from the crankshaft pulley and was fitted for all markets. Its output was controlled by a diverter valve which vented the pump to the atmosphere in conditions of low intake vacuum. The continued efforts of the Environmental Protection Agency in the US also led to the introduction for that market of a new two-way catalytic converter in place of the transverse silencer or muffler. Californian cars continued to require Exhaust Gas Recirculation (EGR). The two-way converter was replaced in 1980 by a three-way unit and, combined with a new oxygen sensor linked to the fuel injection system, eliminated the need for the air injection pump – and the pump was soon dropped on European models as well. A Lambda sensor accurately measured the oxygen content of the exhaust and then adjusted the injection to provide the correct fuel/air mixture to suit the load conditions.

US models also used a simplified fuel evaporative control system, without a line from the charcoal filter to the fan housing. From 1977, engine fumes were piped back from the crankcase directly to the oil tank instead of into the air cleaner as on earlier models. Another pipe connected the oil tank breather to the ribbed throttle housing upstream of the air flow sensor.

The 1980 engines were 'optimised', to use the factory's description. The improvements that led to

By 1979, when this car was built, the two-pedal Sportomatic transmission was available only on special order. This novel but half-way house automatic shift was deleted the following year.

an extra 8bhp in Rest of the World markets were revised ignition and camshaft timing, a tightening of design tolerances in certain areas of the engine, and an increase in compression ratio to 8.6:1. As well as more power, there was a claimed 10 per cent improvement in fuel consumption.

In the US, power was held at 180bhp in 1980, but the compression ratio was increased to 9.3:1 and, combined with the ignition timing improvements, the effect was to make the new model American SCs more flexible and lively.

In January 1981, the power deficiency of emissions-equipped SCs widened when Rest of the World cars received yet another output rise. The engine was uprated to 204bhp, but fuel consumption improved still further. On 1982 and '83 models the engine changes were minor: the camshaft sprockets were attached to the cams by bolts rather than nuts and for the US the oxygen sensor was upgraded.

Transmission

The 915 five-speed gearbox became standard for all markets on the introduction of the SC. It differed from the transmission in the Carrera by having even taller ratios, to take advantage of the flatter torque curve and to benefit emissions by reducing engine speed. A new design of clutch hub with a rubber centre overcame low-speed gear chatter. This would, in time, prove to be more trouble than it was worth, as the rubber centre tended to part with the rest of the clutch. Clutch adjustment was simplified on the SC and a new transmission mounting for the linkage overcame some reliability problems found with the earlier design.

Sportomatic was now offered only as a special order, but its popularity was waning and the stick shift semi-automatic was deleted altogether after the 1979 model year.

The addition of a brake servo was a significant improvement for the 911SC. Its effect was most noticeable around town when the discs were cold. The bulk of the assembly seriously reduced the usefulness of the luggage compartment.

Electrical Equipment & Lighting

On 1978 US models, a 770-watt alternator charged a single 66Ah battery, but for the 1979 model year the alternator became the 980-watt unit that was already in use on Rest of the World Cars. In 1982, the alternator received an integrated voltage regulator and output went up to 1050 watts for all markets.

Suspension & Steering

A performance option for the 1978 SC Targa was Bilstein gas shock absorbers, but when these were fitted they tended to accentuate the fact that the Targa had a fairly flexible bodyshell. The following year, in markets where the Bilsteins had been offered as part of a performance package on the Targa, they were replaced by the Boge struts that had been fitted to earlier models.

The 1981 model SCs had slightly stiffened rear suspension with torsion bar size increasing from 23mm to 24mm.

Brakes

The big braking change on the SC was the introduction of a Hydrovac servo, lightening the pedal significantly and making the 911 less attractive to those who wore gold medallions around their necks. The attraction of the servo was that it did not make the brakes ultra-light, but just assisted them. The improvement was most noticeable around town, especially when the big ventilated disc brakes were cold. The disc diameters were now 287mm (11.2in) front and 295mm (11.5in) rear, and the cast iron calipers were the A-type front and the M-type rear.

Wheels & Tyres

The standard specification for the SC were the ATS 'cookie-cutter' wheels with Dunlop SP Super tyres, sizes being 6J × 15 wheels with 185/70VR tyres at the front and 7J × 15 wheels with 215/60VR tyres at the rear. The UK Sport came with 16in diameter forged alloy Fuchs wheels with Pirelli P7 tyres, sizes being 6J wheels with 205/55VR tyres at the front and 7J wheels with 225/50VR tyres at the rear – these sizes were an option in other markets. The Fuchs wheels of the 1982 models had highly polished rims with black gloss centres.

Special Editions

The 'Martini' model was never actually a mainstream variant of the SC because any 911SC from 1978 could be specified with option number M42, which gave the owner a set of side stripes similar to those first seen on the 1976 British Motor Show 911 Turbo. That car had been a 'special', to celebrate the combined victories in the World Manufacturers' Championship (with the 935) and the World Sports Car Championship (with the 936). It was also the fourth season that the factory racing team had been

'Weissach' models were available in Black Metallic or, as here, Platinum Metallic. The centres of the Fuchs alloy wheels were colour-coded to the body.

supported by the Italian drinks company Martini & Rossi. The stripes proved so popular on the Motor Show Turbo that they were quickly made available as a factory-fit or retro-fit option, usually on cars in Grand Prix White. The numbers shown in the 'Production Data' table (page 78) refer to cars that had M42 applied at the factory.

A total of 408 'Weissach' limited edition models were produced solely for the American market in the 1980 model year. With the option number M439, the standard SC was embellished with special paint – half were in Black Metallic and half in Platinum Metallic. The interior was full leather in Doric Grey with Burgundy piping. Otherwise, the specification was similar to a UK market Sport model, with a flexible lip added to the front air dam and a whaletail rear spoiler added to the rear

Bilstein dampers gave a firmer ride, and special Fuchs wheels with Platinum Metallic centres were used irrespective of body colour. These wheels were fitted with Pirelli CN36 tyres of sizes 185/70VR15 front and 215/60VR15 rear, on 6in and 7in rims respectively. Other decorations included a passenger door mirror, electric sunroof, fog lights below the front bumper and an electric aerial with speakers fitted in the doors and on the rear shelf.

The 911SC 'Ferry Porsche', a special model to celebrate 50 years of the Porsche company, was finished in Meteor (grey with a tint of purple) metallic paint and had a full burgundy leather interior. Other trim was in burgundy/grey striped material with cut-pile velour carpet in burgundy. These models carried a 'Ferry Porsche' autograph on the head restraint area of the seat backs, and were to a high general specification, equipment including a rear wiper, an electric aerial and colour-coded 7J and 8J Fuchs wheels using 185/70VR15 and 215/60VR15 tyres. A total of 200 were built from the start of the 1982 model year.

The paint code plate on the left-hand front door pillar notes the special Platinum Metallic finish of the 'Weissach' model.

Data Section

IDENTIFICATION

Model year	Model	Engine	Gearbox	Chassis numbers	Engine numbers
K-programme					
1978	911SC	930/03	915/44	9118300001-9118302438	6380001 onwards
	911SC Targa	930/03	915/44	9118310001-9118311729	6380001 onwards
	911SC US49	930/04	915/61	9118200001-9118202436	6280001 onwards
	911SC Cal	930/06	915/61	9118200001-9118202436	6580001 onwards
	911SC US49 Targa	930/04	915/61	9118210001-9118212579	6280001 onwards
	911SC Cal Targa	930/06	915/61	9118200001-9118212579	6580001 onwards
	911SC Japan	930/05	915/15	9118309501-9118309804	6180001 onwards
L-programme					
1979	911SC	930/03	915/62	9119300001-9119303318	6390001 onwards
	911SC Targa	930/03	915/62	9119310001-9119311874	6390001 onwards
	911SC US49	930/03	915/63	9119200001-9119202013	6290001 onwards
	911SC Cal	930/06	915/63	9119200001-9119202013	6590001 onwards
	911SC US49 Targa	930/04	915/63	9119210001-9119211965	6290001 onwards
	911SC Cal Targa	930/06	915/63	9119210001-9119211965	6590001 onwards
	911SC Japan	930/05	915/63	9119309501-9119309873	6190001 onwards
A-series					
1980	911SC	930/09	915/62	91A0130001-91A0134831	6300001 onwards
	911SC US	930/07	915/63	91A0140001-91A0144272	6300001 onwards
	911SC Japan	930/08	915/63	91A0130001-91A0134831	6308001 onwards
B-series					
1981	911SC	930/10	915/62	WPOZZZ91ZBS100001-3181	6310001 onwards
	911SC Targa	930/10	915/62	WPOZZZ91ZBS140001-1703	6310001 onwards
	911SC US	930/16	915/63	WPOAA091BS120001-1573	6410001 onwards
	911SC US Targa	930/16	915/63	WPOEA091BS160001-1407	6410001 onwards
	911SC Japan	930/17	930/63	WPOZZZ91ZBS129500-9622	6318001 onwards
	911SC Japan Targa	930/17	930/63	WPOZZZ91ZBS169500-9510	6318001 onwards
C-series					
1982	911SC	930/10	915/62	WPOZZZ91ZCS100001-3307	63C0001 onwards
	911SC Targa	930/10	915/62	WPOZZZ91ZCS140001-1737	63C0001 onwards
	911SC US	930/16	915/63	WPOAA091CS120001-2457	64C0001 onwards
	911SC US Targa	930/16	915/63	WPOEA091CS160001-2426	64C0001 onwards
	911SC Japan	930/17	915/63	WPOZZZ91ZCS109501-9628	63C8001 onwards
	911SC Japan Targa	930/17	915/63	WPOZZZ91ZCS149501-9562	63C8001 onwards
D-series					
1983	911SC	930/10	915/62	WPOZZZ91ZDS100001-2995	63D0001 onwards
	911SC Targa	930/10	915/62	WPOZZZ91ZDS140001-1258	63D0001 onwards
	911SC Cabriolet	930/10	915/62	WPOZZZ91ZDS150001-2406	63D0001 onwards
	911SC US	930/16	915/63	WPOAA091DS120001-2559	64D0001 onwards
	911SC US Targa	930/16	915/63	WPOEA091DS160001-1430	64D0001 onwards
	911SC Cabriolet	930/16	915/63	WPOEA091DS170001-1718	64D0001 onwards
	911SC Japan	930/17	915/63	WPOZZZ91ZDS109501-9645	63D8001 onwards
	911SC Japan Targa	930/17	915/63	WPOZZZ91ZDS149501-9562	63D8001 onwards

General notes

Chassis numbering 1980 chassis numbers were to a new 10-digit formula: the first two digits were the model type, the third the model year (A is 1980, B is 1981, etc), the fourth the plant code (0 is non-descriptive on 1980-only models), the fifth the last digit of the model type (1 for 911, 0 for 930), the sixth the engine code number (eg, 3 for RoW 3-litre, 4 for US 3-litre, 7 for 930 RoW 3.3-litre, etc) and the last four digits were the build number. For the 1981 model year, the 17-digit VIN system was started. For instance, consider WPOZZZ91ZBS100001: WPO is the world make code. ZZZ is the US VSD code, 91 is the first two digits of the model number (911), Z is a test number, B refers to the model year (B=1981), S refers to the plant code (for Stuttgart), the next digit is the third of the model type (911), followed by the body code number, the last four digits are the build number. Model years are identified as follows: A 1980, B 1981, C 1982, D 1983, E 1984, F 1985, G 1986, H 1987, J 1988, K 1989, L 1990, M 1991, N 1992, P 1993 (note no 'O'), R 1994, etc.

1980 models For this model year coupés and Targas shared the same chassis number series, but defined between RoW (including Japan) and the US.

US specification For 1978-79, US specification models are divided into '49-state' cars (US49 above) and California cars (Cal above). For 1980, there was just a single US specification. For 1981-83, cars for Canada also shared US specification.

Japanese specification Japan had its own engine type with specific exhaust emissions equipment: 1978-79, 930/05; 1980, 930/08; 1981-83, 930/17.

Sportomatic Engine codes for this transmission were as follows: for 1978-79, RoW 930/13, US 930/14, Japan 930/15; for 1980, engine was always 930/19; a '9' as the fourth digit of the engine number denotes special mountings for the Sportomatic. Gearbox type was 925/16. Not listed after 1980.

PRODUCTION CHANGES

Aug 1977 START OF K-PROGRAMME
911SC introduced with 3-litre 930 engine of 2994cc (bore 95mm, stroke 70.4mm); valves 49mm inlet, 41.5mm exhaust; ports are 39mm and 35mm respectively for all markets; softer cams, new crankshaft with larger main and con rod bearings; die-cast aluminium crankcase; Nikasil barrels; new camshafts; 11-blade 226mm diameter cooling fan, running at 1.8:1 speed; new capacitor discharge and contactless ignition; runs on 91 RON fuel and all models have air injection pump; Hydrovac 7in brake servo introduced; front anti-roll bar 20mm, rear 18mm; rear torsion bar now 24mm instead of 23mm; clutch pedal spring assistance improved again; rubber torsion damper in centre of clutch reduces transmission noise at low speed; 7000rpm rev counter fitted; front opening window vents deleted from Targa; in UK, SC Sport model given following extras – front and rear spoilers, 6J front and 7J rear Fuchs wheels with 205/55VR16 and 225/50VR16 tyres, sports seats, uprated shock absorbers, Porsche stereo with electric aerial; M42 option specified Martini stripes.

Aug 1978 (START OF L-PROGRAMME)
No major changes from K-programme except for colours, fabrics and carpets. Gear ratios (915/44) – first 0.314, second 0.546, third 0.793, fourth 1.000, fifth 1.217, reverse 0.301, final drive 0.571. Sportomatic ratios (925/09 or 12 or 13) first 0.407, second 0.700, third 1.080, reverse 0.553, final drive 0.296.

Aug 1979 (START OF NEW A-SERIES)
Centre console becomes standard; new checkerboard Pascha upholstery available; UK models have Panasonic stereo and electric aerial as standard; in US many previous options made standard and include air conditioning, power windows, black-look window trim, leather-covered 380mm three-spoke steering wheel; 911SC becomes a '50-state' car in US with three-way catalytic converter and Lambda sensor meaning EGR is shelved; US models go to 9.3:1 compression ratio, vacuum advance and retard distributors, and have a new suction venturi attachment to the oil pump (with mesh filter) to assist oil scavenging in the crankcase; US models have an 85mph speedo; flush-fitting headlamp washers introduced; Sportomatic discontinued; new design of brass tube oil cooler in front wing for RoW but US models keep serpentine type cooler; automatic light for engine compartment; clutch pedal pressure reduced (improved mechanism); new timing chain idler arm and slimmer body to sealed tensioner unit, and all models receive stiffer lower valve covers with horizontal double ribs; longer fifth gear (from 1.217 to 1.273) in gearbox (becomes 915/62) for RoW models; cylinder head inlet port size drops to 34mm, exhaust to 35mm (all models); special model finished in pewter metallic paint with doric grey leather interior and russet cut pile carpets, known in US as 'Weissach' special edition and receives whaletail and extension spoiler at front, sport dampers, etc; alarm is offered for first time as a special option.

Aug 1980 (START OF B-SERIES)
New Berber tweed upholstery, rear seats cloth-fronted; double-peak domed pistons raise compression ratio to 9.8:1 on RoW models, power rises to 204bhp, torque unchanged; Bosch K-Jetronic fuel injection improved (capsule valve for better snap throttle opening and new cold-start injector spray added to air box); non-adjustable fuel distributor on US models, with improved cold running mixture control; now uses 97 RON fuel (not 91 RON) and braided fuel lines replaced by seamless steel tubes; gearing raised slightly in fifth (0.796 from 0.821); improved diaphragm springs fitted to clutch; side repeater flashers on front wings; improved sports seats optional; anti-corrosion warranty increased to seven years; 915 transmission casing now pressure die-cast in aluminium; US models' anti-roll bars now of 20mm front, 18mm rear.

Aug 1981 (START OF C-SERIES)
Special 'Ferry Porsche' model finished in meteor metallic (grey with a tint of purple) with burgundy leather, burgundy/grey striped material and cut pile velour carpet in burgundy; camshaft sprockets fastened with a hex bolt instead of a hex nut; alternator has integrated voltage regulation and rises to 1050W output; options include the front and rear (tea-tray) spoilers of the 911 Turbo.

PRODUCTION DATA

Model year	Model	Power (bhp DIN@rpm)	Torque (Nm@rpm)	Compression ratio	Weight (kg)	Number built
1978	911SC	180@5500	265@4200	8.5:1	1160	2438
	911SC Targa	180@5500	265@4200	8.5:1	1210	1729
	911SC US	180@5500	237@4200	8.5:1	1190	2436
	911SC US Targa	180@5500	237@4200	8.5:1	1240	2579
	911SC Japan	180@5500	237@4200	8.5:1	1190	304
1979	911SC	180@5500	265@4200	8.5:1	1160	3319
	911SC Targa	180@5500	265@4200	8.5:1	1210	3319
	911SC US	180@5500	237@4200	8.5:1	1190	2013
	911SC US Targa	180@5500	237@4200	8.5:1	1240	1965
	911SC Japan	180@5500	237@4200	8.5:1	1190	373
1980	911SC	188@5500	265@4200	8.6:1	1160	4831
	911SC US	180@5500	244@4200	9.3:1	1190	4272
	911SC 'Weissach' US[1]	180@5500	244@4200	9.3:1	1250	408
1981	911SC	204@5900	267@4300	9.8:1	1160	3181
	911SC Targa	204@5900	267@4300	9.8:1	1210	1703
	911SC US	180@5500	244@4200	9.3:1	1190	1573
	911SC US Targa	180@5500	244@4200	9.3:1	1240	1407
	911SC Japan	180@5500	244@4200	9.3:1	1190	132
1982	911SC	204@5900	267@4300	9.8:1	1160	3307
	911SC Targa	204@5900	267@4300	9.8:1	1210	1737
	911SC US	180@5500	244@4200	9.3:1	1190	2457
	911SC US Targa	180@5500	244@4200	9.3:1	1240	2426
	911SC Japan	180@5500	244@4200	9.3:1	1190	190
	Slant-Nose[2]	180@5500	244@4200	9.3:1	1250	4
1983	911SC	204@5900	267@4300	9.8:1	1160	2995
	911SC Targa	204@5900	267@4300	9.8:1	1210	1258
	911SC Cabriolet	204@5900	267@4300	9.8:1	1210	2406
	911SC US	180@5500	244@4200	9.3:1	1190	2559
	911SC US Targa	180@5500	244@4200	9.3:1	1240	1430
	911SC US Cabriolet	180@5500	244@4200	9.3:1	1240	1781
	911 SC Japan	180@5500	244@4200	9.3:1	1190	207
	Slant nose[2]	180@5500	244@4200	9.3:1	1250	1

General note

Weights are DIN kerb weights, but use as a guide only because some are ex-factory (no options) and some are fully equipped.

Numbered notes

[1] 'Weissach' was option number M439 (see page 76) [2] Slant-Nose models refer to 'stock' 911SCs customised in Sonderwunsch (Restoration) Department, and later to become part of the Porsche Exclusiv programme. The 1982/3 Slant-Nose cars had headlights housed in front spoiler; pop-up lights started to appear in 1983.

The introduction of the SC was marked by a new flat-profile script for the model designation. For the first time since the 911's launch, the style adopted the European style of writing the number 1, with a peak.

This factory label shows that the 911SC was comfortably within Californian emissions limits for hydrocarbons, carbon monoxide and oxides of nitrogen.

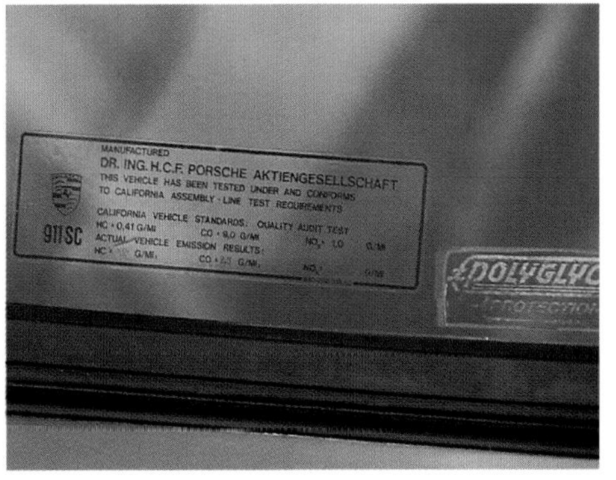

Aug 1982 (START OF D-SERIES)

911 Cabriolet introduced (experimental 'Studie' 4WD cabrio shown at Frankfurt in Sep 1981, European launch at Mar 1982 Geneva Salon), stiffened bodyshell allowing first true open 911; new range of colours and cloths; from Apr 1983, a new stiffer crankcase was used with deleted sump plate and screen and quieter silencer (muffler); heater's manual control deleted; 160mph speedometer standard in all models; lap and diagonal seat belts could be fitted to rear seats; four speakers standard; US/Canada and Japanese models had revised acceleration enrichment controls, an improved Lambda sensor and the brass tube oil cooler first fitted to RoW models from Sep 1979; interesting new options include an electrically heated windshield with graduated tint, Blaupunkt Monterey stereo, 16in wheels with 6in front and 7in rear rims (to take 205 and 225 tyres respectively).

DIMENSIONS

Wheelbase
2271mm
Track (front/rear)
1369mm/1379mm (with standard tyres)
Length
4291mm
Width
1626mm

OPTIONS

Refer to the list of options presented at the end of the chapter on the Carrera 3.2 (see page 90). From 1982 the M numbers were shown on the Vehicle Identification Label (VIL).

COLOUR SCHEMES

1978
Standard body colours
Guards Red (027), Talbot Yellow (106), Continental Orange (107), Apple Green (260), Oak Green Metallic (265), Fern Green (273), Olive Green (274), Light Green Metallic (275), Minerva Blue Metallic (304), Arrow Blue (305), Petrol Blue Metallic (376), Bitter Chocolate (408), Copper Brown Metallic (443), Mocca Brown (451), Cashmire Beige (502), Black (700), Grand Prix White (908), Silver Metallic (936).
Fabrics
Leatherette (999.551.012.40) in Lobster (8AU), Cork (5AU) or Black (7AU); light basket-weave leatherette (999.551.009.40) in Lobster (8AT), Cork (5AT) or Black (7AT); leather (999.551.073.40) in Lobster (8AH), Cork (5AH), Black (7AG), Blue (3AG), Yellow (1AG), Light Green (2AP), Light Red (8AT) or White (9AG); pinstripe velour (999.551.039.40) in Lobster with black stripe (8AK), Cork with black stripe (5AK) or Black with white stripe (7AK); Tartan dress (999.551.083.40) in Beige (4AD), Green (2AC) or Red (8AB).
Carpets
Velour pile (999.551.092.40) in Lobster (8AB), Cork (5AZ), Black (7AZ), Yellow (1AY) or Light Red (8AZ).

1979
Standard body colours
Guards Red (027), Talbot Yellow (106), Oak Green Metallic (265), Olive Green (274), Light Green Metallic (275), Light Blue Metallic (30T), Minerva Blue Metallic (304), Arrow Blue (305), Petrol Blue Metallic (376), Bitter Chocolate (408), Copper Brown Metallic (443), Moccha Brown (451), Casablanca Beige Metallic (Opal, 463), Tobacco Metallic (464), Cashmire Beige (502), Lilac (Flieder, 601), Black (700), Black Metallic (708), Grand Prix White (908), Silver Metallic (936).
Fabrics
Leatherette (BSP) in Brown (40A), Cork (5AU) or Black (7AU); light basket-weave leatherette (999.551.009.40) in Brown (4AT), Cork (5AT) or Black (7AT); leather in blue (3AG), Brown (40A), Dark Green (20B), Yellow (1AG), Light Red (8AT), Cork (5AH), Black (7AG) or White (9AG); pinstripe velour colours as 1978.
Carpets
Cut-pile velour (999.551.098.40) in Brown (4AC), Dark

Green (2AC) Yellow (1AC), Light Red (8AC), Cork (5AC) or Black (7AC).

1980
Standard body colours
As 1979 models
Fabrics
Leatherette in Beige (50B), Brown (40A) or Blue (30B); leather (EHS) in Beige (50B), Brown (40A), Dark Blue (30B), Blue (30A), Dark Green (20B), Yellow (10A), Cork (40D), Light Red (80B), Black (70A) or White (99A); checkerboard velour (TPB) in Beige/Brown (54A), Blue/Black (37A), Brown/Black (47A) or Grey/Black (67A); Tartan dress fabrics as 1978.
Carpets
Cut-pile velour (TFK) in Beige (50B), Brown (40E), Dark Blue (30B), Dark Green (20E), Yellow (10A), Cork (41D), Red (80B) or Black (70E).

1981
Standard body colours
Guards Red (027), Chiffon White (182), Mint Green (20A), Moss Green Metallic (20C), Light Blue Metallic (30T), Pacific Blue Metallic (31G), Minerva Blue Metallic (304), Arrow Blue (305), Mocha Brown (451), Rosewood Metallic (474), Bamboo (523), Caramel (524), Platinum Metallic (for special, 055), Black (700), Black Metallic (708), Wine Red Metallic (895), Grand Prix White (908), Zinc Metallic (956).
Fabrics
Leatherette (BPE) in Beige (50B), Brown (40A), Blue (30B) or Black (70A); leather (EHS) in Beige (50B), Brown (40A), Dark Blue (30B), Red (80S), Hannibal Grey (60S), Papyrus White (95S), Mint Green (20S), Black (70A) or Doric Grey (for special, 6AD); checkerboard velour (TPB) in Beige/Brown (54A), Blue/Black (37A) or Grey/Black (67A); textured cloth (TPU) in Beige (50C), Blue (30C) or Black (70F); Berber tweed (TPB 000 000 00 plus code) in Beige (54B), Blue/Black (37B) or Grey/Black (67B).
Carpets
Cut pile velour (TFK) in Beige (50B), Brown (40E), Dark Blue (30B), Mint Green (20S), Black (70E) or Russet (for special, 8AY).

1982
Standard body colours
As 1981 models but Platinum Metallic (655) now available for all models, plus special model in Meteor Metallic (961).
Fabrics
Leatherette (BPE) in Beige (50B), Brown (87S), Blue (30B) or Black (43S); leather (EHS) in Beige (50B), Brown (3NG), Dark Blue (30B), Red (80S), Hannibal Grey (60S), Papyrus White (95S), Mint Green (20S), Black (1AJ) or Burgundy (for special, 2LB); checkerboard velour, textured cloth and Berber tweeds as 1981 models; special model burgundy/grey stripe design (TPC).
Carpets
As 1981 models, plus cut-pile velour Burgundy (TKF) for special model.

1983
Standard body colours
Guards Red (027), Moss Green Metallic (20C), Glacier Blue (32Z), Pewter Metallic (655), Slate Blue Metallic (661), Quartz Grey Metallic (662), Black (700), Ruby Red Metallic (810), Kiln Red Metallic (811), Grand Prix White (908), Zinc Metallic (956), Light Bronze Metallic (966), Chiffon White (182).
Fabrics
Leatherette (BSP) in Burgundy (3MK), Brown (87S), Blue (30B) or Black (43S); leather (EHS) in Burgundy (7LD), Grey Beige (6FL), Brown (3NG), Black (1AJ), Blue (30B), Red (80S), Pearl White (8YD), Dark Green (6JD) or Champagne (1VD); cloths with wavy stitch pattern (TPU) in Brown (7NU), Blue (30C), Black (70F), Grey Beige (8FU) or Burgundy (5MU); Berber tweeds (TPE) in Beige/Brown (54B), Blue/Black (37B), Grey/Black (67B), Burgundy/Grey (6LB) or Grey-Beige/Grey (1FB); checkerboard velour (TPB) in Light Grey/Black (4FH), Brown/Grey (5RH), Blue/Grey (7GH) or Burgundy/Grey (9LH).
Carpets
Cut-pile velour (TFK) in Light Grey (60A), Brown (40E), Dark Blue (30B), Dark Green (6JD), Black (70E), Grey/Beige (2FL), Red (80S), Burgundy (80E) or Champagne (1VD).

UK Sport specification, seen on Peter Foskett's 1982 911SC, included front spoiler chin extension, 'whale-tail' rear spoiler, Bilstein gas dampers, 16in alloy wheels, Pirelli P7 low-profile tyres and sports seats.

THE CARRERA 3.2 (1984-89)

The late 1970s had seen Porsche shrug off doubts that such a small firm could profitably run three separate and very different product lines for the 911, the 924 and the 928. The company was coming back strongly from yet another world oil crisis and, once again, the racing team was winning, this time with the 911-derived 935. By 1983, the new 956 Group C endurance racing car, also using an engine derived from the 911's flat-six, had won Le Mans at its first attempt. Through the 1980s and into the 1990s the 956 and its derivative, the 962, would become the most successful racing car family ever, still winning 12 years later.

Success on the track combined with the ever-broadening appeal of the 911 – there were now three body styles with the Coupé, the Targa and the new Cabriolet – would lead to Porsche's best ever trading years in the mid-1980s. But it was a time when the company's followers realised that development was slowing. In order to increase production volumes ever higher, engineering staff were working on factory problems as a top priority, and there was relatively little forward thinking about what new models would be required by the end of the decade. Was it a question of make money now and tomorrow would look after itself?

If life at Porsche to the outsider still seemed good early in the decade, inside all was not well. Chief Executive Officer Dr Ernst Fuhrmann was apparently happy to accept a waiting list that stretched to over a year on the basis that exclusivity was still important. It was his view that the 911 was finished and that the future lay with the new 924 and 928 models. Production of 911s had eased from some 45 911SCs per day at Zuffenhausen through 1981, but Fuhrmann's strategy to phase out the 911 and replace it with the 928 was stalling because the 18-year-old 911 was outselling the V8-engined car two to one. It was clear that stopping development of the 911 was out of the question.

Fuhrmann's reluctance to accept that the 911 was still needed in part led to his early retirement at the

EVOLUTION OUTLINE

Aug 1983	Carrera 3.2 (207bhp US, 231bhp Rest of the World) replaces 911SC; engine increased in size to 3.2-litres with Motronic engine management.
Aug 1985	New dashboard with larger side window and central vents; 'Turbo-Look' model launched.
Aug 1986	G50 five-speed gearbox with hydraulic clutch operation; US engines re-mapped for 217bhp; unique Australian Carrera (207bhp) introduced.
Aug 1987	Telephone dial wheels replaced by Fuchs forged alloys.
Sep 1987	Speedster Club Sport study at Frankfurt Show.
Aug 1988	Celebration 911 limited edition.
Jan 1989	Speedster limited edition.

Andy Frost's 1985 model year 3.2 Carrera in Guards Red, probably the most popular Porsche colour of the 1980s, shows off the controversial 'telephone dial' wheels that were the standard fitting until the 1988 model year.

The 1987 Carrera Club Sport was about 50kg lighter than the standard Carrera. Combined with a new engine management chip, this lightness gave slightly better performance. This is photographer John Colley's own car.

end of 1981. He would make way for new blood, something that was seen by the Porsche and Piech families as the only way to revive falling 924 and 928 sales, and save the 911. Only the 911 was selling steadily and that was not enough. A successor had to be found.

Outsiders would have gone for Ferdinand Piech, the brilliant manager who had led the development of the 911 up to the 2.4-litre versions and had been controversially responsible for developing the prototype racers of the late 1960s and early 1970s. By 1980 he was head of engineering at VW-Audi, where he had led Quattro development, and with hindsight he would have been absolutely the right choice for Porsche's new boss. But internal politics got in the way. Piech was part of the family, and the family had stepped out of the day to day running in 1972. They blocked his election and chose Peter Schutz, a German-American head-hunted from a German subsidiary of Caterpillar, the truck maker.

Martini stripes (option M42) on a Grand Prix White 911 made a bold statement about the owner's enthusiasm for the company's racing successes. It was possible to specify the 'Turbo-Look' for the Cabriolet version as a special order from 1984.

Schutz brought a pure market-led management style to Porsche, in contrast to the technology-driven style of his predecessors. For the 911 and for Porsche, this would have excellent short-term business results as volumes started to climb steadily through the first half of the 1980s, for Schutz threw all the profits into upgrading the production facilities, and volumes hit all-time highs. The improvement in production efficiency was desperately needed, but more of the profit should have been spent on development and some of it was wasted on, for instance, over-lavish improvements of staff facilities. Moreover, one of the company's cornerstones of success, exclusivity, was being undermined in a dash for increased volume.

Enthusiast customers, who still made up the core of Porsche business, noted that Porsche's attitude seemed to be to get away with the minimal amount of development needed to justify ever-rising prices. Improvements to the 911 slowed because the engineers were occupied with the limited edition 959 project or were being seconded to production to

The 'Turbo-Look' (above) became a standard Carrera model from 1985. This is Terry Davison's 1987 example. Note the Turbo tea-tray rear spoiler, with its deep underside. The 1989 Speedster (left) – this one is owned by Mike Flannery – offered open-air 911 motoring in a leaner form. The most obvious difference from the standard cabriolet is the lower line of the hood, resulting in changes to the windshield and side windows. The absence of a model designation was a no-cost option.

keep the lines running. But those production lines were producing 911s at a rate never seen before. In 1985, the peak year, some 21,000 of the new 3.2 Carreras were made.

The 911 was now selling to a new type of customer who wanted a Porsche just for its image and who could not care less about anti-roll bar stiffness or maximum torque figures. What the factory could not – or would not – see was that the new breed of customer was fickle. In time, the 'yuppie' tag was virtually to destroy that all important image of sporting purity and exclusivity...

But back in 1982, in his first year as Chairman of Porsche, Schutz immediately set about giving the 911 a boost. He approved the Cabriolet's development, but a four-wheel drive proposal was made a low priority in deference to an agreement between Porsche and VW-Audi (which was developing the Quattro at the same time). Most importantly, Schutz set in motion the engineering work that would lead to the replacement for the 911SC – the 3.2 Carrera – in late 1983. He also realised that the 911 would need a facelift to improve its aerodynamics, but that work was not approved until much later.

'Telephone dial' wheels were one feature of Porsche's attempt to update the Carrera 3.2's appearance without excessive cost. Another external difference was that the front driving lights became more integrated into the shape of the front spoiler.

An enduring feature of the 911 has been that customers could always buy a car that was not covered in aerodynamic hardware. The Carrera script on the engine lid returned to its original style.

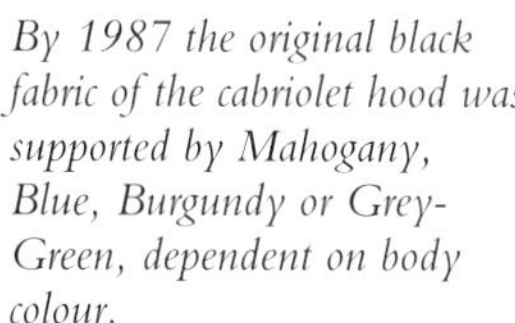

By 1987 the original black fabric of the cabriolet hood was supported by Mahogany, Blue, Burgundy or Grey-Green, dependent on body colour.

The Cabriolet hood stowed neatly under a tonneau. On the Cabriolet the folding rear seats were smaller in order to make room for the hood.

The first public sign of the new development effort was a special 3.3-litre SC that the factory press department used in 1982. But as far back as 1976, 3.5-litre engines had been tested by the engineers at Weissach and subsequently used by development head Helmut Bott as personal transport. The experience was broadened in racing from 1979 when the twin turbo 935 had a capacity of 3164cc – the same as the subsequent production Carrera of 1984.

The revised model was targeted for launch in September 1983 and brought back the hard-worked Carrera name, surrendering again the exclusivity of that title for marketing expediency. The marketing men had come to appreciate the cachet of the name with the 2.7-litre and 3-litre models of the 1970s. The new 1984 model Carrera came out with 3.2-litres, and its engine was the most impressive development on the new 911.

BODYSHELL

There were no major changes in the bodyshell for the 3.2 Carrera, save for detail revisions to improve manufacturing efficiency. This enabled an easy transition of the three bodyshell types – Coupé, Targa and Cabriolet – to the new Carrera specification. The optional 'Turbo-Look' Coupé and Targa followed for 1985.

The guarantee against rust perforation was extended to ten years for 1986. The Cabrio received the long-awaited power hood in September 1986, for the 1987 model year. The operation of this hood was fully automatic, with two small electric motors in the windshield frame locking the front of the hood into place.

The introduction of a larger clutch in 1987 meant that the pick-up points for the rear semi-trailing arms had to be repositioned. This was achieved using a new torsion bar tube, with a profiled cast iron centre section to clear the clutch housing.

Three major new developments of the 911 theme became available during the life of the 3.2 Carrera. These were the Turbo-Look, Club Sport and the Speedster models, all of which are described later in this chapter (see pages 87-89).

BODY TRIM & FITTINGS

The new model received a new front spoiler with integrated fog lamps and was identified by 'Carrera' in script on the engine cover. The new Carrera Targa was given the better-fitting weather seals (with rain channels) for 1987 that had been developed for the Cabrio, to reduce high-speed wind noise. Heater output on all models was improved not only by a new heat exchanger design and a larger main fan, but also by booster fans at each side of the dashboard where the air was drawn from the sills. The air conditioning pump, driven from the end of the crankshaft, was uprated and ran faster.

For the 1985 model year, the radio aerial, previously electrically-operated and fitted to the front wing, became integrated into the windshield and central locking became an option. But if you preferred a conventional aerial, you could separately specify a graduated tint to the top of the windshield or a Securiflex laminated type. The windshield washers were more powerful and were heated. For 1986 central locking became standard, while for 1987 the single rear fog lamp was joined by another

The pinstripe style is one of Porsche's best interiors, being both practical and smart. New features for the 1985 model year, one year after the Carrera 3.2's introduction, included a four-spoke steering wheel, taller seat backrests, and seat release catches on both sides of the backrests.

and both were integrated into the reflective strip between the tail lights; the reversing lights were also integrated into the strip. From September 1987 the passenger door mirror (already standard on the Cabrio) and headlight washers became standard.

Incidentally, in 1987 the Sport package was renamed in the UK and cars became known as the 911 with Sport Equipment (to complement the Turbo-Look or SE). As well as the ubiquitous rear spoiler and front spoiler extension, there were Bilstein shock absorbers and 16in forged alloy wheels with black centres with 205/55 front tyres on 6J wheels and 225/55 rear tyres on 7J wheels. By this stage sports seats were no longer part of the package.

From September 1988, an alarm system was linked to the operation of the central locking circuit and the tempostat heating control system was improved.

INTERIOR TRIM

Leather was a standard fit on the well-equipped US models from 1984. Sport option cars still had special seats with height adjustment, this feature being a no-cost option on the standard cars.

For 1985 there was a new leather steering wheel with four horizontal spokes and the first electrically operated seats, with new switches for height/squab angle and recline. The seat belt buckles were now on the seats themselves and the back rest release catches were fitted on both sides of the seats for the first time. Seat heating was an option. The new seats are identified by the headrests being 40mm (1.6in) taller than those on the earlier seats. For 1985 and 1986 there were successive reductions in gear lever travel of 10 per cent, to make the 911's gearchange more contemporary in feel. Electric height adjustment was an option on sports seats from the 1986 model year, this feature becoming standard for 1988 (with lumbar adjustment as well). Electric operation became

The ventilation system was improved again for the 1986 model year, with larger face level and side window vents. The headlamp level adjustment was introduced for 1987. The non-standard slot next to the sunroof rocker switch is the keyhole for an after-market engine immobiliser.

The seats on the Carrera 3.2 have electric adjustment for height, cushion angle and recline, with this control panel set on the side of the cushion.

became standard on the passenger seat for 1988.

A wider selection of materials was presented for the 1984 model year and extended in 1985. These are listed in the 'Colour Schemes' section at the end of this chapter (page 91).

The interior was changed in detail for the 1986 model year, particularly the seats. The front seats were lowered by 20mm (0.8in) and given extra front-to-back travel. Heating control was improved and a new temperature sensor was mounted on top of the dash instead of between the sun visors. The switchgear was revised and the sun visors were given covered vanity mirrors.

The 25th Anniversary Carreras had special Recaro seats with Dr Porsche's signature monogrammed into the head restraints.

Dashboard & Instruments

There were only detail changes from the 911SC to the Carrera in 1984, one being the addition of a brake pad wear indicator. In 1986, a new dash panel had larger and restyled fresh-air vents and there were new switches and better heat regulation. For 1987, headlamp beam height could be adjusted from the dashboard.

Luggage Compartment

The luggage capacity of a Cabrio could be improved by replacing the rear seats with optional lockers, which also added to security when the hood was down. The fuel tank increased in size from 80 litres (17.60 Imperial gallons, 21.14 US gallons) to 85 litres (18.70 Imperial gallons, 22.46 US gallons) for 1985, and for 1986 the luggage area carpets were colour-coded to match the interior carpets.

Digital Motor Electronics came to the 911 for the 1984 model year, improving performance and reducing fuel consumption by 10 per cent.

Engine

The 3.2-litre production engine was claimed to be 80 per cent new although its basis was still the proven 3-litre assembly, coded 930/20 for Rest of the World models or 930/21 for the US, Canada and Japan. It used the 95mm (3.71in) Nikasil barrels from the SC and the 74.4mm (2.90in) stroke crankshaft from the Turbo, giving a displacement of 3164cc (193.0cu in). The core engine parts were the same for all markets, only the compression ratio and the emissions devices varying – Porsche was moving towards one model for all its markets.

For Rest of the World markets, the compression ratio rose from 9.8:1 to 10.3:1 by using higher crowns to the new forged pistons and a lower roof height for the combustion chamber. For the US, Canada and Japan the compression ratio was 9.5:1. Valves were unchanged from the 911SC, but there were larger port diameters of 40mm (1.56in) inlet and 38mm (1.48in) exhaust, and cam timing was revised. Fuel remained 93 RON for Rest of the World models or lead-free 91 RON for catalysed versions. As on the Turbo, no head gasket was used.

The new 911 Carrera Rest of the World engine's specific power figure of 73bhp/litre was the highest since the 2.7 Carrera RS's 78.2bhp/litre. Overall output was 231bhp at 5900rpm, with maximum torque of 284Nm at 4800rpm. The trade-off for the catalysed engine with its lower compression ratio was 207bhp at 5900rpm and maximum torque of 260Nm at 4800rpm. Australia, Sweden and Switzerland had special engines tuned for low hydrocarbon emissions and low noise.

For the first time on a 911, the ignition, fuel and ambient engine parameters were mapped using a microprocessor control unit. The system also measured engine temperature from a ceramic sensor fitted within the cylinder head. This Digital Motor Electronics (DME or Motronic 2) system was the main reason for power increasing on the 3.2 Carreras, in tandem with a 10 per cent improvement in fuel consumption. This was due in some part to the overrun fuel cut-off, improved cold starting and better cold start stabilisation.

The fuel injection system was now termed by Bosch as LE-Jetronic rather than the previous K-Jetronic. The inlet manifold pipework was redesigned to provide charge-boosting resonance to improve the fuel/air dynamics. The Motronic system also provided protection against over-revving by cutting the fuel injection at precisely 6520rpm, removing the need for a mechanical device in the distributor. Other features of the engine were a more stable idle response to accessory loads and overrun fuel cut-off above 1200rpm. No air injection pump was required – and the engine compartment seemed much less cluttered without it!

New heat exchangers (with silencer or muffler) had larger pipework and more efficient silencing. To reduce heat loss the exchangers were given double-skinned construction. The 930/21 engine for the US, Canadian and Japanese engines was fitted with an improved Lambda sensor and a three-way catalytic converter.

The 3.2 engines were the first to be fitted with the 'mother of all chain-tensioners' – the engine oil-fed hydraulic type. These new tensioners effectively closed the story on the 911's famous weakness. The feed pipes to the tensioners were taken off the external oil supply pipes to each cylinder head bank.

For the 1986 model year, the major engine and transmission parts were guaranteed for five years or 50,000 miles; this will not bother any readers of this book but it shows Porsche's confidence in the powertrain's reliability. Emissions-equipped models received an upgrade in 1987, when the engine (930/25) was re-mapped and 95 RON fuel was specified, taking power up to 217bhp at 5900rpm and torque to 265Nm at 4800bhp. A policy statement at the start of the 1987 model year said that all new models would offer the same power whether or not they were catalysed – by September 1987 85 per cent of new Porsches were delivered with catalytic converters as standard.

TRANSMISSION

The decision not to make the new Carrera engine 3.3-litres, which could have been achieved simply by using the Turbo's barrels as well as its crankshaft, was due to the torque limitations of the 915 gearbox. The transmission's durability was extended by fitting a gearbox oil pump and circulating hot oil through a tube-type cooler mounted beside the casing.

For the 3.2 Carrera, fourth and fifth gears were lengthened, becoming 0.966:1 (28:29) and 0.763:1 (29:38) respectively with a crown wheel/pinion ratio of 8:31. US models used a shorter fifth gear of 0.790:1 (30:38).

In 1987, the 915 was replaced by the Getrag-built G50 five-speed gearbox, with its Borg Warner synchromesh system. The G50 is easily distinguished from the 915 because reverse is to the left and away, whereas on the older gearbox it was to the right and back. The gear lever was revised, becoming more slender. The main reason for the change was that the 915 gearbox was expensive compared to other units, especially now that it needed its own oil cooling system. The G50 gearbox used on the 3.2 Carrera had a maximum torque capacity of 300Nm and did not need separate oil cooling. The clutch was enlarged to the 240mm (9.4in) size of the Turbo and still used the large rubber damper at its centre. The clutch was now hydraulically operated, which made for less tiring operation.

Underside of a Club Sport (top) reveals the Getrag-built G50 gearbox (centre left) that was introduced for the 1987 model year. The new gearbox offered the durability needed to cope with the engine's increasing torque. Timing chain tensioners had always been a weak point in the reliability of the 911 engine (above). The new Carrera 3.2 received a new design which used engine oil to maintain hydraulic pressure on the timing chain idler. The new tensioners were recognisable from the outside by the small feed pipes branching from the cylinder head oil supply.

ELECTRICAL EQUIPMENT & LIGHTING

The 1984 models were fitted with a larger 92A/1260 watt alternator with additional cooling guides at its centre. A central rear stop light came to US models in 1986: it started at the top of the window, found a new home at the lower edge in 1987, and returned to the top again in 1988. Rear fog lights were integrated into the reflective strip, with the reversing lights, in 1987. The quartz halogen headlamp power remained a total of 110-watt dipped and 120-watt main beam, but at last the US cars received headlamps that looked like those fitted to the rest of the world's 911s. For some markets, integrated front fog lights were fitted below the front bumper line.

SUSPENSION & STEERING

The new Carrera carried over the suspension of the outgoing SC, but Boge's new gas dampers became the standard fitting from 1985.

Club Sports had (green) Bilstein gas dampers as standard. All Carrera 3.2s were given larger versions of the familiar A-type cast iron calipers and the brake discs were thicker (at 24mm) than those on the SC.

The 1986 models had stiffer anti-roll bars, diameter increasing from 20mm to 22mm at the front and from 18mm to 21mm at the rear. The shock absorbers were uprated and the rear torsion bars increased in diameter from 24mm to 25mm.

With the introduction of the G50 gearbox, the rear torsion bar tube had to be revised to clear the larger clutch bell-housing. The new cast iron support for the semi-trailing arms used the Turbo's geometry, incorporating anti-squat characteristics.

BRAKES

The 304mm (11.8in) diameter front brake discs on the 1984 Carrera increased in thickness from 20.5mm (0.80in) to 24mm (0.94in), giving more air circulation between the faces. At the rear disc thickness rose from 20mm (0.78in) to 24mm (0.94in) on a 309mm (12.1in) diameter. The total pad area was 78sq cm (12.1sq in) for the A-type front calipers and 52.5sq cm (8.1sq in) for the cast iron M-type rear calipers – the same calipers had been fitted to the outgoing SC.

The Hydrovac servo, of 8in diameter, was common with the Turbo. A pressure-limiting valve was introduced into the rear brake circuit and reduced the chances of wheel lock-up under heavy braking. A new brake pad wear sensor was also fitted.

Most Club Sports were finished in Grand Prix White with these decals on the sides and a small logo on the front lid. The wheel centres were normally colour-coded to the decal colours, but white and black centres were available.

WHEELS & TYRES

At the time of its introduction, the Carrera's standard wheels were the 'telephone dial' cast alloy type with five oval holes around the centre. The familiar Fuchs alloys were still available as an option (now with locking wheel nuts) and their centres could be ordered in white or platinum as well as black.

There were numerous changes in wheel specification during the life of the Carrera 3.2. From 1984, the standard 15in wheel sizes were 6J with 185/70 tyres at the front and 7J with 215/60 tyres at the rear. An option was 7J at the front (with 205/55ZR tyres) and 8J at the rear (with 225/50ZR tyres) on 16in Fuchs wheels. In 1987 the standard front tyres grew to 195/65VR, still on the 6J rims, and in 1988 the standard wheel sizes went to 7J × 15 front and 8J × 15 rear, the Fuchs forged alloy type replacing the 'telephone dials'. The 16in wheels remained an option with the same tyre sizes as before, although they were standard on the Club Sport.

For the final model year of the 3.2 Carrera, 1989, the standard wheels were 6J × 16 front and 8J × 16 rear, with 205/55ZR and 225/50ZR tyres respectively.

CARRERA TURBO-LOOK

From 1984, Carreras could be ordered optionally with the Turbo Coupé bodyshell, and this was announced as a regular model from September 1985. The specification included the Turbo's flared front and rear wheel wings, tea-tray wing and front spoiler extension. The Turbo's suspension and brakes – including perforated discs and 917-type calipers – were used without change, as were 7J/9J front/rear wheels. Cornering was improved with the wider track, stiffer rear torsion bars and a softer rear anti-roll bar. Ride height dropped from 108mm (4.2in) to 94mm (3.7in). Inside the only trim options were leather/cloth or leather throughout.

The Turbo-Look's extra weight, about 50kg (110lb) more than the regular Carrera, affected the acceleration, and the increased frontal area also contributed to the top speed being approximately 12mph slower – a point that explains why some customers specified the turbo engine in the Carrera bodyshell. But the Turbo-Look looked good and cost much less than a real Turbo!

The Targa and Cabrio became available in Turbo-Look form from 1986, the year in which 245/45VR rear tyres on 9J × 16in Fuchs wheels became a special option. In the UK the Turbo-Look model was known as the Carrera with Sport Equipment (SE) for the 1986 model year and the Carrera Super Sport from September 1986.

CARRERA CLUB SPORT

Available from September 1987, the Club Sport was a stripped-out Sport Equipment model, the deleted features including electric windows, electric front seats, rear wiper, central locking, radio (but the windshield antenna remained), passenger sun visor,

Part of the stripped-down specification of the Club Sport was the deletion of the automatic heater control and the return of the older two-lever manual control next to the handbrake. In the absence of electric seat adjustment, the manual levers for fore/aft movement are also grouped near the handbrake. Note the shift pattern of the G50 gearbox.

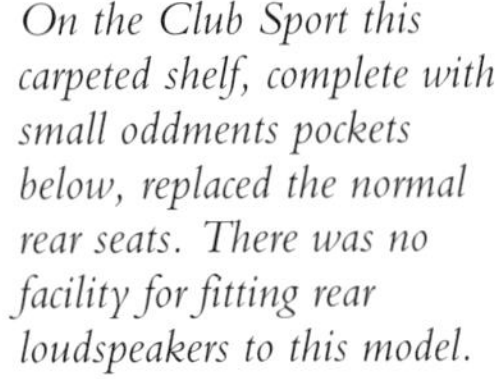

On the Club Sport this carpeted shelf, complete with small oddments pockets below, replaced the normal rear seats. There was no facility for fitting rear loudspeakers to this model.

During 1988 a special anniversary model was released to celebrate 25 years of production of the 911, as shown by a factory-fitted dashboard plaque. Anniversary specification could be ordered on any model in the 911 range.

rear seats, sound insulation (except for engine bay and roof liner) and air conditioning (where fitted as standard). Club Sport models carried the internal option number M637.

The finish inside was not austere, however, the rear seat area having fitted carpeting and the seat trim being leather/cloth or full leather. A shorter-throw gearshift was fitted and the alarm system of the regular Carrera was used. Other detail omissions included the automatic heater control, lockable oddments bin, door pocket lids and the trim panels for the rear bulkhead and sides, while the door trims were simplified. Oddly, items that remained were headlamp washers and (on UK cars) electric exterior mirrors.

Although the cars were prepared in Grand Prix White with optional red Carrera CS side script, it is known that at least one car in the UK was finished in red, so left-hand drive cars in other colours probably exist. All were Coupés, except one – a special order Targa made for a favoured German customer who paid an extra DM7000 for the privilege. Red wheel centres were normal, but wheels could also be supplied with white or black centres. Where no PVC sealer was applied to the underside, the anti-corrosion warranty was reduced from ten years to two. For most markets it was deleted, but UK cars generally had this treatment.

The claimed weight saving was about 50kg (110lb) on the regular Carrera, but only 23kg (51lb) on UK cars according to *Motor* magazine. At first Club Sports were given 6J × 15 and 7J × 15 wheels using Pirelli P6 tyres in sizes 195/65VR and 215/60VR. Later models received 6J × 16 and 7J × 16 wheels and Dunlop D40 tyres in sizes 205/55VR and 225/50VR. Bilstein gas dampers were fitted all round.

The engine was allowed to run to 6840rpm as opposed to the standard car's maximum of 6520rpm by re-chipping the Motronic system and using hollow intake valves. The rev counter was red-lined from 6600rpm as opposed to the regular Carrera's 6200rpm. Although maximum power was unaffected, the engine tweaks and lighter weight combined to improve acceleration, particularly above 60mph. The Club Sport could cover 0-60mph in 5.2sec compared with the standard car's 5.6sec (*Autocar* figures) while top speed rose from 148mph to 151mph.

The Club Sport was discontinued in September 1989 after 340 cars had been delivered. It is believed that only 28 were sold in the US, with 50 going to Britain.

ANNIVERSARY CARRERA

For the 1988 model year, an exclusive run of Carreras in all body styles and with special Marine Blue metallic paint was made to celebrate 25 years of production of the 911. By coincidence it also marked the completion during the summer of 1987 (on 3 June to be precise) of the 250,000th 911. The interiors were finished in blue metallic crushed leather with 'F. Porsche' signatures on the headrest area of the two front seats. Special silver blue silk velour carpet completed the luxurious interior of the anniversary models, and the short gear lever first seen on the Club Sport was used. The cars carried no model designation on the engine lid. Of the 875 Anniversary Carreras made, 300 went to the US (120 Coupés, 100 Cabrios and 80 Targas), 250 were sold in Germany, and 50 went to the UK (30 Coupés, 10 Cabrios and 10 Targas).

The Anniversary 911s had various unique features, including metallic blue crushed leather for the seats and an 'F. Porsche' signature on the headrest area. This car is owned by Roger Wynne.

Speedster interior shows manual window winders and the smaller sun visors used to suit the lower windscreen.

The Speedster's large glass-fibre hood cover moulding hinges backwards and remains in place all the time, precluding the fitting of rear seats.

The Anniversary models were painted in Marine Blue Metallic with matching wheel centres.

SPEEDSTER

This model had first been proposed to Peter Schutz when he took over at Porsche in late 1981, but the body style chosen at that time was the Cabriolet. The Speedster prototype was shown at the Frankfurt Show in 1987 and production models went on sale in January 1989, using the Cabrio bodyshell without any additional stiffening. As with the Cabrio, the Speedster could be ordered in most markets with the Slant-Nose or Turbo-Look body styles, but only the latter was sold in Germany and the US. The Turbo-Look accounted for 1894 of the 2065 Speedsters made between January and September 1989; 63 right-hand drive Speedsters were officially imported to the UK and 823 went to the US.

Visual distinction was provided by the aluminium-framed windscreen being raked down by five degrees and accompanied by frameless side windows. There was a new simplified hood, termed an emergency or temporary hood by the factory to reinforce the message that it was not built to the same high standards of comfort as the Cabrio hood – it was claimed that the Speedster was designed 'for friends of open-air motoring'. The hood was stowed under a colour-coded polyurethane moulding that was designed to improve the aerodynamics of the open car, but made the rear look awkwardly bulky. Customers were warned that the hood might not be water-proof and were advised that the Speedster should not be taken through a car wash. Before purchase could proceed, buyers were asked to sign a disclaimer that they would accept 'a degree of wind noise and water ingress from the seal areas in inclement conditions'. A removable (and hand-fitted at the factory) alloy hard top with heated rear window was listed as an option, but it is unclear whether any were delivered to customers.

There really were no frills on the Speedster. The windows and the heater were manually controlled. The seats were dropped to accommodate the lower roof line, although 20mm (0.8in) spacers were used at the front of the seats to provide better thigh support. The lower part of each seat was the basic non-electric version with a Sport seat back fitted, as used on the Club Sport. The rear seats were removed and the area carpeted. The M419 factory option provided a permanently installed storage box with two lockable lids in the rear seat area.

The factory claimed a 70kg (154lb) weight saving over the Coupé, but on the road it was more like 40kg (88lb), a difference that was cancelled out on the Turbo-Look version. Quoted performance was 0-100kph (0-62mph) in 6.0sec, but 0.1sec could be added for the Turbo-Look and 0.2sec to either model if a catalytic converter was fitted.

As a tailpiece, this Speedster was the last 911 model to be built in the old Zuffenhausen factory on a bodyshell based on the original 1963 design. The Carrera 4 was built on a new production line.

Data Section

The Speedster was conceived as a pure open-air car, following in the footsteps of its 356 namesake. The raked windscreen gives the 911 yet another interpretation. This is Mike Flannery's 1989 model.

PRODUCTION CHANGES

1984 (START OF E-SERIES)
Engine increased to 3164cc with longer-throw crankshaft of 3.3 Turbo and Nikasil barrels of 911SC; Bosch Motronic 2 engine management with LE fuel injection (and engine temperature sensing on cylinder head); 10.3:1 compression ratio with higher crown pistons (and 96 RON fuel); off-accelerator fuel cut-off above 1200rpm, improved idle speed control and Lambda adjustment on US, Canada and Japanese engines; new cam timing (advanced by 3 degrees); cylinder head gasket deleted; larger inlet (38mm) and exhaust (40mm) ports; hydraulically damped spring chain tensioners fed by engine oil; new heat exchanger design with larger pipe diameters, two-stage silencing (on 'RoW' models) and resonant charge boost air intake manifolding; US, Canada and Japan engines use 91 RON lead-free fuel, with 9.5:1 compression ratio, using new three-way catalytic converter in place of first silencer (muffler); oxygen sensor now pre-heated; new final silencer, with 10 per cent improved flow rate; engine weight rises from 190kg to 210kg; gear ratios (US) – first 3.181, second 1.778, third 1.261, fourth 1.000, fifth 0.790, reverse 3.325, final drive 3.875; gear ratios ('RoW') – first 3.181, second 1.833, third 1.261, fourth 1.000, fifth 0.763, reverse 3.325, final drive 3.875; sunroof air deflector revised; Turbo's heater controls fitted and in certain markets central locking is standard; 24mm thick brake discs with larger calipers front and rear; brake pressure limiter to prevent panic front wheel locking; brake servo now 8in; motor-driven vacuum assistance for brake servo maintains brake pressure over longer period.

1985 (START OF F-SERIES)
Production actually started on Oct 1, due to metal workers' strike in Germany; wing-mounted oil cooler changed from brass tube to matrix type; lower front spoiler has slot to improve oil cooling air flow; gear lever travel shortened by 10 per cent; radio antenna now in windshield; windshield washers heated; active carbon filters in breather system prevent escape of fuel vapour; electric adjusted front seats with part leather and cloth or full leather inlay; headrests 40mm taller, backrest release on both sides of seat back.

1986 (START OF G-SERIES)
Swiss models receive more effective silencer; revised shock absorbers and new anti-roll bars; revised rear torsion bars; optional 10 per cent (again) shorter gear shift; all models now have the same gear ratios – first 3.5:1, second 2.059:1, third 1.409:1, fourth 1.125:1, fifth 0.889:1, reverse 3.325:1, final drive 3.444:1; front seats lowered by 20mm and with greater adjustment; new dash panel with larger face-level and side window fresh air vents, and temperature sensor; new switches and better heat regulation; digital self-seek radio with balance control standard; sun visors receive covered vanity mirrors; Sports seats are a no-cost option.

1987 (START OF H-SERIES)
Motronic system on US/Canada/Japan engines re-mapped (new 930/25 engine code) and fuel grade raised to 95 RON, giving output of 217bhp (DIN) and maximum torque of 265Nm; front-mounted oil cooler gets thermostatically controlled fan on these models; Australia gets its first unique model, 207bhp and equipped as previous US models (930/21), with timing retarded to run 91 RON fuel (as opposed to 95); all other 'RoW' models (non-catalysed) run on 98 RON; Swiss models fitted with rear spoiler (and front chin spoiler) to improve engine compartment air circulation, which had been reduced by an acoustic shield mounted under the engine; additional air injection pump fitted to Swiss cars (930/26), power as 930/20 'RoW' engine; all models fitted with Getrag G50 gearbox and hydraulic clutch operation, with these ratios – first 3.5:1, second 2.059:1, third 1.409:1, fourth 1.074:1, fifth 0.861:1, reverse 2.857:1, final drive 3.444:1; clutch size increased to 240mm diameter; new rear torsion bar housing centre section in cast iron; standard front tyres now 195/65VR16; exterior mirror adjustment switch re-positioned; seats now adjustable in three planes; headlight beam adjuster mounted on dash; anti-corrosion warranty extended to ten years; new rear panel has reflective script and fog lights; door handle contains 'point of light' to assist finding it in the dark; Targas get improved weather sealing, with rain gutters; powered Cabrio hood now standard.

1988 (START OF I-SERIES)
Standard 'telephone dial' wheels replaced by 15in diameter 7J front and 8J rear Fuchs forged alloys (with 195/65VR and 215/60VR tyres); the following items, previously options, become standard – passenger door mirror, electric passenger seat, central locking, headlight washers, intensive wash for the windshield; emergency crank provided for electric windows; optional eight-speaker plus booster sound package (hi-fi pack), crushed leather upholstery and provision for subsequent mobile 'phone installation; all brake pads, clutch facings and seals for engine and gearbox are asbestos-free.

1989 (START OF J-SERIES)
Fuchs wheels go up one size all round to 6J × 16in front, 8J × 16in rear; minor change to the fifth speed gear assembly to reduce noise; anti-roll bars now 22mm front, 21mm rear; car alarm fitted and linked to central locking, marked by flashing red diodes in the lock buttons; optional seat heating for both passenger and driver and a radio with CD player.

DIMENSIONS

Wheelbase
2271mm

Track (front/rear)
1398mm/1405mm (standard), 1432/1500mm (Turbo-Look to 1986), 1434mm/1526mm (Turbo-Look from 1986)

Length
4291mm

Width
1650mm (standard), 1829mm (Turbo-Look)

OPTIONS

The following is a list of equipment options used from the introduction of the 911SC in 1978 through to 1992. Porsche Cars North America is among the references for this listing, which is all that can be obtained from official sources. Regrettably it is not possible to date these options, so this list must also apply to the chapters on the 911SC (1978-83) and the 3.6-litre Carrera 4 & 2 (1989-93). Many M numbers were standard for a particular market and will not be shown on the Vehicle Identification Label (VIL). The hundreds of detail options are not shown here, and some M numbers represent a group of options for a particular model.

M09 Three-speed Sportomatic; M18 Sport steering wheel with elevated hub; M20 Speedometer with two scales (kph/mph); M26 Activated charcoal canister; M030 Sport suspension for Carrera 2 (1992/3); M68 Bumpers with impact absorbers; M70 Tonneau cover – Cabriolet; M97-99 Anniversary model 1989; M103 Adjustment of shock absorber strut; M126 Digital radio 1982; M139 Seat heating (left); M148 Modified engine 930/66; M152 Engine noise reduction; M154 Control unit for improved emissions; M155 Motronic unit for cars with catalytic converters; M156 Quieter silencer; M157 Oxygen sensor and catalyst; M158 Radio Monterey (1986) or Reno (1987); M160 Radio Charleston; M167 Bridgestone tyres; M176 Oil cooler with fan; M185 Automatic two-point rear seat belts; M186 Manual rear seat belts; M187 Assymetric headlamps; M190 Increased door side strength; M195 Prepared for cellular telephone; M197 Higher amperage battery (88Ah); M218 Licence brackets, front and rear; M220 Locking differential (40 per cent); M240 Version for countries with inferior fuel; M261 Passenger external mirror, flat glass; M286 High intensity windshield washer; M288 Headlight washer; M298 Prepared for unleaded fuel – manual transmission; M326 Radio Blaupunkt Berlin; M327 Radio Blaupunkt Koln; M328 Radio Blaupunkt Bremen; M328 Radio Blaupunkt Symphony; M329/330 Radio Blaupunkt Toronto; M335 Automatic three-point rear seat belts; M340 Seat heating (right); M341 Central locking; M351 Porsche CR stereo radio/cassette Type DE, manual antenna, loudspeakers; M375 Asbestos-free clutch lining; M377/378 Combination seat (left/right); M378/380 Series seat, electric vertical adjustment (left/right); M383/387 Sports seats, electric vertical adjustment (left/right); M389 Porsche CR stereo US radio/cassette, manual antenna, loudspeakers; M391 Stone guard decal; M395 Light metal wheels 6J × 15in front and 7J × 15 in rear, forged, with 205 and 225 tyres; M399 Air conditioning without front con-

IDENTIFICATION

Model year	Model	Engine	Gearbox	Chassis numbers	Engine numbers
E-series					
1984	911 Carrera	930/20	915/67	WPOZZZ91ZES100001-4033	63E00001 onwards
	Carrera Targa	930/20	915/67	WPOZZZ91ZES140001-1469	63E00001 onwards
	Carrera Cabrio	930/20	915/67	WPOZZZ91ZES150001-1835	63E00001 onwards
	Carrera Japan	930/21	915/68	WPOZZZ91ZES109501-9717	64E00001 onwards
	Carrera Targa Japan	930/21	915/68	WPOZZZ91ZES149501-9564	64E00001 onwards
	Carrera Cabrio Japan	930/21	915/68	WPOZZZ91ZES159501-9577	64E00001 onwards
	Carrera US	930/21	915/68	WPOABO91ES120001-2282	64E00001 onwards
	Carrera Targa US	930/21	915/68	WPOEBO91ES160001-2260	64E00001 onwards
	Carrera Cabrio US	930/21	915/68	WPOEBO91ES170001-1191	64E00001 onwards
F-series					
1985	911 Carrera	930/20	915/69	WPOZZZ91ZFS100001-3529	65F00001 onwards
	Carrera Targa	930/20	915/69	WPOZZZ91ZFS140001-1435	65F00001 onwards
	Carrera Cabrio	930/20	915/69	WPOZZZ91ZFS150001-1583	65F00001 onwards
	Carrera Japan	930/21	915/70	WPOZZZ91ZFS109501-722	64F00001 onwards
	Carrera Targa Japan	930/21	915/70	WPOZZZ91ZFS149501-564	64F00001 onwards
	Carrera Cabrio Japan	930/21	915/70	WPOZZZ91ZFS159501-575	64F00001 onwards
	Carrera US	930/21	915/70	WPOABO91FS120001-1959	64F00001 onwards
	Carrera Targa US	930/21	915/70	WPOEBO91FS160001-1942	64F00001 onwards
	Carrera Cabrio US	930/21	915/70	WPOEBO91FS170001-1050	64F00001 onwards
G-series					
1986	911 Carrera	930/20	915/72	WPOZZZ91ZGS100001-4031	63G00001 onwards
	Carrera Targa	930/20	915/72	WPOZZZ91ZGS140001-1758	63G00001 onwards
	Carrera Cabrio	930/20	915/72	WPOZZZ91ZGS150001-2358	63G00001 onwards
	Carrera Japan	930/21	915/73	WPOZZZ91ZGS109501-733	64G00001 onwards
	Carrera Targa Japan	930/21	915/73	WPOZZZ91ZGS149501-579	64G00001 onwards
	Carrera Cabrio Japan	930/21	915/73	WPOZZZ91ZGS159501-580	64G00001 onwards
	Carrera US	930/21	915/73	WPOABO91GS120001-2619	64G00001 onwards
	Carrera Targa US	930/21	915/73	WPOEBO91GS160001-1976	64G00001 onwards
	Carrera Cabrio US	930/21	915/73	WPOEBO91GS170001-1986	64G00001 onwards
H-series					
1987	911 Carrera	930/20	950/00	WPOZZZ91ZHS100001-3381	63H00001 onwards
	Club Sport	930/20	950/00	WPOZZZ91ZHS105001-081	63H00001 onwards
	Carrera Targa	930/20	950/00	WPOZZZ91ZHS140001-1354	63H00001 onwards
	Carrera Cabrio	930/20	950/00	WPOZZZ91ZHS150001-1464	63H00001 onwards
	Carrera Japan	930/25	950/01	WPOZZZ91ZHS109501-808	64H00001 onwards
	Carrera Targa Japan	930/25	950/01	WPOZZZ91ZHS149501-579	64H00001 onwards
	Carrera Cabrio Japan	930/25	950/01	WPOZZZ91ZHS159501-585	64H00001 onwards
	Carrera US	930/25	950/01	WPOABO91HS120001-2916	64H00001 onwards
	Carrera Club Sport US	930/25	950/01	WPOABO91HS125001-300	64H00001 onwards
	Carrera Targa US	930/25	950/01	WPOEBO91HS160001-2232	64H00001 onwards
	Carrera Cabrio US	930/25	950/01	WPOEBO91HS170001-2653	64H00001 onwards
I-series					
1988	911 Carrera	930/20	G50/00	WPOZZZ91ZJS100001-3580	63J00001 onwards
	Club Sport	930/20	G50/00	WPOZZZ91ZJS105001-148	63J00001 onwards
	Carrera Targa	930/20	G50/00	WPOZZZ91ZJS140001-1281	63J00001 onwards
	Carrera Cabrio	930/20	G50/00	WPOZZZ91ZJS150001-1501	63J00001 onwards
	Carrera Japan	930/25	G50/01	WPOZZZ91ZJS109501-930	64J00001 onwards
	Carrera Targa Japan	930/25	G50/01	WPOZZZ91ZJS149501-586	64J00001 onwards
	Carrera Cabrio Japan	930/25	G50/01	WPOZZZ91ZJS159501-581	64J00001 onwards
	Carrera US	930/25	G50/01	WPOABO91JS120001-2066	64J00001 onwards
	Carrera Club Sport US	930/25	G50/01	WPOABO91JS125001-082	64J00001 onwards
	Carrera Targa US	930/25	G50/01	WPOEBO91JS160001-1500	64J00001 onwards
	Carrera Cabrio US	930/25	G50/01	WPOEBO91JS170001-2116	64J00001 onwards
J-series					
1989	911 Carrera	930/20	G50/00	WPOZZZ91ZKS100001-3532	63K00001 onwards
	Carrera Targa	930/20	G50/00	WPOZZZ91ZKS140001-1063	63K00001 onwards
	Carrera Cabrio	930/20	G50/00	WPOZZZ91ZKS150001-2787	63K00001 onwards
	Club Sport	930/20	G50/00	WPOZZZ91ZKS105001-090	63K00001 onwards
	Speedster	930/20	G50/00	WPOZZZ91ZKS153000-4242	63K00001 onwards
	Carrera US	930/25	G50/01	WPOABO91KS120001-1156	64K00001 onwards
	Carrera Targa US	930/25	G50/01	WPOEBO91KS160001-0860	64K00001 onwards
	Carrera Cabrio US	930/25	G50/01	WPOEBO91KS170001-1361	64K00001 onwards
	Speedster US	930/25	G50/01	WPOEBO91KS173001-823	64K00001 onwards
	Club Sport	930/25	G50/01	WPOEBO91KS125001-007	64K00001 onwards

General notes

Chassis numbering Model years are identified by a letter for the 10th character of 'RoW' models or the ninth character of US models, as follows: E 1984, F 1985, G 1986, H 1987, J 1988, K 1989.

Engines 930/26 was supplied alongside 'RoW' models as a special model for Switzerland from 1985 and Sweden from 1987; 930/25 was supplied to Austria from 1987. 930/26 was as 930/20, plus an air pump and extra noise reduction.

Gearboxes Note change of designation for G50 gearbox for 1988, from 950 to G50; G50/02 was supplied to Switzerland. Option M220 (locking differential) was available on all 1988 G50 gearboxes.

densor; M401 Light metal wheels; M403 50 year anniversary model (1982); M406 Front wheel housing protection (1983-86); M407 Rear seats with static belts; M409 Sport seats in leather (left/right); M410 Sport seats in leatherette/cloth (left/right); M419 Rear luggage compartment instead of seats; M424 Automatic heating control; M425 Rear wiper; M437/438 Comfort seats (left/right); M439 Cabriolet top, electric operation; M440 Manual antenna, two loudspeakers in doors and suppression; M441 Electric antenna (right), two loudspeakers in doors and suppression; M443 Tinted front and side glass, heated windshield; M444 Cabriolet; M446 Targa build kit; M451 Prepared for radio for sport group; M454 Cruise control; M461 Electric antenna (right); M462 Sekuriflex laminated windshield; M463 Clear windshield; M464 Without compressor and tyre pressure gauge; M467 External driver's mirror, convex; M468 Graduated windshield tint, green side glass; M469 Black headlining; M470 Without spoilers; M473 With spoilers; M474 Sport shock absorbers; M475 Brake pads without asbestos; M482 Engine compartment light; M483 Right-hand drive; M487 Connection for foglight from parking light; M490 HiFi sound system; M491 Turbo Look body; M492 H4 headlights for left-hand traffic; M494 Two speakers on rear shelf; M496 Black-look external trim, colour-coded headlamp rims; M498 Without rear model designation; M503 Speedster variant of Cabriolet; M505 Slant nose (USA); M506 Slant nose (RoW); M513 Lumbar support (right seat); M525 Alarm with continuous sound; M526 Cloth door panels; M528 Passenger side external door mirror, convex; M533 Alarm system; M559 Air conditioning; M565 Safety steering wheel in leather, 380mm diameter; M566 Rectangular front fog lights; M567 Graduated green tint windshield; M568 Tinted windshield and side glass; M573 Air conditioning; M577 Heated and tinted windshield; M586 Lumbar support, left seat; M590 Centre console; M592 Anti-lock brakes (Bosch-Teves); M592 Brake fluid warning system; M593 ABS – Bosch; M594 ABS – Wabco; M602 Third brake light, top of rear screen; M605 Vertical headlight adjustment; M630 Police equipment; M637 Club Sport model; M650 Electric sunroof; M651 Electric windows; M652 Intermittent wipe; M656 Manual steering; M659 Front fog lights (1979); M659 On-board computer; M666 Without lacquer preservation and chrome preservation; M673 Prepared for lead-sealed odometer; M684 One-piece rear seat; M686 Radio Blaupunkt Ludwigsburg; M688 Radio Blaupunkt Boston; M690 CD player CD10 with radio; M691 CD player (CD01 for 1988, CD02 from 1989) with radio; M701 Slant nose; M702 High performance engine (930/66); M930-935/945/947/948 Seat covers; M970 Floor mats; M974 Velour carpet in luggage compartment; M980 Seat covering in ruffled leather; M981 All-leather lining; M986 Partial leather lining.

COLOUR SCHEMES

1984 (chart W74-704-2041)

Standard body colours

Guards Red (017), Glacier Blue (32Z), Black (700), Grand Prix White (908), Chiffon White (182)

Special order body colours

Moss Green Metallic (20C), Pewter Metallic (655), Slate Blue Metallic (661), Quartz Grey Metallic (662), Ruby Red Metallic (810), Kiln Red Metallic (811), Zinc Metallic (956), Light Bronze Metallic (966), Platinum Metallic (655).

Fabrics

Leatherette (BPX) in Grey-Beige (4FK), Burgundy (3MK), Cadbury Brown (4RB), Blue (1HH) or Black (43S); leather (EXH) in Can-Can Red (80S), Pearl White (8YD), Dark Green (6JD), Champagne (1VD), Burgundy (7LD), Grey-Beige (6FL), Cadbury Brown (4RB), Black (1AJ) or Blue (30B); textured cloth with wavy line pattern (TPU) in Brown (7NU), Blue (30C), Black (70F), Grey Beige (8FU) or Burgundy (5MU); fabric with in-woven diagonal 'Porsche' script (TPC) in Black (4CR), Brown (6TR), Grey-Beige (8RR), Blue (5HR) or burgundy (2LR); checkerboard velour (TPB) in Light Grey/Black (4FJ), Brown/Grey (5RH), Blue/Grey (7GH) or Burgundy/Grey (9LH); pinstripe velour (TPB) in Brown/Beige (3NN), Black/White (7BN), Grey-Beige/White (9FN), Blue/White (8GJ) or Burgundy/White (1MJ).

Carpets

Cut pile velour (TFK) in Light Grey (60A), Brown (40E), Dark Blue (30B), Dark Green (6JD), Black (70E), Grey-Beige

PRODUCTION DATA

Model year	Model	Power (bhp DIN@rpm)	Torque (Nm@rpm)	Compression ratio	Weight (kg)	Number built
1984	911 Carrera	231@5900	284@4800	10.3:1	1160	4033
	Carrera Targa	231@5900	284@4800	10.3:1	1210	1469
	Carrera Cabrio	231@5900	260@4800	10.3:1	1210	1835
	Carrera Japan	207@5900	260@4800	9.5:1	1250	217
	Carrera Targa Japan	207@5900	260@4800	9.5:1	1300	64
	Carrera Cabrio Japan	207@5900	260@4800	9.5:1	1250	77
	Carrera US	207@5900	260@4800	9.5:1	1250	2282
	Carrera Targa US	207@5900	260@4800	9.5:1	1300	2260
	Carrera Cabrio US	207@5900	260@4800	9.5:1	1300	1191
1985	911 Carrera	231@5900	284@4800	10.3:1	1160	3529
	Carrera Targa	231@5900	284@4800	10.3:1	1210	1435
	Carrera Cabrio	231@5900	260@4800	10.3:1	1210	1583
	Carrera Japan	207@5900	260@4800	9.5:1	1250	222
	Carrera Targa Japan	207@5900	260@4800	9.5:1	1300	64
	Carrera Cabrio Japan	207@5900	260@4800	9.5:1	1300	75
	Carrera US	207@5900	260@4800	9.5:1	1250	1959
	Carrera Targa US	207@5900	260@4800	9.5:1	1300	1942
	Carrera Cabrio US	207@5900	260@4800	9.5:1	1300	1050
1986	911 Carrera	231@5900	284@4800	10.3:1	1210	4031
	Carrera Targa	231@5900	284@4800	10.3:1	1260	1758
	Carrera Cabrio	231@5900	260@4800	10.3:1	1260	2358
	Carrera Japan	207@5900	260@4800	9.5:1	1260	233
	Carrera Targa Japan	207@5900	260@4800	9.5:1	1310	79
	Carrera Cabrio Japan	207@5900	260@4800	9.5:1	1310	80
	Carrera US	207@5900	260@4800	9.5:1	1300	2619
	Carrera Targa US	207@5900	260@4800	9.5:1	1350	1976
	Carrera Cabrio US	207@5900	260@4800	9.5:1	1350	1986
1987	911 Carrera	231@5900	284@4800	10.3:1	1210	3381
	Club Sport	231@5900	284@4800	10.3:1	1172	81
	Carrera Targa	231@5900	284@4800	10.3:1	1260	1354
	Carrera Cabrio	231@5900	284@4800	10.3:1	1260	1464
	Carrera Japan	217@5900	265@4800	9.5:1	1260	308
	Carrera Targa Japan	217@5900	265@4800	9.5:1	1310	79
	Carrera Cabrio Japan	217@5900	265@4800	9.5:1	1310	85
	Carrera US	217@5900	265@4800	9.5:1	1250	2916
	Carrera Targa US	217@5900	265@4800	9.5:1	1300	2232
	Carrera Cabrio US	217@5900	265@4800	9.5:1	1300	2653
1988	911 Carrera	231@5900	284@4800	10.3:1	1210	3580
	Carrera Targa	231@5900	284@4800	10.3:1	1260	1281
	Carrera Cabrio	231@5900	284@4800	10.3:1	1260	1501
	Carrera Japan	217@5900	265@4800	9.5:1	1260	430
	Carrera Targa Japan	217@5900	265@4800	9.5:1	1310	86
	Carrera Cabrio Japan	217@5900	265@4800	9.5:1	1310	81
	Carrera US	217@5900	265@4800	9.5:1	1250	2066
	Carrera Targa US	217@5900	265@4800	9.5:1	1300	1500
	Carrera Cabrio US	217@5900	265@4800	9.5:1	1300	2116
	Club Sport	231@5900	284@4800	10.3:1	1172	148
	Club Sport US	217@5900	265@4800	9.5:1	1210	21
1989	911 Carrera	231@5900	284@4800	10.3:1	1210	3532
	Carrera Targa	231@5900	284@4800	10.3:1	1260	1063
	Carrera Cabrio	231@5900	284@4800	10.3:1	1260	2787
	Speedster	231@5900	284@4800	10.3:1	1210	1242
	Carrera US	217@5900	265@4800	9.5:1	1250	1156
	Carrera Targa US	217@5900	265@4800	9.5:1	1300	860
	Carrera Cabrio US	217@5900	265@4800	9.5:1	1300	1361
	Speedster	217@5900	265@4800	9.5:1	1210	823
	Club Sport	231@5900	284@4800	10.3:1	1172	83
	Club Sport US	217@5900	265@4800	9.5:1	1210	7

General notes

The restoration workshop produced a handful of slant-nose Carrera conversions between 1984-87: one in 1984, two in 1985, one in 1986 and five in 1987. For the 1988 model year the slant-nose became a production model but only on the Turbo. The 1987 remapped 930/25 engine for the USA (214bhp DIN) is more frequently quoted with its SAE maximum power of 217bhp. The Club Sport (M637) was discontinued in September 1989. On the subject of weights, there was a large difference between factory homologation weights and the dry weight of equipped cars. Different markets offered different levels of basic equipment, and others (especially US, Japan and Canada) had extra emissions equipment. For instance, the homologation weight of the 1984 model was 1207kg, but this rose to 1280kg ready for sale in Germany – and the quoted ex-factory weight of the same model was 1160kg. Quoted weight should be treated as a guide only.

(2FL), Can-Can Red (80S), Burgundy (80E) or Champagne (1VD).

1985 (chart VMA7.84, WVK100520)

Standard body colours

Guards Red (027), Black (700), Pastel Beige (536), Dark Blue (347), Marble Grey (673), Grand Prix White (908).

Special order body colours

Garnet Red Metallic (822), Crystal Green Metallic (33N), White Gold Metallic (539), Prussian Blue Metallic (33X), Moss Green Metallic (20C), Iris Blue Metallic (33P), Nutmeg Brown Metallic (492), Meteor Metallic (961), Silver Metallic (936).

Fabrics

Leatherette as 1984, excluding Grey-Beige (4FK) but with addition of Grey-Green (4JX); leather as 1984 excluding Grey-Beige (6FL) but with addition of Grey-Green (5JX), Wild Buffalo (dark brown, 5NW) and Ocean Blue (6GX); checkerboard velour deleted for 911; pinstripe velour (TPB) in Brown/White (3NN), Black/White (7BN), Blue/White (8GJ), Burgundy/White (1MJ) or Grey-Green/White (3JV); pinstripe (narrow) flannel (TPC) in Black (8BF), Brown (2TF), Grey-Green (9JF), Blue (6GF) or Burgundy (1MF); fabric with in-woven diagonal 'Porsche' script, more prominent than 1984 (TPC), in Black (2CZ), Brown (7NZ), Blue (6HZ), Burgundy (5LZ) or Grey-Green (1JK); Cabrio hoods in Black, Dark Brown, Dark Blue, Burgundy or Grey-Green.

Carpets

As 1984, except Grey-Green (8JK) replaces Grey-Beige and White (2YN) added – a good colour for a car carpet!

1986

Standard and special order body colours

As 1985.

Fabrics

Leatherette as 1985, but with Grey-Beige (4FK) reinstated; leather as 1985, but with Grey-Beige (6FL) reinstated; pinstripe velour as 1985, but with addition of Grey-Beige/White (9FN); pinstripe flannel and 'Porsche' script fabric as 1985, but including Grey-Beige (5UY) in the latter.

Carpets

As 1985, but with Grey-Beige (2FL) reinstated.

1987 (chart VMAP6/86, WVK102721)

Standard body colours

Guards Red (027), Black (700), Summer Yellow (10W), Caramel Beige (499), Carmine Red (80F), Grand Prix White (908), Dark Blue (347), Turquoise (21M).

Special order body colours

Lagoon Green Metallic (35Y), Granite Green Metallic (699), Nougat-Brown Metallic (40B), Espresso Brown Metallic (40D), Diamond Blue Metallic (697), Marine Blue Metallic (35V), Silver Metallic (980), Cassis Red Metallic (80D), Venetian Blue Metallic (35U).

Fabrics

Leatherette (BPX) in Linen (4WX), Burgundy (3MK), Mahogany (1MX), Black (43S), Grey-Green (4JX) or Blue (1KX); leather (YDX) in Burgundy (7LD), Mahogany (2LX), Brown (4RB), Black (1AJ), Blue (7JX), Grey-Green (5JX), Linen (7VX), Plum Red (1MC), Silver-Grey (3VC), Caramel (4UC), Venetian Blue (7KC) or Champagne (1VD); pinstripe velour (TPB) in Black/White (7BN), Mahogany/White (6LN), Blue/White (8GJ), Burgundy/White (1MJ), Grey-Green/White (3JV); pinstripe flannel (TPC) in Mahogany (9LF) Anthracite (8BF), Grey-Green (9JF), Blue (6GF) or Burgundy (1MF); fabric with in-woven diagonal 'Porsche' script as 1986, but less Brown and add Mahogany (4MR); Cabrio hoods in Black, Mahogany, Blue, Burgundy or Grey-Green.

Carpets

Cut pile velour (TFK) in Mahogany (5MF), Blue (3KF), Linen (2XF), Burgundy (80E), Black (70E), Grey-Green (8JK), Champagne (1VD), Plum Red (4MM), Silver-Grey (7VM), Caramel (5UM) or Venetian Blue (3KM).

1988 (chart VMAP7/87, WVK102720)

Standard and special order body colours

As 1987.

Fabrics and carpets

Special materials available for 25-year Anniversary model, painted in Marine Blue Metallic (35V); ruffled leather (YDS 8HF) in Blue Metallic with 'Ferry Porsche' signature on the headrest area of the two front seats; silk velour carpet (TLV 6HM) in Silver Blue.

THE 3.6-LITRE CARRERA (1989-93)

Ian King's Carrera 4 Targa shows the new design of front bumper and side skirt, with a much more squared-off lower edge to the 911's classic curves. This car is fitted with five-spoke 'Cup Design' wheels.

When recession hit in the late 1980s, the 'yuppies' deserted Porsche in their droves. The 3.2 Carrera suddenly seemed to be rather out-dated as the competition, especially from Japan, targeted the sports car market that Porsche had dominated for so long. In 1987 911 Carrera sales had slipped back to around 17,000 and at the end of that year Schutz was gone, replaced by well-trusted Porsche finance man Heinz Branitzski. He was briefed to find Porsche a new direction – again.

Porsche's problems were compounded by the fact that its loyal customers, who had previously bought a 911 because it was something special and not likely to be seen in every town centre in the land, had deserted the marque too. Branitzski's task was to re-establish the trust of the core customers and somehow take the company forward from a much-reduced trading position. He had a very difficult job. In the last year of the 3.2 Carrera, 1989, just under 7000 were made. There was a cold window blowing at Porsche...

Management instability continued as Porsche plunged into recession on a scale that the company was not prepared for. In March 1990, another new Chief Executive Officer in the form of Arno Bohn, formerly of the Nixdorf computer business, was given the task of rescuing the company. There are stories of bitter boardroom battles over the direction Porsche should take in its struggle to survive. There were several director-level resignations and Bohn gained a reputation for being outspoken in his conflict with the controlling Porsche and Piech families. By September 1992, he too was gone, to be replaced by former Production Director Wendelin Wiedeking, then aged 39.

Wiedeking's declared objective was to slash Porsche's cost base by 30 per cent by 1995. From the

EVOLUTION OUTLINE

Aug 1989	Carrera 4 introduced as new four-wheel drive 911 model; re-style of bodyshell, twin spark, 3.6-litre engine (250bhp), coil spring over shock absorber suspension, ABS brakes.
Oct 1989	Carrera 2 announced (rear-wheel drive only); Tiptronic automatic transmission launched at same time.
Aug 1991	Turbo-Look body style for Carrera 2 Coupé and Cabriolet.
Oct 1991	Carrera 2 RS with 260bhp and up to 170kg lighter than Carrera 2.
Aug 1992	RS America (entry-level Carrera 2) for North America; America Roadster (Turbo-Look Cabriolet Carrera 2).
Oct 1992	Carrera 2 Speedster launched.
Feb 1993	Carrera 2 Speedster production starts; 911 Celebration (30 years of the 911).
Dec 1993	Carrera 2 and 4 discontinued; Targa deleted; 911 (993) Carrera introduced in Coupé and Cabriolet forms.

Mike King's Carrera 2 Tiptronic, again fitted with the attractive 'Cup Design' wheels.

moment he took over, Herr Wiedeking had to counter continuous external comment that the firm was up for sale. This was strenuously rejected at every turn, but it was clear that some major surgery was going to be necessary on a company that had grown complacent of its position. This would appear not to have been the most conducive environment from which to stage a recovery, but Wiedeking was to lead a whirlwind of change.

The new broom started sweeping. In 1993 alone, the workforce was reduced by 15 per cent, and by 1994 nearly 40 per cent of the original management had been laid off. Many new initiatives improved productivity. Wiedeking's production training brought massive dividends, which started with Japanese specialists introducing state-of-the-art *kaizen* (constant improvement) production methods. The savings in production were startling: the new 1994 Carrera took 40 hours less to build, quality improved by 15-20 per cent, the amount of space needed to assemble each vehicle was reduced by 21 per cent, and the stock inventory – such a drain on the company's liquidity – by 43 per cent. And business did indeed improve, turning round the record loss of 239 million D-marks in 1992/93 on the strength of both cost savings *and* rising sales.

The recovery was led by the new 993, but the 964 played its part. At the start of the 1994 model year the 993 was available only in two-wheel drive coupé form and 3690 964s were sold during the model year – Carrera 2 Speedsters, Cabriolets, Carrera 4s and Turbos. But 16,693 993s were sold too, demonstrating forcefully how the new model had captured the imagination of the marketplace in a way the 964 had not. It was a very different picture from 1993, when a total of just 12,500 Porsches were sold.

Production of the 964 ceased in spring 1994, with completion of orders for the Turbo. The end of the 964 also marked the passing of the Speedster, as this model was not a feature of the 993 range.

Let us return to 1989 and the new Carrera 4, because this was the car that was to win back Porsche's loyal customers, to show them that owning a 911 was indeed something special. With its back to the wall, the company resolved to fight its way out of trouble with the one major asset that had hauled it back from the brink in previous hard times – the engineering team at Weissach.

That Porsche's engineers managed to pull still more innovations from the 911 ideas pile in the late 1980s is astonishing, but the extravagant 959 programme had given them a healthy reserve of technology to draw upon. The 959 was a wonder-car with many technological marvels of industry-leading standard, but Porsche did not make as much as it might have with the car. The 283 959s were all pre-sold, and by the time of delivery to a booming market they seemed grossly under-priced. A buoyant grey market sprung up around the 959, for a speculative owner who paid some £180,000 could re-sell immediately for anything up to £500,000 – and someone reputedly paid $1,000,000 in Japan.

None of this speculative gain went to Porsche, but it was an obvious move for the cash-strapped company to cream off some of the 959's technology into a new range of 911s – the Carrera 4 and Carrera 2. And there was a new factory too, for the strikingly-

In standard form for the first three years of production the Carrera 4 used these new seven-spoke alloy wheels, with 205/55 front tyres and 225/50 rear tyres. Considerable road noise was transmitted into the cabin because tyre pressures were high.

The Cabriolet progressively ate into the Targa's share of the 911 market, to the extent that by 1993 the Targa had virtually disappeared. This 1993 Cabriolet shows off the new Classic Grey hood colour for that year.

painted (in shades of pink) body assembly plant at Zuffenhausen would build the latest 911s. To these models would fall the task of keeping Porsche afloat until the new direction could fire the excitement of those much sought new customers.

Officially announced in November 1988 but leaked to the press as much as a year earlier, the Carrera 4 was a very significant development for Porsche. Whereas all previous 911s were part of a continuous development stream that could be traced back to 1963, the Carrera 4 was 87 per cent new, and as such it should be judged the first stage of the second generation. And as had happened so many times, the changes on the four-wheel drive Carrera 4 were understated by the factory. The bits that remained unchanged were those that everyone could see: roof, front wings, front compartment lid, doors and seats – and of course that famous profile. Inevitably the word 'facelift' crept into press reports by the less well-informed, but anyone who looked closely could see that the '87 per cent new' tag had real credibility – the engine, suspension, brakes and transmission were all new. Under the skin, the 911 had been truly transformed. The changes were major enough for the car to be given a new internal factory designation of 964. And the joke on the cynical press – there were many at the time because it was fashionable to knock Porsche in 1989 – was that there were still those who talked about the 'wayward handling' of the rear engine design. For normal road use, the 911 had been tamed long before.

The Carrera 2 followed early in 1990, replacing the 3.2 Carrera. The new two-wheel drive 911 used most of the Carrera 4's equipment, but with a simpler and lighter transmission. With the basic models of the second generation established, Porsche then set about widening the appeal of the 911 in the way that had proved successful in the later years of the 3.2 Carrera. The Turbo-Look, the Speedster and another Anniversary model (marking the 911's 30th birthday) enhanced a range which had to take the company through its worst ever trading situation in the period 1991-93. Deliveries of the Carrera 4 and Carrera 2 ran out in 1993, to be replaced with the 993 model.

BODYSHELL

The structure of the Carrera 4 was entirely new. It was made, as previously, from hot zinc-dipped steel, but considerable efforts had been made to improve manufacturing efficiency by using highly automated methods. In terms of the bodyshell generally, it had been important to retain the classic 911 profile, yet to improve the aerodynamics and the styling. These goals were achieved elegantly with new front and rear bumpers, combined with a much smoother, enclosed underbody and a movable rear spoiler.

The bumpers were made from deformable thermoplastic supported on an aluminium sub-frame. For US models the sub-frames were carried on telescopic dampers, to provide 'collision recovery' ability. For 'Rest of the World' models, the supports were simple deformable structures. The driving lights were styled into the new bumpers, so that changes of line in the bodyshell profile were less abrupt than on the earlier models. At the rear the exhaust tailpipe exited on the right-hand side, the opposite to the 3.2 Carrera.

The rear spoiler was a particularly neat solution to the potential conflict between retaining the classical 911 shape yet providing improved stability at higher speeds. The spoiler was raised by an electric motor when the car exceeded 50mph (80kph), and retracted when speed fell below 6mph (10kph). Since the spoiler was housed in a larger opening in the engine cover, cooling was improved when the car was stationary. The moving spoiler might not have been as effective aerodynamically as a whaletail, but it was successful from the visual point of view.

Aerodynamic improvements were applied to most details of the bodyshell. The gap between the top of the rear window glass and the roof was reduced. The front windshield was glued into a much lower profile rubber seal, which in turn was glued to the bodyshell. The rising drip rails next to the windshield were reduced in size. The oil cooler was still in the right front wing, ahead of the wheel, but aligned differently to benefit from air ducted into the wheelarch from under the bumper, hot air being ducted out just ahead of the front wheel. The condenser for the air conditioning system (where one was fitted) was sited in the same manner in the left front wing.

The Carrera 4 bodyshell was shared by the Carrera 2, which was announced a year later, in October 1989, in Coupé, Targa and Cabrio forms. Sales of the Targa model, however, were dwindling and the Carrera 2 would be the last 911 to be offered with this style of open motoring. For the 1992 model year the Turbo-Look Cabrio was also offered for the Carrera 2. From the 1993 model year, all models carried the chassis number on the A-pillar, so that it was visible from outside the car – this was in the interests of better security.

BODY TRIM

The Carrera 4 was notable in having very little superfluous body trim. New plastic sill extensions squared off the sides of the car, but other trim – including door mirrors and windshield wipers – was carried over from the 3.2 Carrera. The sunroof received a new wind deflector at the leading edge, while the addition of the movable spoiler required the rear wiper to be mounted through the window glass instead of on the engine lid.

The heating system was effectively completely new, the new undertray incorporating new ducting and servo-operated fans to reduce temperature fluctuations. The new design also took account of air conditioning, although this remained an option. The revised heating and ventilation went a long way to providing the 911 with a contemporary climate control equivalent to other luxury – and water-cooled – GT cars. The system was further improved for 1992 and at the same time the Turbo-Look Cabrio received the automatic control of the closed models. From 1993 the air conditioning refrigerant was CFC-free.

INTERIOR TRIM

The higher central driveshaft tunnel for the four-wheel drive system was the only obvious difference between the old 3.2 Carrera and the new Carrera 4. New door loudspeakers were fitted and new trim choices were available (see 'Colour Schemes' on pages 107-108). A footrest was also provided alongside the clutch for the first time on a 911. On right-hand drive models, the front compartment lid release lever moved conveniently to the driver's side.

From the 1990 model year, driver and passenger airbags were fitted for specific markets and became standard across the left-hand drive range from April 1991. Right-hand drive cars were equipped with a driver's airbag from 1993. When a passenger airbag was fitted, the glovebox moved to a new position below the dashboard. For the 1991 model year a time delay on the interior light and new rear seat back releases (with a button on the top of the seat back) were introduced.

DASHBOARD & INSTRUMENTS

The main dash was carried over from the outgoing 3.2 Carrera, but there were detail revisions. All the instruments were revised in appearance from the earlier Carrera and were back-lit. Most changed were the oil level and oil pressure gauges, which now had 'external' indicator needles, meaning that the needles no longer extended from behind a hidden pivot. The gauges also included an array of 13 warning

The Carrera 4 introduced an electrically-operated rear spoiler (far left) which deployed automatically above 50mph and retracted when speed fell below 6mph. In the wake of the Carrera 4, the Carrera 2 was introduced (left) early in 1990 to replace the old Carrera 3.2. More sporting than the four-wheel drive model, it was modified to great effect by the factory's racing department.

Apart from new trim choices and door loudspeakers, the only significant change in this Carrera 4's interior architecture compared with the old Carrera 3.2 is the higher central tunnel necessary for the four-wheel drive system.

The instruments were totally updated for the new models (above). The figures and indicator needles were now backlit at night and the oil combination gauge now contained an array of warning lights. This car does not have the airbag steering wheel. The instruments continued to be developed (right) and by 1992 the clock even carried its own complement of warning lights. The speedometer contained a shift indicator on Tiptronic models.

lights, which finally ensured that even the most long-standing 911 driver was forced to look in the handbook to find out what they all meant. A 7600rpm rev counter was fitted and the speedometer was calibrated to 180mph or 300kph. New climate controls, mounted in the middle of the dash, were taken from the 944 series.

The dashboard was carried over to the new Carrera 2, but obviously without the controls for the four-wheel drive transmission. The Carrera 4 had the differential lock control mounted on the centre console, ahead of the gear lever.

From the 1990 model year, Tiptronic-equipped cars had an on-board computer which gave the driver the following information: journey distance on fuel remaining, daily kilometre total, average fuel consumption, digital speed read-out, average journey speed and outside air temperature. Also from 1990, the position of the electrically-operated rear spoiler could be manually controlled by a switch on the centre console, although the speed-controlled movement remained.

Luggage Compartment

The luggage compartment was re-shaped and reduced in size to accommodate the Carrera 4's front differential and driveshaft assemblies. For the same reason, fuel tank capacity was reduced from 85 litres (18.70 Imperial gallons, 22.46 US gallons) to 77 litres (16.94 Imperial gallons, 20.34 US gallons), including a reserve of 10 litres (2.20 Imperial gallons, 2.64 US gallons). A new option from 1993 was a 92-litre tank (20.24 Imperial gallons, 24.31 US gallons) for those who wanted extended range.

The factory said the Carrera 4 was 87 per cent new under the skin, and here's some of the evidence. The luggage compartment has a completely different layout, with the plastic fuel tank now moved upwards and backwards to accommodate the front differential below, the fuse panel moved to the left-hand rear of the compartment, and the new ABS equipment under the cover to the rear of the battery.

The Carrera 4 and Carrera 2 shared a new 3.6-litre engine developing 250bhp. A notable feature of the new models was the distinctive whine, like the sound of a jet aircraft turbofan, made by the revised curved-blade cooling fan while cruising.

ENGINE

The Carrera 4 engine – and subsequently that of the Carrera 2 – was termed the M64/01 and had a capacity of 3600cc (219.6cu in). It developed 250bhp at 6100rpm and maximum torque of 310Nm at 4800rpm for all markets.

It was a design goal for the Carrera 4 that its performance should exceed that of the 3.2 Carrera, so power had to be increased to compensate for the weight of the four-wheel drive equipment. Increased capacity was achieved by enlarging the bore from 95mm (3.70in) to 100mm (3.90in) and the stroke from 74.4mm (2.90in) to 76.4mm (2.98in). The cylinder heads used ceramic port liners: ceramic is a poor conductor of heat and in this application it reduced the transfer of heat from the exhaust gas to the cylinder head. The cylinder heads

Great attention was paid to the aerodynamics of the Carrera 4. A full-length undertray to the rear of the engine not only helped air flow but also contributed to lower noise levels. Note the NACA duct below the gearbox area.

ran up to 40°C cooler in the region of the exhaust ports, allowing the deletion of the sodium-cooled exhaust valves that had been present from the first 911s. Sodium cooling, however, was now used on the intake valves in order to allow heat to transfer from the head to the valve and so help cold starting; it also reduced noise between valves and followers when cold.

New forged pistons with dished crowns ran in slightly conical cylinders, so that the cylinder walls became perfectly parallel when the engine was hot. The two centre cylinders carried anti-knock sensors, each one connected to the adjacent cylinders by a metal strap to detect the onset of detonation. The crankcase was revised to accommodate the wider-spaced cylinder head bolt attachments and a new, lighter crankshaft was used (but with all major bearing dimensions carried over from the 3.2-litre engine) with a vibration damper at the pulley drive end. A new 12-blade cooling fan was driven at the same 1.6:1 ratio as on the 959. The crank drove the cooling fan in the familiar way, but now with a belt different from that driving the alternator.

A twin-spark ignition system with double distributors (the second one was driven by a small toothed belt from the first) allowed the ignition timing to be retarded by 6 degrees compared with the 3.2 engine. This in turn allowed the compression ratio to increase to a standard 11.3:1 for all markets, despite a decrease in the octane requirement from 98 RON to 95 RON. These improvements were made possible by a revised Motronic programme. A new two-stage resonant intake manifold ensured good low speed response.

A primary objective of the new engine was to reduce noise, and the cam timing chain tensioners were completely redesigned for this purpose. Considering one side only, the new hydraulic tensioner bears onto the rear of a large polyamide lever, which is pivoted at the other end of its length. The end of the lever, which is shaped to bear onto the trailing part of each double-row chain, also carries a mounting for a connecting rod to a second (also pivoting) chain ramp on the other side of the chain. This way the tensioner works on both the driven and driving lengths of the chain.

The engine oil cooler, present on all previous 911s, was deleted, and the oil radiator in the right-hand front wing was enlarged accordingly. The intake system for the new engine was completely new, utilising pulsed air theory to ensure the best filling of the cylinders. The new Motronic injection used sequential fuel injection, which was timed on crankshaft position and controlled by parameters such as engine temperature, engine speed and oxygen sensing (Lambda) in the exhaust. The Motronic system also controlled any tendency for the engine to pre-detonate by retarding the spark in 3-degree steps when using low-grade fuel or under load.

The big breakthrough with the Carrera 4 was that it truly became a car for all markets. Every engine had the same power and torque, whether or not it was fitted with a three-way catalytic converter – this alone says a lot about the clever design of the converter-equipped exhaust system. The catalyst itself was all-metal (with no ceramic core) and so was more compact. All Carrera 4s had an active charcoal filter to absorb vapour from the fuel tank.

From 1993 all Porsche models leaving the factory were filled with Shell TMO full synthetic engine oil.

TRANSMISSION

A prototype four-wheel drive Cabrio study had been shown at the 1981 Frankfurt Show, and the 959 had pioneered four-wheel drive in production at Porsche. The Carrera 4's transmission was much simpler than that on the 959, however, and owed more to the system used on the Paris-Dakar four-wheel drive cars of 1984.

The five-speed gearbox was known as the G64/00 and was derived from the G50 used on the 3.2 Carrera. The drive to the front wheels was taken from the front of the gearbox, via a centre epicyclic differential that divided the torque transmitted from the engine to the front (31 per cent) and back (69 per cent) wheels. A rigid torque tube containing a propeller shaft and the gear linkage took the drive to the front axle, where a front differential distributed drive to the wheels. The rear wheels were driven from the centre differential via a shaft through a hollow gearbox output shaft to another differential. The slip of both differentials was controlled by multi-plate clutches. Control of the differentials was electronic and linked to the ABS sensors in each wheel, so that the correct amount of torque could be split between each axle or each wheel if slip was detected. The centre and rear differentials could also be locked manually – for traction in extreme conditions – by means of a 'traction' switch in the centre console; this locking facility would disengage above 25mph. For the Swiss market, a variant with longer fourth and fifth speeds (G64/01) was used to meet local noise control requirements.

The transmission of the new Carrera 2 was based on the G50 design, with changes to the ratios. The 9:31 ratio of the crown wheel and pinion was unchanged from the 3.2. On export models to the US, Canada, Japan and Australia, fourth and fifth gears were shortened (32:36 from 35:38 for fourth, 37:33 from 38:33 for fifth), mainly for noise reasons. This gearbox was known as the G50/01, with Switzerland again receiving its own G50/02 variety.

For the 1990 model year, a double mass flywheel containing a rubber damper was fitted. This was termed ZMS (*Zweimassenschwungrad*) in technical documentation. The new flywheel assembly reduced the transmission of low-speed torsional vibration from the engine to the gearbox.

Tiptronic 'dual-function' transmission was introduced with the Carrera 2 at the start of 1990. This transmission, the result of a joint study by ZF and Bosch, comprised four speeds selectable entirely automatically or in a semi-automatic sequential mode. The gearbox was described as 'intelligent' in that a computer calculated the right gear for the loading on the transmission. The other feature – and the big improvement over previous automatic gearboxes – was its ability to give ratio changes without interruption of the driving torque, termed by the factory as a power-flow change.

The Tiptronic selector offered the driver a gear shift with two operating planes. In the first plane a conventional P-R-N-D-3-2-1 automatic shift was available, but if the lever was moved to the second plane (to the right) the driver had a sequential 'adaptive' shift. Pushing the lever forward would change to a higher gear and pulling it back would change to a lower gear. If the car's speed did not match the desirable speed range for that ratio, the control unit would retain the shift command until the appropriate moment by assessing vehicle speed, accelerator actuation speed, engine speed and lateral and longitudinal acceleration. The system was intended to prevent unwanted gear shifts in corners and to be responsive to 'sporting' driving by sensing fast accelerator movements.

Despite all the hype about its electronic brains and so on, performance of the Tiptronic was down on a manual Carrera 2, 0-62mph (0 100kph) taking 6.6sec as opposed to 5.7sec. But let that not detract from the Tiptronic; it has been an outstanding improvement in automatic transmission technology, and its value is in its flexibility for town and country driving.

The Tiptronic system for the US and Canada was improved for the 1992 model year with a revised 9:32 final drive ratio and with the addition of the Keylock/Shiftlock control system to prevent accidental selection of an incorrect ratio. This was extended to Tiptronic models for all markets the following year.

Two new rotary controls were found on the Carrera 4 centre console (top). The left-hand switch is a manual override for deploying or retracting the automatic rear spoiler, while the right-hand one allows the centre and rear differentials to be locked in poor weather conditions. Tiptronic was introduced to the Carrera 2 (above) as the next-generation automatic transmission for Porsches. On the left-hand side of the gate the driver had the choice of clutchless (and intelligent) manual shifting or a fully automatic regime. Moving the lever to the right-hand side of the gate offered a push/pull shift option.

ELECTRICAL EQUIPMENT & LIGHTING

The alternator on the Carrera 4 was uprated to 1610 watt/115A and charged a 72Ah battery. The new front deformable bumper had integrated driving lights and fog lights. The new headlamps were sealed

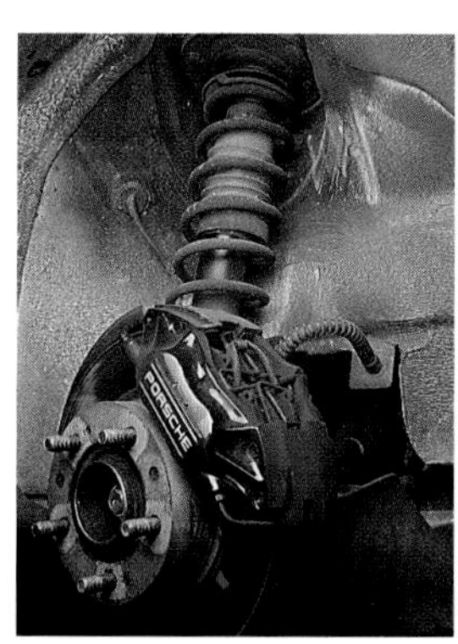

The front suspension discarded the 911's time-honoured torsion bars and adopted conventional coil springs over the shock absorbers. A significant redesign of the front chassis was necessary to accommodate four-wheel drive.

beam units, and all markets (except right-hand drive and France) now had the same lights. At the rear, the old style of tail-light was broadly retained, but the lenses were raked with the line of the rear body rather than presenting a vertical face. The rear fog lamps were integrated into a new reflector strip fitted under the engine lid. The number plate lamps were now fitted in the bumper moulding, above the number plate.

Suspension & Steering

The Carrera 4 suspension front and back was completely new and marked the end of torsion bars on the 911 – the front differential and drive shafts meant there simply was not space for them. The MacPherson strut principle was maintained at the front, with concentric coil springs over the struts and cast aluminium lower arms. The new front suspension allowed a degree of front/back movement that had not been possible with the torsion bar arrangement, and this helped to subdue cabin noise on rough surfaces. Negative scrub radius (the 3.2 Carrera had positive scrub) was included in the front suspension geometry. This reflected the contribution of the new ABS to wheel stability under braking and gave the Carrera 4 a degree of automatic steering correction when the front wheels began to slip. A 20mm front anti-roll bar replaced the outgoing 3.2 Carrera's 22mm bar. The front suspension on the Carrera 2 was largely identical to the Carrera 4, except for the absence of drive shafts. The increased weight on the front axle was the main reason for the introduction of power steering on this 911, using the proven rack and pinion design.

At the rear the Turbo's cast aluminium semi-trailing arms were used, with coil springs acting concentrically outside the existing shock absorbers. Rubber mountings allowed some wheel movement to give roll steer in cornering. Rear anti-roll bar size dropped from the 3.2 Carrera's 21mm to 20mm (or 19mm on the Tiptronic). The rear suspension was common to Carrera 4 and Carrera 2.

Brakes

The brakes on the Carrera 4 were completely new, although derived from those on the 928 S4, and were linked to Bosch ABS (Anti-Block System). The brake servo acted in the same way to reduce the effort to move the master cylinder piston, but additional control was placed on the outlet, which included the ABS control unit. A separate hydraulic pump charged a pressure accumulator, which charged the control unit to provide energy to counter brake pedal force and provide the ABS function to each wheel. An ABS sensor was provided for each front wheel and there was a further one for the rear wheels. Under heavy braking, the rear brake pressure would be eased to prevent locking, as on the 3.2 Carreras. As brake pedal pressure was increased and the front wheels began to lock, the ABS would reduce the braking pressure though the control unit.

Brake disc sizes were 298mm (11.6in) front and 299mm (11.6in) rear – a minute difference! – on both Carrera models. The discs had four-piston aluminium calipers all round. The pistons were of unequal size on each face, with the front primary pistons being sized at 40mm (1.56in) diameter and the secondary ones at 36mm (1.40in). The rear calipers were smaller, with 30mm (1.17in) and 28mm (1.09in) diameter pistons. Cooling air for the front brakes was ducted from the twin horizontal slots under the front number plate.

Wheels & Tyres

The looks of the 1989 Carrera 4 were set off by new seven-spoke, smoothly-styled, slightly convex-faced alloy wheels, known as Club Sport wheels. Wheel and tyre sizes were the same as the standard issue on that year's 3.2 Carrera, namely 6J × 16in front wheels with 205/55ZR tyres and 8J × 16in rear wheels with 225/50ZR tyres. Bridgestone RE71 tyres were the preferred factory fit.

From the start of the 1992 model year both the Carrera 4 and 2 received new 'Cup Design' wheels. Derived from the Carrera Cup racing series, these attractive five-spoke alloy designs were unchanged in size and used the same tyres.

Carrera 2 RS

Born out of the successful Carrera Cup racing series, the 'second-generation' Carrera 2 RS was a sports model with little concession to comfort, and was announced at the Geneva Motor Show in March 1991. The output of the re-chipped 3.6-litre engine was increased to 260bhp at 6100rpm, with maximum torque of 325Nm at 4800rpm. Pistons and cylinders were claimed to be matched and a sports flywheel lightened by 7kg was used. The engine mounts were solid rubber and only a single cooling fan drive was used; 98 RON fuel was required and a low-rating 36Ah alternator was fitted.

The standard form of the new RS was the Sport (or Lightweight), claimed by the factory to weigh 1230kg (2712lb). Besides this basic model, three variants of the RS were offered: the Carrera Cup (option M001, for the racing series), the Touring (option M002) and the Competition (option M003, another racing version with small differences over the Carrera Cup model). We shall not discuss the two racing versions here, but a description of how the Touring model differed comes later.

The Carrera 2 RS arrived in late 1991. With no concessions to touring comfort, this car was modified to perform. The suspension was lowered 40mm from standard, instantly giving the car a purposeful stance.

The Sport was a stripped-out version with the sunroof, electric mirrors, electric seats, central locking, alarm and electric windows removed – and the wiring loom to support these items was also largely removed. Recaro sports seats with only fore/aft adjustment were fitted, and these had seat belts colour-coded to the body. There were no rear seats, this area being carpeted and having the RS logo on the firewall. There were simple door trims with door pull straps and manual window winders. There was provision only for a two-speaker radio system and the side windows used thinner glass (3mm instead of 4.7mm). There was no interior sound insulation. Options were a leather-covered steering wheel with extended centre hub, deletion of rear model designation and a basic stereo/cassette at no extra cost.

Special seam welding was used on the bodyshells and the wing edges were rolled to enable larger wheels to be fitted. Underbody sealer was deleted and the body corrosion warranty was only three years as a result. Only the Space-Saver tyre was covered by elementary carpeting in the front compartment which also had a master switch, a 92-litre (20.24 Imperial gallons, 24.31 US gallons) fuel tank and an aluminium lid. The rear bumper was a new lightweight design, with the number plate lamps either side of the plate. Manually-adjusted Turbo style exterior mirrors were fitted.

The bodyshell was lowered by 40mm (1.56in) and stiffer springs and shock absorbers were used – this was not a car to use for touring! The understeering nature of the car was increased by using a 24mm (0.94in) diameter front anti-roll bar, up 4mm (0.16in) on the Carrera 2. The standard car's steel front hubs were replaced by aluminium ones and an adjustable rear anti-roll bar was fitted, reduced to 18mm (0.70in) from the Carrera 2's 20mm (0.78in). The rear suspension was modified to change the roll-steer effect of the standard car and the spring plates allowed more negative camber, of approximately 1 degree all round. Ball-type joints were used for the

The Carrera 2 RS is barely suitable for road use. The spartan interior includes lightened trim and racing bucket seats that are uncomfortable on long journeys. Revised door trims have canvas pulls and manual windows.

Available in the US from 1992, the RS America was a reduced specification Carrera 2, rather than a high-performance special. It has driver and passenger airbags as standard, hence the revised steering wheel.

shock absorber top mountings front and rear. A cross-brace was fitted in the front compartment between the front shock absorber top mountings.

Brakes were from the Turbo at the front and from the Carrera Cup racer at the rear, the latter of 299mm (11.66in) diameter and 24mm (0.94in) thickness. The two-stage ABS was re-adjusted to provide better recovery during hard use.

The Cup Design magnesium alloy wheels were 7.5J × 17 front and 9J × 17 rear with 205/50 ZR and 255/40ZR tyres respectively. No steering servo was fitted to left-hand drive models. The G50 gearbox had closer ratios, with a higher final drive ratio of 3.444:1 and stronger synchromesh than the Carrera 2. The gear lever was shortened and moved close to the driver. A limited slip differential was standard.

The road-going RS variant was the Touring model (option M002), which weighed around 1300kg (2866lb). This better-equipped RS came with a stereo/cassette, central locking, sound proofing, electric windows and the rear panel trim found on the Carrera 2 (but no rear seats). It had Carrera 2 door panels, sports seats with electric height adjustment, and the thinner side glass. It came with the aluminium front compartment lid, the 10-year body warranty (it had under-body protection) and the Carrera 2's wiring harness. Its options were headlamp washers, heated seats, electric sunroof, full interior climate control, a non-tinted windshield, or a tinted windshield with a dark green upper edge.

Performance of the Sport was impressive, with a factory-quoted maximum speed of 162mph (261kph) and a 0-62mph (0-100kph) time of 5.4sec. The RS was not sold in the US because its weight-saving thin glass and lack of door beams did not comply with federal regulations. Porsche's objective was to start production in the summer of 1991 and to make at least 1000 units by the end of the year in order to qualify the car for the racing Group N/GT class. However, a total run of 2051 cars was made to the end of the 1992 model year, of which 76 were

The engine of the RS America was the standard 250bhp Carrera 2 unit. Note the air conditioner compressor pipes leading directly out of the engine compartment to the remotely mounted condenser. The mechanism for the moving electric spoiler of the regular Carrera 4 and Carrera 2 models had displaced the condenser from its previous position under the engine lid grille.

As with all Carrera 4 and Carrera 2 models, the RS America has no bumper overriders. The bumper is flexible, but it is necessary to park carefully to avoid scraping the paint. The fixed rear spoiler used on this model is the one previously seen on the 3.2 Carrera. The RS America does not have rear seats, but unlike the Club Sport model of 1987 this model has doors to the storage boxes under the shelf.

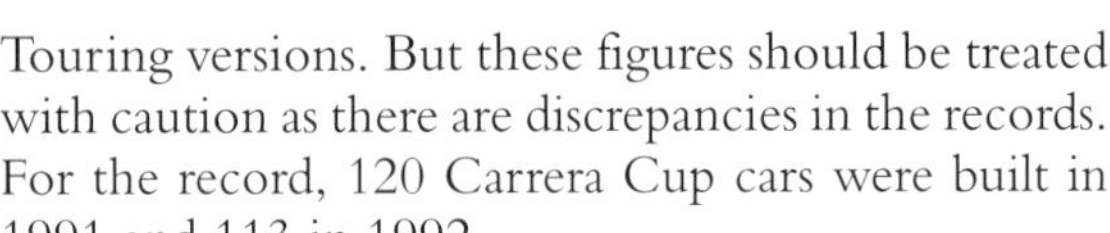

Touring versions. But these figures should be treated with caution as there are discrepancies in the records. For the record, 120 Carrera Cup cars were built in 1991 and 113 in 1992.

RS AMERICA

This model was manufactured solely for the US and Canadian marketplace in 1992-93. The concept of the RS America was similar to that of the European RS, but driver-reaction in the US seemed to fall well short of the ecstatic reception given in Europe to the new Lightweight.

The first impression is that many of the weight-saving measures of the European RS were used on the RS America, but the key to understanding the difference was that the RS America sold for about $10,000 less than a regular Carrera 2, whereas the European RS sold for about $20,000 more! There was a significant amount of detail difference because the European RS was an homologation special for racing, whereas the America was a low specification variant of the regular model.

The RS America saved weight by losing the air conditioning, power steering, electric sunroof and rear seats. Sound insulation was removed from the rear firewall and the rear quarter panels. A lightweight fixed whaletail spoiler replaced the moving rear spoiler of the standard car. Inside the electric windows stayed, but the lightweight door trims, with door pulls, from the European RS were used. A storage compartment replaced the rear seats. In

The Speedster returned in 1993 on the Carrera 2 chassis. Customers were not obliged to have body-colour wheels, as here, but with the Speedster one was making a loud statement anyway...

the front, lightweight fabric replaced the pile carpeting of the Carrera 2.

A sports suspension package was fitted (the same M030 option that was available for the Carrera 2), and the aluminium alloy Cup Design wheels were 7J × 17 with 205/50ZR tyres at the front and 8J × 17 with 255/40ZR tyres at the rear. Anti-roll bar sizes were 22mm (0.86in) front and 20mm (0.78in) rear.

Unlike the RS, the RS America used the standard 250bhp (DIN) engine. The factory's 0-62mph (0-100kph) time was 5.4sec and the top speed was 162mph (261kph). Weight was 1340kg (2955lb) compared with 1398kg (3083lb) for the Carrera 2. Some 240 RS America models were sold before the start of the 1993 model year (in August 1992). These all carry the 1993 'P' designator in their chassis numbers, however, with engine numbers retaining the 1992 'N' designator.

America Roadster

This was a Turbo-Look Cabrio for the 1992 model year with the Carrera 2's normally aspirated 3.6-litre engine. It came complete with Cup Design wheels, as did all 1992 models. It had the fully automatic folding hood of the standard Cabrio and could be ordered with manual or Tiptronic transmission. Brakes were the Turbo's cross-perforated discs with a diameter of 322mm (12.56in) at the front and 299mm (11.66in) at the rear. The standard car's anti-roll bars were changed to 21mm (0.82in) front and 22mm (0.86in) rear, except that the rear bar was reduced to 21mm (0.82in) when Tiptronic was specified. Factory figures gave performance as 0-62mph (0-100kph) in 5.5sec and a top speed of 158mph (254kph). A total of 250 cars were made.

Carrera 2 Speedster

Announced in October 1992, the new Speedster was based on the Carrera 2. The changes from the Coupé were based around the shortened windshield and simplified hood concept seen on the 1989 model. Interestingly, the Speedster was not offered from its introduction in Turbo-Look, which had been far and away the most popular version in 1989.

Inside, the bucket Recaro seats from the RS were used, the backs of these being colour-coded to the exterior body. Optionally, Sports seats that were electrically adjustable for height or the Carrera 2 multi-function seats with heating could be specified. Also colour-coded inside were the door pull straps, the gear lever and handbrake boots, and the instrument mounting facia.

As before, the Speedster was well-equipped and was available in five-speed manual or Tiptronic forms. The standard Cup Design wheels were 6J × 17 front (with 205/55ZR tyres) and 8J × 17 rear (with 225/50ZR tyres) and these could be ordered with body colouring as well. The hood design benefited from improved windshield locks. Manually adjustable external mirrors from the Carrera 2 RS were used. Although a run of 3000 Speedsters was planned for 1993, only 936 were actually built. Unlike the 1989 Speedster, the 1993 model had unique chassis number identification (see page 108).

The Speedster interior featured a colour-coded instrument surround and Recaro bucket racing seats.

911 CELEBRATION

This model was a limited edition Carrera 4 with the Turbo-Look bodyshell. However, the running gear remained standard Carrera 4, so these cars are not full Turbo-Look models, with the Turbo brakes and suspension.

The Celebration was introduced in March 1993 on the anniversary of 30 years of continuous 911 production of the 911. The specification was like the 1993 Carrera 4, but with special paint and an interior featuring full leather and '30 Jahre 911' badges. It came with a 92-litre fuel tank (20.24 Imperial gallons, 24.31 US gallons) and a stylised 911 badge on the engine cover with its underline embossed with the words '30 Jahre'. The number of these cars manufactured was 911...

RS 3.8

The RS 3.8 was a limited edition series that was intended to qualify the car for GT racing in 1993. These Weissach-built cars (about 100 were made) were distinguished by their large, adjustable biplane rear wing on a full Turbo-look bodyshell. The engine (M64/04) had a capacity of 3746cc and was not turbocharged. It produced 300bhp at 6500rpm and maximum torque of 360Nm at 5250rpm. The compression ratio was 11.0:1 and Bosch Motronic 2.1 engine management was used. The Speedline 9J × 18 front wheels were fitted with 235/40ZR Dunlop tyres, the 11J × 18 rears with 285/35ZR tyres. Weight was reduced to 1140kg (without fuel), enabling 0-62mph (0-100kph) acceleration in 4.9sec and a top speed of 170mph (274kph).

A very limited-edition 911 (below) for the road was the RS3.8. Developed from the Carrera 2 RS, this 300bhp sprinter was an homologation special for GT racing in 1993. Note the biplane wing and the horizontal splitter protruding from the front spoiler. To celebrate the 30th anniversary of the 911 in 1993, a commemorative run of Carrera 4s with the Turbo bodyshell was produced. Apart from special paint, the main external distinguishing feature is this '30 Jahre' style of 911 logo (below left) on the engine lid.

Data Section

PRODUCTION DATA

Model year	Model	Power (bhp DIN@rpm)	Torque (Nm@rpm)	Compression ratio	Weight (kg)	Number built
1989	Carrera 4	250@6100	310@4800	11.3:1	1450	2068
	Carrera 4 US	250@6100	310@4800	11.3:1	1450	1117
1990	Carrera 2/4	250@6100	310@4800	11.3:1	1350/1450	3957
	Carrera 2/4 Targa	250@6100	310@4800	11.3:1	1400/1500	322
	Carrera 2/4 Cabrio	250@6100	310@4800	11.3:1	1400/1500	895
	Carrera 2/4 US	250@6100	310@4800	11.3:1	1350/1450	1317
	Carrera 2/4 Canada	250@6100	310@4800	11.3:1	1350/1450	80
	Carrera 2/4 Targa US	250@6100	310@4800	11.3:1	1400/1500	158
	Carrera 2/4 Targa Canada	250@6100	310@4800	11.3:1	1400/1500	61
	Carrera 2/4 Cabrio US	250@6100	310@4800	11.3:1	1400/1500	673
	Carrera 2/4 Canada	250@6100	310@4800	11.3:1	1350/1450	61
1991	Carrera 2/4	250@6100	310@4800	11.3:1	1350/1450	7840
	Carrera 2/4 US	250@6100	310@4800	11.3:1	1350/1450	1608
	Carrera 2/4 Targa	250@6100	310@4800	11.3:1	1400/1500	1196
	Carrera 2/4 Targa US	250@6100	310@4800	11.3:1	1400/1500	746
	Carrera 2/4 Cabrio	250@6100	310@4800	11.3:1	1400/1500	3886
	Carrera 2/4 Cabrio US	250@6100	310@4800	11.3:1	1400/1500	2207
1992	Carrera 2/4	250@6100	310@4800	11.3:1	1350/1450	4844
	Carrera 2/4 US	250@6100	310@4800	11.3:1	1350/1450	715
	Carrera 2/4 Targa	250@6100	310@4800	11.3:1	1400/1500	597
	Carrera 2/4 Targa US	250@6100	310@4800	11.3:1	1400/1500	211
	Carrera 2/4 Cabrio	250@6100	310@4800	11.3:1	1400/1500	2885
	Carrera 2/4 Cabrio US	250@6100	310@4800	11.3:1	1400/1500	992
	Carrera 2 RS	260@6100	325@4800	11.3:1	1250	2051
	RS America	250@6100	310@4800	11.3:1	1340	298
1993	Carrera 2/4	250@6100	310@4800	11.3:1	1350/1450	3249
	Carrera 2/4 US	250@6100	310@4800	11.3:1	1350/1450	520
	Carrera 2/4 US 718[1]	250@6100	310@4800	11.3:1	1350/1450	280
	Carrera 2/4 Targa	250@6100	310@4800	11.3:1	1400/1500	419
	Carrera 2/4 Targa US	250@6100	310@4800	11.3:1	1400/1500	137
	Carrera 2/4 Targa US 718[1]	250@6100	310@4800	11.3:1	1400/1500	81
	Carrera 2/4 Cabrio	250@6100	310@4800	11.3:1	1400/1500	1414
	Carrera 2/4 Cabrio US	250@6100	310@4800	11.3:1	1400/1500	600
	Carrera 2/4 Cabrio US 718[1]	250@6100	310@4800	11.3:1	1400/1500	138
	RS America	250@6100	310@4800	11.3:1	1340	450
	RS America 718[1]	250@6100	310@4800	11.3:1	1340	68
	Speedster	250@6100	310@4800	11.3:1	1350	509
	Speedster US	250@6100	310@4800	11.3:1	1400	427

General notes

US models are frequently quoted with a maximum power output of 247bhp, but this refers to the SAE net horsepower as opposed to the German standard DIN figure. US/Canada models after May 1993 were listed as 1994 (R-programme) models.

Numbered notes

[1] Option M718 refers to a 1993 mid-year specification change.

PRODUCTION CHANGES

1989 (START OF K-SERIES)

Engine capacity 3600cc with 100mm bore and 76.4mm stroke; sodium-filled 42.5mm intake valves, hollow 49mm exhaust valves; engine oil capacity reduced to 12 imperial pints (11.4 litres); new free-flow (all-metal) catalytic converter with low noise silencer (muffler); G64/00 five-speed gearbox, driving through torque-splitting centre epicyclic differential; ratios as follows – first 3.5:1, second 2.118:1, third 1.444:1, fourth 1.086:1, fifth 0.868:1, reverse 2.857:1, final drive 3.444:1; drive shaft forward to front differential (in torque tube) and rearwards through hollow shaft in gearbox to rear differential; centre differential linked to Bosch ABS provides four-wheel drive with torque sensing at each wheel; brakes are 298mm/28mm front and 299mm/24mm rear; new underbody with centre tunnel to accommodate torque tube, new heating and ventilation system; speed-controlled electrically-operated rear spoiler; new front and rear bumpers, detail body changes to improve aerodynamics; coil spring suspension all round; new 77-litre fuel tank and front suspension changes shape of luggage compartment; asbestos-free materials now used on all models.

1990 (START OF L-SERIES)

Two-mass flywheel lowers interior noise levels; ten-speaker fitment; headlamp height adjustment standard; new option of on-board computer, giving outside temperature, fuel consumption and speeds, with read-out integrated into rev counter; Carrera 4 now available in Targa and Cabrio (with electrically-operated roof) forms; Carrera 2 replaces 3.2 Carrera, based on Carrera 4 but rear-wheel drive only, with same power, suspension and brakes; available from launch as Coupé, Targa or Cabrio; Carrera 2 offered with Tiptronic automatic gearbox; final drive ratios 3.444:1 (manual) or 3.667:1 (Tiptronic).

1991 (START OF M-SERIES)

Airbags standard for driver and passenger on left-hand drive cars from Apr 1991; interior light delay switch introduced on all models; new seat back release buttons on seat top; new control unit for the central locking allows doors to be locked and front luggage compartment then to be opened (and armed again after closing); sports suspension pack available for Carrera 2 (new shock absorbers, springs and front anti-roll bar); manual gear ratios altered slightly to first 3.5:1, second 2.059:1, third 1.407:1, fourth 1.086:1, fifth 0.868:1; new Tiptronic ratios of first 2.479:1, second 1.479:1, third 1.000:1, fourth 0.728:1, final drive 3.667:1.

1992 (START OF N-SERIES)

Carrera 2 RS, RS America and Turbo-Look Cabrio introduced for new model year; on Carrera 4 and 2, new Cup Design wheels replace seven-spoke CS design; new style external mirrors; new interiors.

1993 (START OF P-SERIES)

Carrera 2 Speedster introduced; 911 Celebration model; otherwise no significant changes.

DIMENSIONS

Wheelbase
2271mm

Track (front/rear)
1379mm/1374mm

Length
4250mm

Width
1651mm

OPTIONS

See listing in Carrera 3.2 (1984-89) chapter (page 91).

COLOUR SCHEMES

1989 (charts VDA 7/88, WVK 10720)

Standard body colours
Guards Red (80K), Black (700), Linen Grey (60M), Apricot Beige (548), Murano Green (22C), Grand Prix White (908), Dark Blue (347)

Special order body colours
Forest Green Metallic (22E), Cognac Brown Metallic (40L), Coral Metallic (81K), Baltic Blue Metallic (37B), Slate Grey Metallic (22D), Velvet Red Metallic (81L), Diamond Blue Metallic (697), Linen Grey Metallic (55), Silver Metallic (980), Stone Grey Metallic (693).

Fabrics
Leatherette (BPX) in Linen Grey (4WX), Burgundy (3MK), Blue (1KX), Mahogany (1MX), Black (43S) or Cashmire Beige (7RT); leather (YDX) in Burgundy (7LD), Mahogany (2LX), Venetian Blue (7KC), Black (1AJ), Blue (7JX), Cashmire Beige (2WH), Velvet Red (4MT), Linen Grey (7VX), Silk Grey (5VT), Slate Grey (2WT) or Caramel (4UC); pinstripe velour (TPC) in Linen Grey/White (4WJ), Black/White (7BN), Mahogany/White (6LN), Blue/White (8GJ), Burgundy/White (1MJ) or Cashmire Beige/White (4TN); multi-colour studio check (TPD) in Black (2VV), Mahogany (8XV), Blue (9JV), Burgundy (1MV), Linen Grey (6UV) or Cashmire Beige (5TC); fabric with in-woven diagonal 'Porsche' script (TPC) in Black (2CZ), Cashmire Beige (7TH), Mahogany (4MR), Blue (6HZ), Burgundy (5LZ) or Linen Grey (5WZ); Cabrio hoods in Black, Mahogany, Blue or Burgundy.

Carpets
Silk velour (TFK) in Mahogany (5MF), Blue (4KV), Linen Grey (2XF), Burgundy (8MD), Black (5FV), Slate Grey (3WT), Cashmire Beige (8UT), Velvet Red (9MT), Silk Grey (7VT), Caramel (5UM) or Venetian Blue (3KM).

1990 (charts WVK 102020, WVK 103815)

Standard body colours
As 1989 plus Marine Blue Metallic (35V).

Special order body colours
Satin Blue Metallic, Oak Green Metallic, Venetian Blue

IDENTIFICATION

Year	Model	Engine	Gearbox	Chassis numbers	Engine numbers
K-series					
1989	Carrera	M64/01	G64/00	WPOZZZ96ZKS400001-2068	62K00001 onwards
	Carrera 4 US	M64/01	G64/00	WPOABO96KS450001-1117	62K00001 onwards
L-series					
1990	Carrera 4	M64/01	G64/00	WPOZZZ96ZLS400001-3957	62L00001 onwards
	Carrera 4 Targa	M64/01	G64/00	WPOZZZ96ZLS410001-0322	62L00001 onwards
	Carrera 4 Cabrio	M64/01	G64/00	WPOZZZ96ZLS420001-0895	62L00001 onwards
	Carrera 4 US	M64/01	G64/00	WPOAB296LS450001-1317	62L00001 onwards
	Carrera 4 Canada	M64/01	G64/00	WPOAB096LS459001-9080	62L00001 onwards
	Carrera 4 Targa Canada	M64/01	G64/00	WPOBB296LS460001-0158	62L00001 onwards
	Carrera 4 Targa US	M64/01	G64/00	WPOBB096LS469001-9061	62L00001 onwards
	Carrera 4 Cabrio US	M64/01	G64/00	WPOCB296LS470001-0673	62L00001 onwards
	Carrera 4 Cabrio Canada	M64/01	G64/00	WPOCB096LS479001-9061	62L00001 onwards
	Carrera 2	M64/01	G50/03	As Carrera 4	62L00001 onwards
	Carrera 2 Tiptronic	M64/01	G50/01	As Carrera 4	62L00001 onwards
	Carrera 2 US	M64/01	G50/01	As Carrera 4	62L00001 onwards
M-series					
1991	Carrera 4	M64/01	G64/00	WPOZZZ96ZMS400001-7840	62M00001 onwards
	Carrera 4 US	M64/01	G64/00	WPOAB296MS410001-1608	62M00001 onwards
	Carrera 4 Targa	M64/01	G64/00	WPOZZZ96ZMS430001-1196	62M00001 onwards
	Carrera 4 Targa US	M64/01	G64/00	WPOBB296MS440001-0746	62M00001 onwards
	Carrera 4 Cabrio	M64/01	G64/00	WPOZZZ96ZMS450001-3886	62M00001 onwards
	Carrera 4 Cabrio US	M64/01	G64/00	WPOCB296MS460001-2207	62M00001 onwards
	Carrera 2	M64/01	G50/03	WPOZZZ96ZMS400001-7840	62M00001 onwards
	Carrera Cup	M64/01	G50/03	WPOZZZ96ZMS409001-120	62M00001 onwards
N-series					
1992	Carrera 4	M64/01	G64/00	WPOZZZ96ZNS400001-04844	62N00001 onwards
	Carrera 4 US	M64/01	G64/00	WPOAB296NS420001-0715	62N00001 onwards
	Carrera 4 Targa	M64/01	G64/00	WPOZZZ96ZNS430001-0597	62N00001 onwards
	Carrera 4 Targa US	M64/01	G64/00	WPOBB296NS440001-0211	62N00001 onwards
	Carrera 4 Cabrio	M64/01	G64/00	WPOZZZ96ZNS450001-2885	62N00001 onwards
	Carrera 4 Cabrio US	M64/01	G64/00	WPOCB296NS460001-0992	62N00001 onwards
	Carrera 2	M64/01	G50/03	WPOZZZ96ZNS400001-04844	62N00001 onwards
	Carrera 2 RS	M64/03	G50/10	WPOZZZ96ZNS490001-1992	62N80001 onwards
	Carrera 2 RS America	M64/01	G50/05	WPOAB296PS418001-18298	62N00001 onwards
P-series					
1993	Carrera 4	M64/01	G64/00	WPOZZZ96ZPS400001-3249	62P00001 onwards
	Carrera 4 US	M64/01	G64/00	WPOAB296PS420001-0520	62P00001 onwards
	Carrera 4 US (718)	M64/01	G64/00	WPOAB296RNS420001-0280	62P00001 onwards
	Carrera 4 Targa	M64/01	G64/00	WPOZZZ96ZPS430001-0419	62P00001 onwards
	Carrera 4 Targa US	M64/01	G64/00	WPOBB296PS440001-0137	62P00001 onwards
	Carrera 4 Targa US (718)	M64/01	G64/00	WPOBB296RS440001-0081	62P00001 onwards
	Carrera 4 Cabrio	M64/01	G64/00	WPOZZZ96ZPS450001-1414	62P00001 onwards
	Carrera 4 Cabrio US	M64/01	G64/00	WPOCB296PS460001-0600	62P00001 onwards
	Carrera 4 Cabrio US (718)	M64/01	G64/00	WPOCB296RS460001-0138	62P00001 onwards
	Carrera 2	M64/01	G50/03	WPOZZZ96ZPS400001-3249	62P00001 onwards
	Carrera 2 US	M64/03	G50/05	As Carrera 4	62P80001 onwards
	Carrera 2 Tiptronic	M64/01	A50/02	As Carrera 4	62P50001 onwards
	Carrera 2 Tiptronic US	M64/01	A50/03	As Carrera 4	62P50001 onwards
	Carrera 2 RS America	M64/01	G50/05	WPOAB296PS418001-450	62P00001 onwards
	Carrera 2 RS America (718)	M64/01	G50/05	WPOAB296PS418001-068	62P00001 onwards
	Speedster	M64/01	G50/00	WPOAB296PS418001-509	62P00001 onwards
	Speedster US	M64/01	G50/00	WPOAB296PS418001-427	62P00001 onwards
	Carrera RS 3.8	M64/04	G50/10	WPOZZZ96PS497001-129	62P85001 onwards

General notes

Manual gearbox The Carrera 4 gearbox (G64/00) was the same for all markets except Switzerland (G64/01). From 1991, the Carrera 4 gearbox for Taiwan was G24/02. On the Carrera 2, the Swiss gearbox was G50/02 with a longer fourth and fifth gear (for less noise). The Carrera 2 gearbox with limited slip differential was G50/03 (or G50/04 for Switzerland). Gearboxes carried serial numbers (eg, G5005 1 0 00001): the first five digits refer to the gearbox type, here G50/05; the next digit refers to whether a limited slip differential (lsd) is fitted (1 or 2 = yes, 0 = no), with type 1 referring to the optional C2 40 per cent unit and type 2 to the C2 RS 20-100 per cent unit.

Tiptronic Engines from 1991 were in the series 62M50001 onwards; the Tiptronic gearbox type number was A50, with serial numbers in the series A50011001945 onwards. The 1991 Tiptronic was A50/01 only, but for 1992 there was A50/02 for 'RoW' cars (serial numbers start A5001-) or A50/03 for US and Taiwan (serial numbers start A5003-).

Carrera 2 RS 1992 basic version was the Sport/Lightweight/Basic model. Options on this were Carrera Cup (M001), Touring (M002) or Competition (M003). The chassis numbers shown above for the RS are only the production series, not build numbers (see page104). The 1992 Carrera Cup cars had chassis numbers starting WPOZZZ96ZNS499001; M003 versions were assigned chassis numbers starting with WPOZZZ96ZNS498001. There is conflict in the numbering for the 1992 RS types, so treat the data presented here with caution. 1992 RS America was option number M504.

Miscellaneous 1990 US Carreras were delivered with airbag, Canadian examples without airbag are shown with a 9 as the 13th character in the chassis number (instead of a 0). 1993 Speedster is option M503 on Cabrio chassis. US/Canada models after May 1993 were listed as 1994 (R-series) models.

Metallic, Violet Blue Metallic, Cassis Red Metallic, Tahoe Blue Metallic, Granite Green Metallic, Turquoise Metallic, Lagoon Green Metallic, Zermatt Silver Metallic.

Fabrics
As 1989.

Carpets
As 1989.

1991 (charts VMK 8/90, WVK 127410)

Standard body colours
Guards Red* (80K), Black* (700), Rubystone Red* (82N), Maritime Blue *(38B), Grand Prix White* (908), Signal Green (22S), Mint Green (22R).

Special order body colours
Cobalt Blue Metallic (37U), Oak Green Metallic (22L), Polar Silver Metallic* (92E), Slate Grey Metallic (22D), Black Metallic (738), Horizon Blue Metallic (37X), Midnight Blue Metallic* (37W), Coral Red Metallic (82H), Amethyst Metallic* (38A), Amazon Green Metallic (37Z). * indicates colours available on Carrera 2 RS.

Fabrics
Leatherette (BPX) in Classic Grey (5WH), Cobalt Blue (5ZF), Light Grey (3ZT), Magenta (9WX), Black (43S) or Cashmire Beige (7RT); Leather (YDS) in Classic Grey (6XL), Light Grey (8ZL), Black (8YR), Cobalt Blue (9YL), Cashmire Beige (4YU), Magenta (6YL), Sherwood Green (J25), Carrera Grey (D35) or Matador Red (M05); multi-colour studio check (TPD) in Black (2VV), Classic grey (9WT), Cobalt Blue (9YD), Magenta (1MV), Light Grey (6UV) or Cashmire Beige (5TC); fabric with in-woven diagonal 'Porsche' script (TPC) in Black (2CZ), Cashmire Beige (TH), Light Grey (7TH), Classic Grey (6WC), Cobalt Blue (7ZK) or Magenta (9YC).

Carpets
Silk velour (TLV) in Classic Grey (4XR), Light Grey (6YR), Magenta (8WZ), Cobalt Blue (4ZN), Black (5FV), Matador Red (M33), Cashmire Beige (8UT), Carrera Grey (D13) or Sherwood Green (J23).

1992 (chart WVK12742192)

Standard body colours
Black (A1), Guards Red (G1), Grand Prix White (P5), Rubystone Red (G4), Maritime Blue (F2), Signal Green (M1), Mint Green (N4).

Metallic body colours
Blue (Z8), Amazon Green (N7) Amethyst (F9), Slate Grey (09), Horizon Blue (F4), Coral Red (G7), Oak Green (N9), Cobalt Blue (F6), Midnight Blue (F8), Polar Silver (A8).

Special order body colours
Satin Blue Metallic (50), Marine Blue Metallic (56), Cassis Red Metallic (52), Violet Blue Metallic (57), Granite Green Metallic (53), Tahoe Blue Metallic, Lagoon Green Metallic (54), Turquoise Metallic (59), Zermatt Silver Metallic (55).

Special body colours for Turbo-Look
(chart WVK126910 10/92)
Raspberry Red Metallic (with Red interior), Wimbledon Green Metallic (with Green interior), Lavender Blue Metallic (with Grey interior).

Fabrics
Multi-colour studio check in Blue, Light Grey, Cashmire Beige, Classic Grey, Light Grey or Cobalt Blue; other Porsche fabrics unchanged; leather in Black, Light Grey, Cashmire Beige, Light Grey or Cobalt Blue; custom leather in Matador Red, Carrera Grey, Sherwood Green; Cabrio hoods in Black, Dark Blue, Cobalt Blue or Magenta.

Carpets
As 1991.

1993 (charts WKV 127 42093, VMK 8/92)

Standard body colours
As 1992, excluding Rubystone Red.

Special order body colours
As 1992, excluding Metallic Coral Red, but with addition of Violet Blue Metallic (57), Wimbledon Green Metallic (B5), Raspberry Red Metallic (A7) and (in early 1993) Speed Yellow.

Fabrics
As 1992, but Cabrio hoods now include Classic Grey.

Carpets
As 1991.

THE TURBO (1975-93)

If any one model of Porsche 911 comes to the mind of the proverbial man-in-the-street, then it is an image of a black Turbo, crouched low on wide wheels clothed with big wing extensions. The Turbo conjures up fantasies of raw power and elegance, of high automotive technology and style. And in 1974, in post oil-crisis Europe, it was a bold and courageous statement of defiance about the future that delighted the automotive industry and Porsche's customers alike.

The Turbo's pedigree and its character were faultless. Turbocharging had made its name on Porsche racing cars with the CanAm 917-10s and 917-30s of 1972-73. These huge open sports cars, with flat-12 turbocharged engines developing up to 1100bhp, had crushed their opposition.

The road car's origins can be traced back to a prototype 911 study shown at the 1973 Paris Salon. A year of intensive development followed, during which the company agonised internally about whether such a powerful car had a place on roads which were, at that time of the Middle East oil crisis, restricted to meagre speed limits. But Ernst Fuhrmann's leadership gave the Turbo a clear direction and in October 1974 the new production model was unveiled. Code-numbered 930 internally, the Turbo was instantly given the status of company flagship and demonstrated new levels of 911 luxury and technology. Incidentally, the original official designation for the car was 911 Turbo, not 930 Turbo.

The marketing people initially wanted the Turbo to be a stripped-out lightweight, expecting demand to be as strong as that seen previously with the 1973 Carrera RS. And like the RS, the Turbo was playing its part in the racing homologation game, the original plan having been to build a series of 500 over the allowed period of two years. The salesmen keenly sold the early Turbos on the basis that the model would remain a limited edition, but with all the development involved it seems unlikely that Fuhrmann and his directors shared this view. In any case, the Turbo's popularity was such that the planned 500 production run was more than doubled – the Turbo's future was assured.

The Turbo featured a completely reworked flat-six engine of 3-litres, and introduced a whole new set of design margins. At a stroke, this countered some suggestions that, in growing from 2-litres to 2.7-litres, the original engine was fully stretched and conceding some of its original reliability. The 3-litre was a superb engine and laid the foundation for Porsche's 911 engine programmes right through to the present day.

EVOLUTION OUTLINE

Oct 1974	3.0 Turbo announced with 260bhp (US models 245bhp from 1975); extended wheelarch flares and tea-tray spoiler; four-speed gearbox.
Oct 1976	Martini limited edition.
Aug 1977	3.3-litre model (300bhp or 265bhp for US); intercooler and 917 brakes.
Jul 1979	Turbo discontinued in US.
Aug 1982	Improvements to exhaust for reduced air pollution and noise.
Aug 1985	Engine upgraded with Motronic engine management; production resumed for US; Turbo SE/930S (slant-nose) limited edition; Turbo now available in Targa and Cabriolet forms.
Oct 1988	G50 five-speed gearbox introduced.
Jul 1989	Turbo discontinued.
Mar 1990	New Turbo announced, using chassis of Carrera 2 (3.3-litres with 320bhp).
Oct 1992	Engine enlarged to 3.6-litres (360bhp).

The Turbo's dramatically flared wheelarches and large rear spoiler caught the imagination of enthusiasts the world over. This is an early production car from 1974.

Alan Stein's lovely UK-specification 3-litre 911 Turbo (above). The right-hand drive version did not become available until September 1975, so it featured all the 1976 model year benefits such as a zinc-coated bodyshell and new electrically-operated door mirrors. Jim Boyden's 1986 US Turbo (left) is a fine example of the car that was re-introduced to the American market after an absence of six years.

The new engine turned out to have immense marketing power. It became a real status symbol to have that little word 'turbo' on your rear deck, and this fashion subsequently spread right across the motor industry. But for all the hype, in bare statistical terms, the Turbo's overall performance was not much better than that of the Carrera RS. This was due to the difficulty of spinning the wheels under hard acceleration (to obtain 0-60mph times), the ratio gaps in the four-speed gearbox and the car's extra weight. The 2.7 Carrera with 210bhp returned a maximum speed of 140mph (225kph) and went to 60mph in 6.3sec. The Turbo with 260bhp managed 153mph (246kph) and reached 60mph in 6.1sec.

Torque was much improved as well, the peak rising from 255Nm at 5100rpm, to 343Nm at 4000rpm. The curve was less peaky and this allowed the engineers to justify only four speeds in the redesigned gearbox. At the time, Porsche told its customers that the engine could pull so strongly from low revs that five speeds were simply unnecessary. As an aside, the presence of the turbo in the exhaust actually made the 911 quieter. The new 3-litre engine, with many improvements over the

By 1986 the rear spoiler was deepened (above right) on its underside to allow the intercooler to exhaust through the engine grille. As a point of detail, the new US cars were no longer termed 'Turbo Carreras'. The body warranty was extended to ten years on 1986 models. Robin Duckitt's 1989 car (right) is a UK-specification limited edition built as a final batch before what was expected to be the Turbo's permanent demise. This car, typical of the customising work performed by Porsche during the late 1980s, features the rear wings of the Slant-Nose model, but with conventional headlamps and a deep front skirt. A new Turbo, however, had arrived within a year.

sometimes not-so-dependable 2.7-litre unit, also proved to be very reliable.

But what really set the Turbo apart was its looks, which were quite unlike those of any other production 911. With a deep front air dam, large rear spoiler and heavily flared wheelarches front and back, the car looked fantastic. Porsche was playing to the exclusivity market with the Turbo in a way that it had not dared contemplate before.

For 1978 the engine capacity was increased to 3.3-litres and the Turbo received the brakes it should have had from the start (early cars are noticeably under-braked). The engine upgrade seemed a big step at the time, but history shows it to have been simply another stage in the relentless enlargement of the flat-six. The 3.3-litre Turbo was hailed by *Motor* in 1978 as the quickest production road car it had ever tested. The Turbo progressively acquired all the most modern technical, environmental and comfort features – and usually received them ahead of the regular 911 range.

Magazine road tests leading up to 1980 clearly carry the message that the 3.3 Turbo was probably going to be the last and the very best of the 911 line.

Derived from the Carrera 2, the new 3.6-litre Turbo of 1993 had a 360bhp engine that delivered shatteringly quick performance.

Fuhrmann was seriously thinking about the end of the 911 series and was not inclined to keep shovelling money into development of a separate Turbo model. It was for this reason that Porsche called a halt to Turbo sales to the US and Japan at the end of 1980. This was to Canada's gain because it received the more powerful European-specification Turbo from 1981.

But the Turbo would not lie down, especially in Europe. Eventually in 1986, the 930 made it back to the US, at least partly compensating for the fact that federal laws had kept the sensational 959 off America's highways. Even the Turbo's second demise in 1989 was strongly challenged by its ardent fans. The discontinuation of the Turbo that year was much over-sold by dealer salesmen. They said it was the last chance to buy one and cleared their showrooms – and lost a lot of respect from regular buyers in the process because a new-shape Turbo was rolled out at the 1990 Geneva Salon. Many buyers of the old model had thought they were getting a last-of-line landmark in 1989. The new model was on sale by the end of 1990.

The new Turbo with the Carrera 2 shape developed 320bhp from its 3.3-litre engine. When the capacity was stretched to 3.6-litres in 1993, however, performance became nothing short of sensational. Two 3.6-litre versions were available. The standard model with 360bhp yielded a maximum speed of 175mph (282kph) and 0-62mph (0-100kph) in 4.8sec. And then there was the 381bhp Turbo S, with a maximum speed of 180mph (290kph) and a 0-62mph (0-100kph) time of just 4.66sec – and these are factory figures, which have always been traditionally conservative.

The text that follows only describes new Turbo fittings or differences from the standard 911 of the same model year.

The 'whaletail' spoiler was derived from the design used on the 1973-74 3-litre RS. The 1975 model has a small secondary engine cooling grille, a style that was used only for one year.

So much heat was generated in the engine compartment, particularly at standstill, that the secondary engine cooling grille was enlarged for 1976.

BODYSHELL

The 911 Turbo was developed from the H-programme (1975 model year) 911 Coupé bodyshell, the impetus behind its revised body shape being aerodynamic development. The front/rear spoiler combination first seen on the 3.0 RS was refined for road use, significantly reducing positive lift at front

For 1978 the 'whaletail' gave way to the 'tea-tray', which had one large grille on its upper surface

The dual functions of the 'tea-tray' grille can be seen with the engine lid raised: the air-to-air intercooler connected into the engine intake manifolding is on the left, while the air conditioning condenser on the right is mounted directly to the grille itself.

This 1986 Turbo has a replacement front air dam, complete with opening for a supplementary oil cooler and integrated mountings for driving lights.

These large intakes in the rear wings of this 1989 car were copied from those of the racing 935, but they were more for appearance than function on the road cars.

and rear. But the new wide wing extensions were bad news aerodynamically: the Turbo's frontal area was greater and so the penetration of the car through the air was poorer when compared to the slim bodyshells of models like the 2.7 Carrera or the 911S. But no-one, except perhaps the aerodynamicists, worried too much about this when the car had an extra 50bhp and looked so good...

From September 1975, when the first right-hand drive cars became available in the UK, the Turbo was covered by the new six-year anti-corrosion warranty on the basic load-bearing platform, for which zinc-coated steel panels were used throughout.

From 1978, the 'whaletail' rear spoiler gave way to a 'tea-tray' – and there is a difference! The 'tea-tray' had a larger area in plan view and was slightly higher in elevation than the whaletail, in order to accommodate the new air-to-air intercooler under the central grille area. The 'tea-tray' was easily spotted from the side by the upturned lip around its rear and side edges.

In 1986 the anti-rust warranty was lengthened to ten years as with the other models. This year also saw the availability of the Turbo in Targa form, and the option of the uprated Turbo 930S in the US or Turbo SE in the UK. The Turbo could be ordered in Cabrio form as well from September 1987 and any of the three body styles could now be specified in a Slant-Nose version.

In March 1990 at the Geneva Motor Show, the new Turbo was launched with the new 911 shape (internal code number 964) first seen on the Carrera 4. The 1991 model year Turbo (as it became) was fitted with a different rear 'tea-tray' spoiler, but no additional front lip spoiler was necessary. The deformable front and rear bumper panels and smooth undertray were as on the Carrera 4. The 3.6 Turbo was announced in October 1992 and was available only in coupé form. It was said that the additional torque would not be suitable for the Cabriolet.

BODY TRIM

The original Turbo in standard form shared with the 2.7 Carrera the new 'black-look' to the windows, door handles and wipers, completely eliminating chrome from the car's trim and complementing the aggressive character that the changed body shape suggested – but chrome trim remained an option. As final styling touches, the headlamp rims were colour-coded and the front parts of the wide rear wheelarches were accented by black protective decals that were supposedly there to stop stone chips, but also told everyone that these 911s were that little bit different. The rear spoiler included a small grille in the high-pressure top section, to feed air to the cooling blower and to help with cooling the engine compartment when at standstill. The main grille supplied the air conditioning condenser.

Aside from the obvious bodywork differences, Turbos could be identified by a small 'turbo' script – or 'Turbo Carrera' on American models – on the lower central section of the engine cover. Headlamp washers, foglamps, rear wiper, tinted glass and electric sunroof were standard. The Turbo shared the 80-

The first Turbos had the full luxury treatment, featuring a new tartan inlay to the leather seats, a four-speaker stereo with speakers in the doors, and an automatic heater control.

The smart Burgundy interior of this 1986 US Turbo features that year's ventilation improvements, with larger face and side window vents, and new switchgear presentation.

Who could fail to become addicted to staring at that little boost gauge? The Turbo's power was nothing special at low revs, but then it arrived all in a rush, that little needle flicking round the dial as the car surged forward. The boost gauge did not become standard on Turbos until the 1977 model year.

The tidy luggage compartment of a 1986 US Turbo (right). The after-market brace between the tops of the MacPherson struts is a well-proven modification to stiffen the front structure of a 911, thereby reducing wheel camber change during hard cornering. When stripped of its carpets (far right), the luggage compartment of the 3.6 Turbo shows how carefully every component has been packaged. The front strut brace is now standard.

litre fuel tank that had been introduced on the previous year's G-programme models. From 1976, an electrically heated and adjustable driver's door mirror was fitted.

The Turbo was the first model to receive new-shape external mirrors and a bonded-in windshield in 1990.

INTERIOR TRIM

The emphasis was on luxury with the original Turbo. The standard package contained the automatic climate control by Behr, leather seats with tartan inlay, special carpets, stereo/cassette with four speakers (normally an option) and extra sound deadening. The rear fan to improve heater performance on the standard 911 was deleted on the Turbo, due to lack of space. Later improvements, which generally led the normally aspirated models, are given in the data section (pages 121-123).

All the refinements introduced on the Carrera 4 and Carrera 2 were given to the 1991 model year Turbo, including the new centre console and underdash glove compartment.

DASHBOARD & INSTRUMENTS

Differences from the normal 911 were minimal: a smaller three-spoke steering wheel was fitted and the rev counter read to 7000rpm instead of 8000rpm. Surprisingly, a boost gauge was not fitted to the Turbo until the 1977 model year. At the same time, the heater controls were lit, a seat belt warning light was added and the handbrake lever mechanism was improved.

ENGINE

The engine (coded 930/50) was developed from the Carrera RS 3.0 unit. Its capacity of 2994cc was achieved with larger barrels of 95mm (3.70in) bore but the 70.4mm (2.75in) stroke was unchanged.

A single KKK Type 3LDZ exhaust-driven turbocharger ran to a maximum speed of between 80,000-100,000rpm and delivered maximum boost of 0.8 bar. An all-new induction/exhaust system was designed for the turbocharger and wastegate installation. The turbo was installed after the heat exchangers, upstream of the silencer (muffler) and fed from both cylinder banks.

An aluminium crankcase with wider-spaced cylinder head studs was used to suit the larger Nikasil barrels with shrouded stud passages and there were new stronger forged alloy pistons on the existing rods and crank. Compression ratio was reduced from 8.5:1 to 6.5:1, but with the turbo at maximum boost the computed ratio became 11.7:1. The pistons were cooled by oil squirters from below, and this cooling requirement, plus the need to maintain a high oil flow through the turbocharger bearings, resulted in the crankcase oil circulation and scavenge pumps being increased in size by 8mm (0.13in), and oil capacity growing to 13 litres. The scavenge pump, driven from the end of the left camshaft, returned oil to the main oil tank.

The camshaft housing design was simplified and the cams now ran in four bearing journals instead of three. There were new cylinder heads with smaller ports (relative to the 2.7 Carrera) and milder cam timing gave better low speed throttle response. The valve included angle was reduced by 2° 15' but the valves themselves were the same size as on the RS 3.0 at 49mm (1.91in) inlet and 41.5mm (1.62in) sodium-cooled exhaust. Fuel of 96 RON was required, but it could be lead-free. Sparks were generated using new breakerless ignition and fuel was controlled from Bosch K-Jetronic injection, fitted with a larger air throttle valve of 110mm instead of 85mm; the throttle valve area contained the vacuum bleed for the new brake servo. The Turbo was also fitted with a faster-running cooling fan, achieved by using different pulleys. The European engine was 32kg (71lb) heavier than the 2.7-litre unit.

Cars for the US, Canada and Japan were fitted with thermal reactors fed by a camshaft-driven air

Twin exhaust tail-pipes were first seen on the 1983 Turbos when the wastegate exhaust was taken directly to atmosphere.

pump. Exhaust gas recirculation was also used from 1977 to reduce emissions. The emissions hardware resulted in a maximum power figure of 245bhp, 15bhp lower than the 'Rest of the World' level.

For the 1976 models, a by-pass valve in the intake manifolding reduced the ferocity of the 'kick' in the back when the accelerator was floored. Previously, around 3500rpm had been the threshold of a rocket-like 'ignition sequence', but now the power came in more progressively, more like an express train, from below 3000rpm.

The Turbo engine had its first major upgrade in 1978, going to 3.3-litres. Bore and stroke were increased to 95mm (3.71in) and 74.4mm (2.90in) respectively, and the main bearings and con rod 'big ends' were also enlarged. Compression ratio was raised to 7.0:1. An air-to-air intercooler, located just under the main engine lid grille area, reduced charge air temperature by 50-60°C and, together with the other changes, resulted in a maximum output of 300bhp, up by 40bhp. Torque increased too, to 412Nm at 4000rpm. The new rubber-centre clutch design also seen on the 911SC that year resulted in the engine being moved back by 30mm (1.17in), which shows how much better the handling had become since the mid-1960s. Also like the new 911 SC, every 1978 Turbo was fitted with an air pump to reduce exhaust emissions. All US Turbo models had thermal reactors, but Californian cars also had an additional vacuum control to retard the ignition timing at full load and so reduce emissions further; this extra vacuum control became standard across the US range in 1980.

Progressive improvements to the Turbo engine in 1983 and 1986 were aimed at reduced emissions and noise, the latter dropping by a claimed 25 per cent (from 82dB to 79dB) on the logarithmic decibel scale. In 1983, maximum torque was edged up to 432Nm at 4000rpm with improvements to the Bosch K-Jetronic fuel injection and the ignition: the injection had a new warm-up regulator and capsule valve in the fuel distributor, while the ignition distributor now had a double vacuum advance/retard and temperature compensation. The revised engine (930/66) had a new exhaust system, with the wastegate exhaust now going directly to atmosphere and the exhausts finishing as a pair of tail-pipes on the left side. For the 1986 model year, the engine was heavily revised again (930/68) to bring it in line with worldwide emissions legislation. This was made possible by the new mapped Digital Motor Electronics (DME, or Motronic as it became known) developed by Bosch. Equipped with this new motor, the Turbo went on sale again in the US.

The 1991 model year Turbo was still 3.3-litres, but offered 320bhp at 5750rpm and a stunning 450Nm of torque at 4500rpm. It featured a revised resonant air intake system with passages designed for minimum flow loss as well as being matched to a new exhaust. The remapped Bosch Motronic system

The first turbo installations were fairly simple compared with what came later. The large duct on the left (complete with wastegate below) is the charge air feed, and the boosted charge returns from the turbo in the other large duct adjacent to it. The turbo itself is mounted below the engine compartment metalwork between the heat exchangers and final silencer.

The busy engine compartment of a 1986 US Turbo. The horizontal radiator is the air-to-air intercooler, placed after the turbocharger in the high-pressure duct to the intake plenum. The intercooler reduces the temperature of the charge air and noticeably improves engine power as a result.

resulted in more power, better fuel consumption and improved emissions. The intercooler was enlarged by a claimed 50 per cent in terms of air volume, and there was a bigger turbocharger with a new impeller for low-speed response and 0.7 bar maximum boost. All markets had all-metal (and very compact) three-way closed loop catalytic converters, the converter and silencer fitted to the wastegate forming the left-side exhaust outlet. The main silencer had increased volume and was now positioned longitudinally on the right-hand side of the engine, with its own outlet on the left. New for the Turbo were hydro-bushings for the engine mountings to reduce internal vibration, and cabin noise was also reduced by a dual mass flywheel.

A turbocharged version of the 3.6-litre engine from the Carrera 4 and Carrera 2 was introduced for the spring of 1993. It used the crankshaft, rods, crankcase, camshaft assemblies and barrels from the Carrera 2, but the pistons and the camshafts themselves (with increased lift and greater overlap) were new. Unlike the Carrera 2 engine, only a single spark plug per cylinder was used, for space reasons. The previous model's early Motronic injection/ignition system was retained. Compared with the 3.3-litre engine, the compression ratio was increased from 7.0:1 to 7.5:1, and maximum boost went up to 0.85 bar. Power rose from 320bhp to 360bhp and Porsche claimed fuel consumption was unchanged, if not better.

TRANSMISSION

There was an all-new four-speed gearbox (coded 930/30) for the original Turbo, designed so that the new, deeply-finned gearbox casing in aluminium (it had been magnesium) was within the same physical envelope as the 915 gearbox. It was designed with a maximum torque capacity of 442Nm – a reasonable margin on the 1975 engine's output of 343Nm. The gear wheels themselves were wider and stronger than the 915 gears. An option was a final drive gear set (the 930/32 gearbox) to balance the drive ratio when optional 225/50 tyres were fitted. The standard final drive was 4.222:1, the option 4000:1.

The clutch diameter was increased from 225mm (8.78in) to 240mm (9.36in) and gave increased pedal pressure but in 1977 an over-centre 'assister' spring reduced pedal effort. In 1978, a new rubber-centred clutch was fitted, while the pressure plate and clutch housing were made from cast iron to improve strength. The new clutch hub eliminated gear chatter at engine idle, but time would show that this clutch design was not very reliable.

In 1989, the Turbo was offered for the first time with a standard five-speed gearbox, based on the new G50 design that had been announced in 1986 for the 3.2 Carrera. The new 1991 model with the Carrera 4 bodyshell carried over this five-speed gearbox, but with revised ratios and the more precise gear shift mechanism seen on the Carrera 2. It also used the double-mass ZMS flywheel introduced on the Carrera 4 and 2 the same year. The limited slip differential became standard on the new 1991 model and was the same type as used on the Carrera 2 RS, namely with as little as 20 per cent locking factor under acceleration and up to 100 per cent lock-up on overrun. The 1993 model used the same G50/52 gearbox as the 1991-92 models.

Electrical Equipment & Lighting

The 1975 Turbo was launched with a 12V/66Ah battery (88Ah optional) with a Bosch 980-watt alternator. Alternator output was raised twice, to 1050-watt/75A in 1982 and to 1260-watt/90A (with a standard 88Ah battery) in 1989. Automatic cabin heat regulation was introduced, using heat sensors in the exhaust and cabin. As on the atmospheric models, the headlamps were H4 with a rating of 60 watts (main beam) and 55 watts (dipped). The heated rear window had two-stage operation.

For the 1991 model year the Turbo received the on-board computer given to the Tiptronic the previous year. By 1993, the battery was 75Ah and the alternator capacity was 1610-watt/115A.

Suspension & Steering

The Turbo's suspension set-up was derived from that of the 3.0 RSR. At the front, there was increased negative camber and reduced castor, making the steering heavier. The front cross-member was cast aluminium and the front suspension had anti-dive geometry, created by raising the rear mounting of the lower wishbones. The front track (on 7in rims) was increased by 60mm (2.34in). The front anti-roll bar was the old 18mm (0.70in) diameter design used on the 1973 911 models, but a new one-piece bar of 20mm (0.78in) was adopted in 1977 and this increased to 22mm (0.86in) for 1985. For the new 964 Turbo of 1991, the front anti-roll bar was reduced to 21mm, staying at that size for the 3.6-litre Turbo. Rear anti-roll bar size from 1975 was 18mm, but from the 1985 model year this was increased to 20mm. For the 964-based Turbo, for 1991, the rear anti-roll bar stayed at 20mm, increasing to 22mm for the 3.6-litre model. Bilstein gas shock absorbers were used all round.

The geometry of the 1975 model rear semi-trailing arms was changed to reduce squat under acceleration and the track (on 8in rims) increased by 120mm (4.68in). These semi-trailing arms were now sand-cast aluminium and the rear wheel bearing carriers were designed to take bearings from the 917 sports racer. Front torsion bar size was 19mm (0.74in) – the same as the regular 911s. Rear torsion bar diameter was 26mm (1.01in), but in 1989 the size increased to 27mm (1.05in). Anti-roll bar diameter started at 18mm (0.70in) in 1975, went to 20mm (0.78in) in 1985, but returned to 18mm (0.70in) in 1989. When the new 964-based Turbo model appeared, the standard Carrera 2 suspension was uprated with stiffer springs and shock absorbers. Steering was power-assisted for the first time on a Turbo, with damping.

The 1991 model steering was servo-assisted and higher-geared. The suspension was also heavily revised, adopting a coil spring over damper layout with MacPherson struts at the front and semi-trailing arms at the rear. The rear swing arms had toe-angle correction in movement to improve stability in a straight line or when changing direction rapidly, particularly when the throttle was closed in a corner.

A mud-spattered 1975 Turbo rear end shows off its Bilstein shock absorber and the engine's lower valve covers newly strengthened by added ribbing. The brake calipers look far too humble for the performance of the car – the Turbo did not receive suitably powerful brakes until the 1978 model year.

Brakes

If the original Turbo's looks and engine received all the development attention, the brakes took a few years to catch up. Although the prototype used cross-drilled and ventilated discs from the 917 sports racing cars at front and rear, it was felt that the long-term reliability of these racing-developed items was insufficiently understood (there had been cracking problems between the drilled holes) to include them on a production car. The brakes for the first Turbo, therefore, were carried over from the 2.7-litre Carrera, and used S-type aluminium front calipers and M-type cast iron rear calipers.

The 917-derived brakes were eventually seen on the 3.3-litre Turbo in 1978 and were the largest so far used on a production 911. The new discs were 304mm (11.86in) diameter and 32mm (1.25in) thick at the front, and 309mm (12.05in) diameter and 28mm (1.09in) thick at the rear. They were mounted on aluminium hubs and used four-piston aluminium calipers with heavy finning to help cool-

By 1986 the sealed beam Hella headlamps fitted to US cars were available with the more powerful H4 filaments.

The 3.6 Turbo runs on special 18in Speedline wheels. The 8J front rims carry 225/40 tyres and the 10J rears have 265/35 tyres – an incredibly low profile.

ing. The new brakes gave the 3.3-litre Turbo huge reserves of stopping power.

A brake servo reduced pedal effort for left-hand drive markets for 1977, and this improvement was carried over to right-hand drive models in 1978. The ratio of the servo was increased from the original 2.5:1 to 3.0:1 on 1985 models, on which a new brake master cylinder contributed to reducing pedal effort by nearly 25 per cent.

ABS anti-lock braking was introduced on the 1991 model Turbo with the adoption of the chassis derived from the Carrera 4. Brake disc diameter changed on the 1991 models to 322mm (12.68in) front and 299mm (11.77in) rear. The brakes fitted to the 1993 Turbo broke new ground in that Brembo, the manufacturer, was able to paint the calipers in a striking, heat-resistant red paint.

The wide wings on this 1976 model housed big 7Jx15 front and 8Jx15 rear Fuchs wheels, and spacers increased the track. The tyres on these first Turbos were usually Pirelli CN36s with 185/70 front and 215/60 rear sizes, which met US bumper height requirements.

Wheels & Tyres

The 1975 models began with Fuchs forged alloy 15in wheels with deep black centres, sizes being 7J front and 8J rear. Production Turbos were generally fitted at first with Dunlop tyres in 185/70VR front and 215/60VR rear sizes, but early press cars and UK models had Pirelli CN36 tyres in the same sizes. Spacers increased the wheel offset front and rear. In the US, these tyres gave a legal bumper height, but elsewhere Pirelli's new low-profile Cinturato P7 tyres were a popular option because they had more grip and lowered the centre of gravity of the car by 18mm (0.70in) – but P7s did not last as long. The P7s, specified at 205/55VR front and 225/50VR rear, became standard in 1976; in 1977 16in wheels were fitted and used the same tyre profiles.

Rear tyre pressures were raised in 1978 from 2.4 bar (34lb psi) to 3.0 bar (43lb psi) to compensate for the engine being moved back, and putting an extra 30kg (66lb) on the rear wheels. The pressure rise increased the 'pyong' sound on poor roads. By 1987, the 16in wheels were carrying 205/55VR tyres at the front on 7J rims, while at the back 245/45VR tyres rode on 9J rims.

The 1991 model Turbo used 17in Cup Design wheels with 7J front and 9J rear rims, tyre sizes being 205/50ZR and 255/45ZR. Unusually, the potential buyer of the 1991 Turbo had three choices for tyres: first Bridgestone, and then Pirelli and Yokohama, were approved for use. The 1993 model Turbo was fitted with three-piece Cup-style wheels made by Speedline. These came in 8J × 18 and 10J × 18 sizes with 225/40ZR and 265/35ZR tyres.

Martini Turbo (1976)

A Martini Turbo was built for the British Motor Show in October 1976. The car was finished in Grand Prix White with racing sponsor Martini's well-known light blue, dark blue and red stripes applied. The show car had special 'Fuhrmann' seats that were claimed to be to an orthopaedic design with padded blocks of red, white and blue leather – but these were too expensive for production models. The British Motor Show car also had special velour carpet and leather-trimmed accessories.

The Martini Turbo, in fact, was never a series production model or even a special edition, but the stripes could be ordered as an option (M42) for Grand Prix White models, whether mainstream 911SCs or Turbos. The suspension and engine were the same as on regular 1977 model year Turbos. Of approximately 200 Turbos delivered worldwide with the stripes, half went to the US.

Turbo SE Slant-Nose (1986-87)

The Slant-Nose had been built as a special order conversion (*Sonderwunschen*) by the restoration shop in Zuffenhausen since 1981 (the first car, chassis number 932BX000619, was delivered on 16 July), but only received official option status (M506) in 1986 (for the 1987 model year) as a special limited edition under the newly-titled Porsche Exclusiv programme. In the UK, the Turbo with Special Equipment (Turbo SE) was available as an official option from early 1986, while in the US the 'official option' model – called the 930S – was not available until March 1987.

Early Slant-Nose custom models had the headlamps in the front air dam, but from 1982 pop-up headlamp versions started to appear (the first was delivered on 6 July) and became the standard offering for the 1985 model year. Behind the headlamp covers, on the wing top surfaces, were vents which allowed high pressure air to escape from the wheel-arch interiors when the car was at speed. The rear wings featured strongly styled air intakes ahead of the wheels. Side skirts, body colour-coded Fuchs wheels and a special front spoiler with integrated driving lights completed the exterior body customising. The S used the same wheel/tyres sizes as the 1986 Turbo.

The interior was in full leather, and came with air conditioning and special electrically adjustable and heated Recaro seats. The controls for these seats were initially on a console on the top side of the seat, not on the sides as on the regular electrically adjustable seats. The custom leather dash panel featured a squared-off version of the instrument pod oval and a colour-coded leather steering wheel.

Engine power was raised to 330bhp at 5500rpm, but maximum torque of 431Nm at 4000rpm was the same as the 1986 Turbo. The power increase came from higher lift cams, a revised exhaust system, higher boost pressure and a larger intercooler. A larger oil cooler was mounted under the front bumper line.

Production numbers of the *Sonderwunsch* (special order conversion) Slant-Nose Turbo models were as follows: 1981, 1; 1982, 38; 1983, 35; 1984, 34; 1985, 44; 1986, 52; 1987, 33. Figures for the production Slant-Nose Turbo are given in the main 'Production Data' table (see page 121).

TURBO S (1992-93)

Shown as a study at the 1992 Geneva Salon, the special edition Turbo S was made to order and 80 cars were built. The car could be ordered in any colour but seemed to be most eye-catching in yellow. The output of the 3.3-litre engine was increased to 381bhp at 6000rpm, and maximum torque was 490Nm at 4800rpm.

The 1987 Turbo Slant-Nose derived its front profile from the 935 racer, but pop-up headlamps were added. Early customised Slant-Nose cars lacked pop-up headlamps, having the lights mounted below the bumper line.

The study was an experimental lightweight in the style of the Carrera 2 RS, and the Turbo S had similar interior treatment. There were Recaro bucket seats, fabric door pulls and wind-up windows. Rear seats and radio were deleted, thin side and rear window glass was used, and the electrical harness was lightened. External features included a one-piece whaletail rear spoiler, air intake scoops in the front bumper in place of driving lights, and air intakes in each rear wing for the brakes. The doors, rear engine lid and front luggage compartment lid were in plastic composite. The prototype carried 'IMSA Supercar Champion' decals. The dry weight was 1290kg (2844lb), approximately 190kg (419lb) less than the standard Turbo.

The suspension was stiffened and new brakes and calipers were used. Speedline three-piece wheels of 8J × 18 front and 10J × 18 rear were fitted with Pirelli P Zero tyres with sizes of 235/40ZR and 265/35ZR respectively.

The 1992 3.3-litre Turbo S was a limited edition of just 80 cars. The chassis specification was broadly similar to the Carrera 2 RS, but different in detail. Engine output of 380bhp gave 0-62mph (0-100kph) acceleration in just 4.7sec.

Data Section

PRODUCTION DATA

Model year	Model	Power (bhp DIN@rpm)	Torque (Nm@rpm)	Compression ratio	Weight (kg)	Number built
1975	930	260@5500	343@4000	6.5:1	1140	284
1976	930	260@5500	343@4000	6.5:1	1195	644
	930 US	245@5500	343@4000	6.5:1	1195	530
1977	930	260@5500	343@4000	6.5:1	1195	695
	930 US	245@5500	343@4000	6.5:1	1195	727
1978	930	300@5500	412@4000	6.5:1	1300	735
	930 US	265@5500	395@4000	7.0:1	1300	461
	930 Japan	265@5500	395@4000	7.0:1	1300	61
1979	930	300@5500	412@4000	7.0:1	1300	820
	930 US	265@5500	395@4000	7.0:1	1300	1200
	930 Japan	265@5500	395@4000	7.0:1	1300	32
1980	930	300@5500	412@4000	7.0:1	1300	840
1981	930	300@5500	412@4000	7.0:1	1300	698
	930 Canada	300@5500	412@4000	7.0:1	1300	63
1982	930	300@5500	412@4000	7.0:1	1300	938
	930 Canada	300@5500	412@4000	7.0:1	1300	89
1983	930	300@5500	432@4000	7.0:1	1300	1015
	930 Canada	300@5500	412@4000	7.0:1	1300	65
1984	930	300@5500	432@4000	7.0:1	1300	804
	930 Canada	300@5500	412@4000	7.0:1	1300	77
1985	930	300@5500	432@4000	7.0:1	1300	1063
	930 Canada	300@5500	412@4000	7.0:1	1300	85
1986	930	300@5500	432@4000	7.0:1	1335	1158
	930 Canada	300@5500	412@4000	7.0:1	1335	88
	930 US	282@5500	390@4000	7.0:1	1335	1424
1987	930	300@5500	432@4000	7.0:1	1335	720
	930 Targa	300@5500	432@4000	7.0:1	1335	69
	930 Cabrio	300@5500	432@4000	7.0:1	1335	142
	930 Canada	300@5500	412@4000	7.0:1	1335	88
	930 US	282@5500	390@4000	7.0:1	1335	1605
	930 Targa US	282@5500	390@4000	7.0:1	1335	87
	930 Cabrio US	282@5500	390@4000	7.0:1	1335	183
	930 S-N US[1]	282@5500	390@4000	7.0:1	1335	200
1988	930	300@5500	432@4000	7.0:1	1335	677
	930 Targa	300@5500	432@4000	7.0:1	1335	136
	930 Cabrio	300@5500	432@4000	7.0:1	1335	242
	930 US	282@5500	390@4000	7.0:1	1335	701
	930 Targa US	282@5500	390@4000	7.0:1	1335	141
	930 Cabrio US	282@5500	390@4000	7.0:1	1335	591
	930 S-N	300@5500	432@4000	7.0:1	1335	18
	930 S-N US[1]	282@5500	390@4000	7.0:1	1335	278
1989	930	300@5500	432@4000	7.0:1	1335	857
	930 Targa	300@5500	432@4000	7.0:1	1335	115
	930 Cabrio	300@5500	432@4000	7.0:1	1335	244
	930 US	282@5500	390@4000	7.0:1	1335	639
	930 Targa US	282@5500	390@4000	7.0:1	1335	109
	930 Cabrio US	282@5500	390@4000	7.0:1	1335	600
	930 S-N	300@5500	432@4000	7.0:1	1335	32
	930 S-N US[1]	282@5500	390@4000	7.0:1	1335	147
1991	964T	320@5750	450@4500	7.0:1	1470	2288
	964T US	320@5750	450@4500	7.0:1	1470	674
1992	964T	320@5750	450@4500	7.0:1	1470	836
	964T US	320@5750	450@4500	7.0:1	1470	309
	964T S[2]	381@6000	490@4800	7.0:1	1470	80
1993	964T	360@5500	520@4200	7.5:1	1470	650
	964T US[3]	360@5500	520@4200	7.5:1	1470	288

Numbered notes

[1] S-N refers to Slant-Nose [2] S indicates special edition Turbo S [3] 1993 US Turbo 3.6 production total includes mid-year specification change models (M718).

PRODUCTION CHANGES

Feb 1975

Production starts, with first UK right-hand drive cars available Sep 1975; engine designated 930/50; Nikasil barrels, forged alloy pistons, aluminium crankcase; compression ratio 6.5:1; cylinder head valve sizes were inlet 49mm and exhaust 41.5mm (sizes later to be adopted for 1978 SC); cooling fan (245mm diameter) ratio increased from 1.3:1 to 1.67:1 to run faster and deliver more air; 96 RON fuel in 80-litre fuel tank; gear ratios (930/30 gearbox) are first 2.250, second 1.304, third 0.893, fourth 0.656, reverse 2.437, final drive 4.000 (or 4.222 in US); standard 'RoW' final drive ratio of 4.000 with 15in wheels fitted, but option for 4.222 when 16in wheels used; aluminium S-type calipers (78sq cm swept disc area) front, cast iron M-type (52.5sq cm) rear; ventilated disc diameter 282mm front and 290mm rear, thickness 20.5mm front and 20mm rear.

1976

Six year anti-corrosion warranty; new electric door mirror; by-pass valve for turbo, plus maximum boost increased to one bar; Pirelli P7 205/50VR15 front and 225/50VR15 rear tyres; 16in wheels optional with final drive ratio 4.222; note the Turbo did not use the five-blade cooling fan adopted on 1976 911 models.

1977

Electrical pressure switch gives boost read-out to new gauge mounted within rev counter; twin fuel pumps, modified pressurised fuel accumulator; Hydrovac brake servo (7in) fitted to LHD cars; additional spring reduces clutch effort; 16in Fuchs alloy wheels standard and final drive ratio now standardised at 4.222; first/second gear synchromesh revised and differential assembly strengthened with two planet wheels instead of four; one-piece front anti-roll bar and two-piece spring plates to allow ride height adjustment; two-stage rear window heater; new centre console and revised heater/fresh air controls (as 911SC).

1978

New 3.3-litre engine (930/60); 95mm bore and 74.4mm stroke gives 3299cc; turbo intercooler mounted over engine; new crankshaft (better dynamic balance) with larger main bearings (bearings 1-7 up from 57mm to 60mm diameter, bearing 8 up from 31mm to 40mm), different connecting rod end bearings (narrower, but diameter up from 52mm to 55mm) and shorter connecting rods (by 0.7mm); head gaskets deleted; 97 RON fuel (or 91 RON unleaded for US with recommendation for 96 RON if driving hard); unequal length cylinder barrel fin layout to balance air cooling from top to bottom of barrel; larger oil pump (pressure port increased from 43mm to 51mm, scavenge port from 58mm to 80mm); flywheel mounting bolts increased from six to nine on a diameter of 70mm (was 44mm); cooling fan drive ratio now 1.8:1; new anti-clockwise rotating breakerless Capacitative Discharge Ignition (CDI); air conditioning condenser repositioned to front of car; lighter and larger turbo; air injection pump driven from end of left camshaft; 930/60 engine is 23kg heavier than original 930/50; rubber-centred clutch means engine moves back 30mm (and needs larger bell-housing); gear ratios (930/34 gearbox) are first 2.000, second 1.304, third 0.893, fourth 1.600, reverse 2.437, final drive 4.222; weight distribution now 37/63 front/rear; rear tyre pressures up from 2.4 bar to 3.0 bar; 917 pattern brakes with cross-drilled discs and four-piston alloy calipers (94sq cm pad swept area); disc diameter increased to 304mm front and 309mm rear, thickness to 32mm front and 28mm rear; larger Hydrovac servo (8in), and now fitted to RHD cars; 80-litre fuel tank.

1979

All changes as for 911SC (see page 77).

1980

Turbo discontinued in US and Japan; 'RoW' models get two exhaust outlets and new brass tube oil cooler.

1981

Alternator rating increased to 1150W; other changes as for 911SC (see page 77).

1982

Fuchs alloy wheels have highly polished rims to highlight their black centres; other changes as for 911SC (see page 77).

1983

New engine designation of 930/66; completely revised

IDENTIFICATION

Model year	Model	Engine	Gearbox	Chassis numbers	Engine numbers
1975	930	930/50	930/30	9305700001-9305700284	6750001 onwards
1976	930	930/50	930/30	9306700001-9306700644	6760001 onwards
	930 US	930/51	930/30	9306800001-9306800530	6860001 onwards
1977	930	930/52	930/33	9307700001-9307700695	6770001 onwards
	930 US	930/53	930/33	9307800001-9307800727	6872001 onwards
1978	930	930/60	930/34	9308700001-9308700735	6780001 onwards
	930 Japan	930/62	930/34	9308709501-9308709561	6782001 onwards
	930 US49[1]	930/61	930/34	9308800001-9308800461	6880001 onwards
	930 California	930/63	930/34	9308800001-9308800461	6881001 onwards
1979	930	930/60	930/34	9309700001-9309700820	6790001 onwards
	930 Japan	930/62	930/34	9309709501-9309709532	6791001 onwards
	930 US49[1]	930/64	930/34	9309800001-9309801200	6890001 onwards
	930 California	930/63	930/34	9309800001-9309801200	6890001 onwards
1980	930	930/60	930/34	93A0070001-93A0070840	6700001 onwards
	930 Japan	930/65	930/34	93A0070001-93A0070840	6708001 onwards
1981	930	930/60	930/34	WPOZZZ93ZBS000001-698	6710001 onwards
	930 Canada	930/60	930/34	WPOJAO93BS050001-0063	6710001 onwards
1982	930	930/60	930/34	WPOZZZ93ZCS000001-938	67C0001 onwards
	930 Canada	930/60	930/34	WPOJAO93CS050001-0089	67C0001 onwards
1983	930	930/66	930/34	WPOZZZ93ZDS000001-1015	67D0001 onwards
	930 Canada	930/66	930/34	WPOJAO93DS050001-0065	67D0001 onwards
1984	930	930/66	930/34	WPOZZZ93ZES000001-0804	67E0001 onwards
	930 Canada	930/66	930/34	WPOJAO93ES050001-0077	67E0001 onwards
1985	930	930/66	930/34	WPOZZZ93ZFS000001-1063	67F0001 onwards
	930 Canada	930/66	930/34	WPOJAO93FS050001-0085	67F0001 onwards
1986	930	930/66	930/36	WPOZZZ93ZGS000001-1158	67G0001 onwards
	930 Canada	930/66	930/37	WPOJAO93GS050001-0088	67G0001 onwards
	930 US	930/68	930/37	WPOJBO93GS050001-1424	67G0001 onwards
1987	930	930/66	930/36	WPOZZZ93ZHS000001-0720	67H0001 onwards
	930 Canada	930/66	930/36	WPOJAO93HS050001-088	67H0001 onwards
	930 US	930/68	930/36	WPOJBO93HS050001-5000	68H0001 onwards
	930 Cabrio	930/66	930/36	WPOZZZ93ZHS020001-0142	68H0001 onwards
	930 Cabrio US	930/68	930/36	WPOEBO93HS070001-0183	68H0001 onwards
	930 Cabrio Canada	930/66	930/36	WPOEAO93HS075001-0183	68H0001 onwards
	930 Targa	930/66	930/36	WPOZZZ93ZHS010001-0069	68H0001 onwards
	930 Targa US	930/68	930/36	WPOEBO93ZHS060001-0087	68H0001 onwards
	930 Targa Canada	930/66	930/36	WPOEAO93HS065001-0087	68H0001 onwards
	930 S-N[2]	930/66	930/36	WPOZZZ93ZHS050001-0087	68H0001 onwards
	930 S-N Targa[2]	930/66	930/36	WPOZZZ93ZHS060001-0087	68H0001 onwards
	930 S-N Cabrio[2]	930/66	930/36	WPOZZZ93ZHS070001-0087	68H0001 onwards
	930 S-N US[2]	930/68	930/36	WPOEBO93HS050001-0087	68H0001 onwards
	930 S-N Targa US[2]	930/68	930/36	WPOZZZ93ZHS060001-0087	68H0001 onwards
	930 S-N Cabrio US[2]	930/68	930/36	WPOZZZ93ZHS070001-0087	68H0001 onwards
1988	930	930/66	930/36	WPOZZZ93ZJS000001-0677	67J0001 onwards
	930 Targa	930/66	930/36	WPOZZZ93ZJS010001-0136	67J0001 onwards
	930 Cabrio	930/66	930/36	WPOZZZ93ZJS020001-0242	68J0001 onwards
	930 NA[3]	930/68	930/36	WPOJBO93JS050001-0701	68J0001 onwards
	930 Targa NA[3]	930/68	930/36	WPOEBO93JS060001-0141	68J0001 onwards
	930 Cabrio NA[3]	930/66	930/36	WPOEBO93JS070001-0591	68J0001 onwards
	930 S-N[2]	930/68	930/36	WPOZZZ93ZJS000001-0591	68J0001 onwards
	930 S-N Targa NA[2]	930/68	930/36	WPOEBO93ZJS010001-0591	68J0001 onwards
	930 S-N Cabrio[2]	930/66	930/36	WPOEAO93JS020001-0591	68J0001 onwards
1989	930	930/66	G50/50	WPOZZZ93KS000001-857	67K0051-1103
	930 Targa	930/66	G50/50	WPOZZZ93KS010001-115	67K0051-1103
	930 Cabrio	930/66	G50/50	WPOZZZ93KS020001-244	67K0051-1103
	930 NA[3]	930/68	G50/50	WPOJBO93KS050001-639	67K0051-1232
	930 Targa NA[3]	930/68	G50/50	WPOEBO93KS060001-109	67K0051-1232
	930 Cabrio NA[3]	930/68	G50/50	WPOEBO93KS070001-600	67K0051-1232
1991	964T	M30/69	G50/52	WPOZZZ96ZMS470001-2298	61M00001
	964T US	M30/69	G50/52	WPOAA296MS480001-674	61M00001
1992	964T	M30/69	G50/52	WPOZZZ96ZNS470001-836	61N00001
	964T US	M30/69	G50/52	WPOAA296NS480001-309	61N00001
1993	964T	M64/50	G50/52	WPOZZZ96ZPS470001-650	61P00001
	964T US	M64/50	G50/52	WPOAC296RS480001-288	61P00001

General notes

Engines 930/54 was the 1977 Turbo engine for Japan (as 930/53); 930/62 was the 1978-79 engine for Japan; 930/64 was the 1979 model run-out for the US; 930/65 was the 195kw 1980-82 engine for Japan (as 930/64).

Miscellaneous 1988 onwards Cabrios carry 'Cb' suffix to chassis number; some number sequences refer to the production series allocated to a particular model and so will not align with the actual number of a specific model built; 964T refers to the new Turbo built on the Carrera 2/4 chassis.

Numbered notes

[1] US49 refers to non-California US specification for '49 States'; [2] S-N refers to Slant-Nose ; [3] NA refers to North American specification (US and Canada).

exhaust system, with wastegate exhaust now going direct to atmosphere; power unchanged, but maximum torque rises from 410Nm to 431Nm; K-Jetronic fuel injection has detail changes, with new warm-up regulator and capsule valve in fuel distributor; 98 RON fuel; new ignition distributor with double vacuum advance/retard and temperature compensation (all injection/ignition changes for low emissions); two boost fans to improve footwell warming (and cooling) at low engine speeds.

1984

Minor safety and comfort changes; anti-theft locking wheel nuts; new interior fabrics with Porsche script; brake pad wear indicators; heating with three-speed fan; alternator rating reduced to 1100W; new pressure-fed timing chain tensioners.

1985

From Oct 1984 because of industrial action; radio antenna in windshield; electrically heated washer nozzles; seats slide electrically, now heated and with taller (by 40mm) head restraints; central locking standard; four-spoke steering wheel, shortened gear lever; leather-covered door handles and storage compartment lid; sports seats are no-cost option, with electric height adjustment only; larger brake master cylinder; anti-roll bars increase to 22mm front and 20m rear; fuel tank now 85 litres.

1986

Turbo re-introduced to US market, 930/68 engine with Digital Motor Electronics (DME) linking exhaust sensors, etc, to injection and ignition; equipped with catalytic converter and Lambda (oxygen) sensor, 95 RON unleaded fuel; all noise and pollution accessories now make engine weight 269kg; for 'RoW' markets new 'clean' DME engine is 930/66; DME associated injection system known as LE-Jetronic; rear wheels now 9J × 16in with 245/45VR tyres (front stays at 7J × 16in with 205/55VR tyres); front seats lower; re-styled dash with larger fascia fresh air vents; sun visors have covered vanity mirrors.

1987

Rear reflector panel has integrated fog lights and includes Porsche script; seats fully adjustable electrically; headlight beam adjustable from dash; perforated discs get bevelled holes to assist with heat dissipation; gear ratios (all markets) are first 2.25, second 1.3043, third 0.8928, fourth

The cars are 10 years apart but the badge script has not changed. The finish is bright on the 1976 car and matt black on the 1986 car.

0.6250, reverse 2.437, final drive 4.222.

1988

Turbo now available as Targa and Cabrio; passenger door mirror and eight-speaker hi-fi installation standard in all markets; electric windows can be raised by emergency manual crank.

1989

Alarm fitted as standard, activates when doors locked; five-speed G50 gearbox standard (and hydraulic clutch) with ratios (all markets) of first 3.154, second 1.789, third 1.269, fourth 0.967, fifth 0.756, reverse 2.437, final drive 3.444; larger rear torsion bars, revised anti-roll bars (22mm front, 18mm rear), firmer shock absorbers; brake, clutch and engine/gearbox seals are asbestos-free; Turbo discontinued Sep 1989.

1991

Turbo re-launched Sep 1990 (first shown Mar 1990), RHD cars delivered from early 1991; new two-wheel drive only Turbo with Carrera 4 Coupé body (type 964) revisions but with usual flared wheelarches and tea-tray rear spoiler; 3.3-litre engine with resonant intake manifold, revised exhaust system, bigger turbocharger and larger intercooler; Maximum boost now 0.7 bar (was 0.8); revised injection and Motronic control; dual mass flywheel; two (left and right) exhaust tail pipe outlets; transmission still five-speed G50 (built by Getrag) with Borg-Warner synchromesh, standard limited slip differential, improved gear shift; smaller external electrically operated mirrors; new 17in Cup Design wheels of 7J front (with 205/50ZR tyres) and 9J rear (with 255/40ZR tyres); stronger semi-trailing arms; anti-roll bars now 21mm front 22mm rear; disc diameter 322mm front, 299mm rear; four-piston calipers (86sq cm pad swept area) have asbestos-free pads and wear indicators; space-saver spare tyre is 155-16 size to clear new brake discs; driver/passenger airbag standard for selected markets (including US); standard features include air conditioning, on-board computer with digital boost indicator; back-lit instruments.

1992

No major changes to specification.

1993

3.6-litre engine with 100mm bore and 76.4m stroke; compression ratio increased to 7.5:1; 360bhp at 5500rpm, maximum torque 520Nm at 4200rpm; stronger clutch and limited slip diff (same as used on Carrera 2 RS); two-spring clutch pedal action; three-piece Speedline wheels of 8J × 18in front (with 225/40ZR tyres) and 10J × 18in rear (with 265/35ZR tyres); tyres are Yokohama A008P; bodyshell lowered 20mm (except US); 12 per cent stiffer springs; locked rear axle control bearing deletes toe-change characteristic found on Carrera 2; Turbo S front brakes with red-painted calipers all round; driver airbag standard for all markets; 1610W alternator with 12V/75Ah battery; fuel tank 77 litres (optional 92 litres); 'Turbo' logos on wheel-hub caps; chromed 'Turbo 3.6' on engine cover and embroidered onto rear firewall carpet; kph speedometers now read to 320 (was 300), mph speedos stay at 180; air conditioner now uses CFC-free refrigerant.

DIMENSIONS

Wheelbase

2261mm (from 1975), 2271mm (from 1990), 2272mm (from 1993)

Track (front/rear)

1432mm/1500mm (from 1975), 1434mm/1526mm (from 1986), 1442mm/1488mm (from 1993)

Length

4318mm (from 1975), 4250mm (from 1990), 4275mm (from 1993)

Width

1829mm (from 1975), 1775mm (from 1990), 1755mm (from 1993)

COLOUR SCHEMES

1975

Body colours

As 911 (see page 66).

Interiors

The new Turbo was offered with a new range of interior fabrics for the seat centres termed 'Tartan Dress' (999.551.081.40) in MacLaughlan (red, 8AB), Black Watch (green, 2AC) or Dress Mackenzie (brown/beige, 4AD); these could be matched with red, black or brown-beige leather; alternatively full leather could be specified.

1976

Body colours

As 911 (see page 66).

Interiors

Unchanged, but Tartan Dress now offered across the whole 911 range.

1977

Body colours

As 911 (see page 66)

Interiors

Grained leatherette (999.551.012.40) and light basket-weave leatherette added for the Turbo, in Black (7AU), Lobster (8AU) or Cork (5AU); pinstripe velour (see 911) join Tartan Dress fabrics and offered in Black/White, Lobster/Black or Cork/Black.

1978

Body colours

As 911 (see page 78)

Interiors

Leather colour options now Lobster (8AH), Cork (5AH), Black (7AG), Blue (3AG), Yellow (1AG), Light Green (2AP), Light Red (8AT) or White (9AG); fabrics were pinstripe or Tartan Dress, as 1977; velour pile carpets in Lobster, Cork, Black, Yellow or Light Red to match the other materials.

1979

Body colours

As 911SC (see page 78)

Interiors

Turbo now offered only with leather (no leatherette), colours as 1979 911SC (see page 78); cloths are as 1978; new cut-pile velour carpets as 1979 911SC.

1980

Body colours

As 911SC (see page 79).

Interiors

Checkerboard velour and textured fabric offered in same range as 1979 911SC (see page 79), leather unchanged from 1979.

1981

Body colours

As 911SC (see page 79).

Interiors

Berber tweed fabric joins others (as 1980 SC).

1982 onwards

Body colours and interiors all as 911 of same model year (see pages 79, 91-92 and 107).

Early right-hand drive Turbo owned by Alan Stein looks purposeful with its wide haunches.

THE 911 CARRERA (1993-98)

If the Carrera 2 and 4 had turned around the core Porsche customers during the recession of the early '90s and got them buying again, then the new Carrera – identified both internally at Porsche and externally as the 993 – re-invented the concept of the 911 and opened up a whole new market. The result proved to be the right car at the right time for Porsche. From the moment of launch in late 1993, the factory struggled to keep up with demand.

Whatever the economic position of the company at the start of the decade, no-one could accuse Porsche of being complacent. There was dynamism in the development of the 911 that had not been seen since the progress of the early cars in the late '60s and early '70s. And the car that headlined that new surge was the 993, a 911 that made every earlier 911 look positively dated.

The 993 was a major investment in the short term

EVOLUTION OUTLINE

Dec 1993	993-bodied 911 introduced with 272bhp 3.6-litre engine and multi-link rear suspension.
Aug 1994	New Carrera 4 with transmission 50% lighter than 964 type. Tiptronic transmission available for rear-wheel drive Carreras.
Feb 1995	Carrera RS with 300bhp, followed by new 993 Turbo with 408bhp engine, twin turbochargers and six-speed gearbox.
Sep 1995	911 Targa and Carrera 4S (wide-body) announced.
Sep 1996	Wide-bodied Carrera S (rear-wheel drive) introduced.
Sep 1997	911 Carrera Coupé (996) replaces rear-wheel drive 993 Coupé and Cabriolet.
Mar 1998	911 Carrera Cabriolet (996) introduced.

The 993 (opposite) was the fourth generation of 911, making striking improvements in the three critical areas of sports car appeal – looks, power and handling. It turned around Porsche's fortunes from 1994, becoming the best-selling 911 ever. Off-roading in the Carrera 4 (above)! Using one of the lightest four-wheel drive systems, and assisted by the traction-controlling Automatic Brake Differential (ABD), the Carrera 4 accelerated faster than the two-wheel drive model, even on firm ground.

for Porsche, born of the high priority to inject the 964 models with wider appeal while consolidating sales to core customers. The 993's task was to sustain the company's recovery from the difficult years of recession until the start of the wholly new model range due in 1996-97. This it did famously.

Porsche's strategy meant the 993 had to combine typical 911 features – high performance and aggressive character – with the kind of improvements that would win new customers from the refined sports saloons offered by the likes of Mercedes and BMW. Consequently, the big effort went into reducing ride harshness and interior noise.

The fourth distinct generation of 911, the 993 was said to be 80% new when it was announced. It was a claim that had been made before, notably on the 968, and often observers had been left asking what had really changed and just what '80%' actually meant. Porsche had no intention of making this mistake again. The 993 made striking steps forward in the three critical areas of sports car appeal – looks, engine and handling.

First impressions were startling. No other car in the price range conveyed the same static presence – a presence that gripped you with simultaneous feelings of retro and high technology, performance and dependability. Briton Tony Hatter had conceived a new visual interpretation of the 911 that injected adrenaline into the lines of the 964, which looked almost bland by comparison. Design department head Harm Lagaay called the new appearance 'muscular' and, indeed, the 911 gave the impression of being on steroids.

Once in the driving seat, the familiar 911 cockpit seemed much the same. The engine remained at 3600cc (219.6cu in), but an extra 22bhp not only compensated for the car's additional 20kg (44lb), but improved performance all round. Acceleration to 62mph (100kph) was 0.1sec better, at 5.6sec, and top speed rose to 168mph (270kph), up 6mph (10kph) on the 964 model.

The effort to improve the ride and handling ensured the real joy of the 993 was to be discovered when you were on the move. There was an immediate realisation that, at any speed, the car was altogether quieter and less anxious in the cabin. There was also less susceptibility to bump and thump over poor road surfaces. This was a new kind of comfort in a 911 and it was easy to understand why drivers who had never considered the car before might be tempted. But there was more.

The real treat came when you pushed this 911 through a series of demanding bends, even in the wet. With earlier 911s, tyre improvements had obscured many of the 911's original tail-happy vices, but in the right (or is it wrong?) conditions, it was still possible to provoke the characteristic power-off tail-slide. This unfriendly behaviour was a product not only of the rearward weight bias but also the semi-trailing arm rear suspension. For the 993, the engineers came up with a completely new multi-link suspension derived from the 'Weissach' axle first seen on the 928. It was a significant and very costly change to make, but the result was a 911 with virtually no handling vices and vastly superior ride quality. When you lifted in the middle of a rain-soaked

The ever-popular Cabriolet followed the coupé in spring 1994. The clean, fulsome lines of the rear were accentuated by a narrower light strip for the 993.

corner to avoid that errant wild animal, the new 911 did not automatically unleash an unwelcome scare as the car swapped ends and dispatched you into the scenery. To provoke the 993 into any sort of tail slide now demanded fairly violent action from the driver.

By August 1995, the 993 was the only model range offered by Porsche. The towel had been thrown in on the struggle to keep interest alive in the four-cylinder 968 and V8-powered 928 ranges. Not for the first time the future of Porsche rested squarely on the 911's shoulders and, happily, the early success of the 993 was sustained. Even the Targa re-emerged alongside the Coupé and Cabriolet. The new Targa caught a wave of excitement in much the same way as had the fresh styling of the Coupé. It was a new concept for an open-roofed fixed-head car.

Another surprise, and an indication that the 993 had indeed successfully penetrated new markets, was the popularity of the Tiptronic automatic transmission option. Even outside the US, where automatics have always been popular, Tiptronics were accounting for up to 60% of 993 sales in the big cities. This was a very different picture to the old days of Sportomatic – and a testament to the aggravation of driving in conditions of ever increasing congestion.

The 1995 Carrera RS addressed the constant niche demand for a hard-edged, no-compromise 911. By virtue of its multi-link rear suspension and 300bhp, the new Carrera RS was far more accomplished than the 964 models – it will rate among the most desirable of hot-rod 911s in years to come. While not being all that suited to everyday traffic, an RS cannot be bettered for fun at the race track.

In 1995 the Turbo returned. For a car used to being described in superlatives, this new version was as outstanding as one could imagine. The 408bhp from its twin-turbo engine was nothing less than racing car performance in a car that offered complete luxury and real refinement.

For the 1997 model year, the 993 was showing no signs of needing replacement. Including the Turbo, there were eight different versions to choose from. Even on the introduction of the new 911 (the 996) in September 1997, a waiting list remained for the older rear-wheel drive model. But while the rear-wheel drive 993s ceased production by the end of 1997, the all-wheel drive and Turbo 993s were planned to continue in production for the remainder of the 1998 model year (until July 1998).

Horst Marchart, Executive Vice-President in charge of Research and Development, has said that survival requires change. He considers that the modern sports car should always be influenced by modern technology, not restrained by traditional solutions. And so the 996 has made a dramatic break with 911 heritage: it is water-cooled, for improved cylinder head cooling and to reduce acoustic noise. It is larger and more comfortable than the 993. It is a Porsche for the new century.

It has been said the 911 is like the proverbial carpenter's hammer. It has had three new heads and four new handles, but it is still the same hammer. The 996 is indeed a wonderful car that is winning many hearts in the technology-conscious age into which it has been born. But it is a human failing to be sentimental. While the concept of the new 996 is perhaps appropriate for its time, it can be difficult for enthusiasts to contemplate a 911 that is water-cooled and more user-friendly.

Time will tell whether the 996 will challenge the 993's status as arguably the greatest sports car of the 20th century.

The Targa, a refreshingly innovative new concept for an old Porsche favourite, lost the dated look of the earlier model and was easily mistaken for a coupé from some angles. Prominent in this view are the new design of 'concave' spoke two-piece wheels.

BODYSHELL

At first glance the body of the 993 appeared to be nothing more than a make-over on the 964 Turbo. But there was much more to the new appearance than the pronounced wheel-arch flares. Following the example started by the 968, there had been considerable effort to replace the previous straight lines of the 964 with, in the industrial designer's vocubulary, 'softer' lines. This trend would reach its peak with the later 996 model. Referring to the 964 Turbo wings as looking like 'big lips' around the wheels, Harm Lagaay considered the bulges on the 993 to be more muscular, and by inference more smoothly integrated. Along with new, lower headlamps, the frontal appearance of the 993 seemed more aggressive.

The 993 was the first 911 to require significant changes to the body-in-white, mainly to accommodate the mountings for the sub-frame that carried the multi-link suspension. The only body parts carried over from the 964 were the roof and bonnet. There were revised door beams for improved side impact protection, and simplified operation of the door mechanisms. The changes resulted in a bodyshell that was said to be 20% stiffer with no increase in weight. The shell was still hot-dip galvanised and the ten-year warranty against rust perforation was maintained. Water-based paints were now used entirely, even for the metallic colours.

This is a 1997 Carrera S, which combined the Turbo chassis and rear-wheel drive transmission to produce a supremely confident package.

The rubber seals that located the windshield were reduced in size, increasing the glass area and improving aerodynamics. Rear side windows were bonded to the outside, reducing wind noise, while new seals reduced the force necessary to shut the doors.

The 993 was available initially only in Coupé form, but the Cabriolet followed in March 1994. But the real surprise came with the return of the Targa for the 1996 model year.

The new Targa design retained the overall shape and character of the 911 while featuring an electrically-operated glass panel that could slide backwards. The Targa was based on the same body-in-white as the Cabriolet, with additional strengthening around the windshield frame. The new variant was only 30kg (66lb) heavier than the Coupé. The new roof design owed nothing to the earlier Targas, having better all-round visibility while achieving increased roll-over protection. In line with the general refinement of the 993, the Targa was notable for its low wind noise – not a strong point of the old Targa!

The feeling inside the Targa was much more open, because there was indeed more glass. Thermally insulated, the glass contained a special UV filter to help keep inside temperatures under control on hot, sunny days. And if you did not like direct sun, a roller blind would glide across the opening at the touch of a switch. The whole design was extremely elegant, both in appearance and operation, and as a result new Targas commanded a premium over the Coupé. Memories of the old and chunky-looking Targas faded fast.

The windshield wiper location was revised, so that each wiper covered some 80% of the glass area. It was considered too expensive to recess the pivots below the bonnet line.

The Targa's roof was thermally insulated and filtered ultra-violet light. The elegance of the design is evident, particularly in the absence of the old rain gutters of the coupé and the new form of the rear side window. The opening glass slid back under the rear window at the touch of a switch, to provide open-air motoring. The panel in front of the sliding roof opened forwards to prevent wind buffeting inside the car.

BODY TRIM & FITTINGS

The front valence was heavily revised to reflect the new style that had first been adopted with the 968, using more flowing break lines where it attached to the wings. As well as significantly larger inlets on the front, small side air exits on either side acted as invisible spoilers ahead of the front wheel profiles, reducing drag at higher speeds.

At the rear, the policy of greater integration of the valence was continued, with accommodation for the twin exhaust outlets and a less pronounced bumper than on the 964. The attention to drag reduction was further evident at the top of the rear window, where a small lip prevented flow breakaway over the recess, and again under the car, where a new underbody sheath was claimed to give the 993 a degree of ground effect. The new engine cover incorporated a movable spoiler that integrated more closely to the cover when closed.

The improvement to detailing was a highlight of the 993's new specification. Of note were the new electrically-operated door mirrors and the colour-coded door handles – both items first used on the 968. The windshield wiper location was revised, with the pivots placed closely together and providing improved sweep of the glass. The pivots were still exposed – it would still have been too expensive to modify the body-in-white to recess these.

The Cabriolet soft-top was significantly stiffer than on the 964 model. The Cabrio also introduced an optional wind deflector behind the front seats. This reduced air turbulence and noise, and also gave some protection to luggage behind the seats.

INTERIOR TRIM

A new interior design was offered for the 993, including new colours and fabrics. There were new door and rear side trims to complement the updated appearance. The electrically-controlled front seats were revised with a new seam pattern and improved upper thigh support. For those in chilly climates, seat heating was available as an option.

The interior received new fabrics and colours, as well as revised door trims and rear side trims. This is a 1997 model coupé in opulent Boxster Red leather. By this time the 911 was winning customers from the more comfort-oriented sports saloons such as BMW and Mercedes. The Cabriolet featured a wind-break (below) behind the front seats to ensure wind-in-the-hair motoring did not become too wild.

The 911 has always had to make the best out of a heating system based around the air-cooled engine. Consistency of heat delivery has been the main problem, especially when the engine is cold. The 993's heating was improved with the adoption of a revised electronically-controlled heating unit, which included an integrated particle filter. The filter improved the interior environment by capturing particles down to a size of 0.005mm, which screens out most flower pollens. Air conditioning was a factory option (standard in some markets) and featured a new 'max cold' control position.

The heated rear window now had automatic time control and the driver had two levels of heating (de-ice and de-fog). After 12 minutes the de-ice circuit switched off automatically, while the de-fog was switched off manually. There was a new type of switch for the external mirror control, located on the door just inside from the driver's mirror.

Dashboard & Instruments

The dashboard was an evolution of the 964 layout, reflecting the new interior colours, but with driver and passenger airbags standard for all markets.

The standard radio fit from the factory was the Blaupunkt Bremen RCM43 radio/cassette player, with a CD player on the options list. Also on the options list was a newly developed ten-speaker system that was fully integrated into the standard fittings. This included a 150-watt amplifier, woofers in the doors, a tweeter below each of the knee bolsters and a pair of two-way speakers on the parcel shelf. Automatic sound regulation was possible with the addition of an optional digital sound processing (DSP) unit fitted in the driver's door armrest. Also optional was an on-board computer which gave read-outs of fuel consumption. Theft protection, as delivered from the factory, improved with the integration of the central locking and alarm with an engine immobiliser.

Luggage Compartment

The shape of the luggage compartment was largely unchanged from the 964, having a capacity of 123 litres. A notable design feature was that the Space Saver spare wheel contributed to the energy-absorbing capability of the car in a frontal impact. It was mounted below and in front of the plastic fuel tank which held 74.5 litres (16.4 Imperial gallons, 19.7 US gallons) of Super Unleaded (98 RON) fuel. A 92-litre (20.2 Imperial gallons, 24.3 US gallons) version was available as an option.

The 3.6-litre engine gained another 22bhp. Despite weighing an extra 20kg, the 993 delivered better all-round performance than the 964. The improved 1996 models (left) used a Varioram induction system and larger valves to produce 285bhp from the last full-scale production version of the air-cooled boxer 'six'.

ENGINE

The 993 engine remained at 3600cc (219.6cu in), but was some 10% more powerful than the 964 version. Maximum power rose to 272bhp at 6100rpm and maximum torque to 330Nm (243lb ft) at 5000rpm. Compression ratio remained at 11.3:1 and fuel consumption was claimed to be about the same.

Internal improvements included lighter pistons and connecting rods, and a strengthened crankshaft. The 993 engine now used many lightweight materials including magnesium for the cooling fan, oil pump housing and timing chain housings. Plastic was used for the intake system, cooling and heating ducting, valve covers and vacuum reservoir.

Induction system airflow sensing was by the hot film method and the Bosch engine management system was upgraded to version M2.10, with knock regulation and control of the sequential, multi-point fuel injection. An important improvement which would lead to reduced servicing costs was the introduction of hydraulic valve adjustment. The exhaust system now had dual exit pipes and separate catalytic converter cores downstream of the individual heat

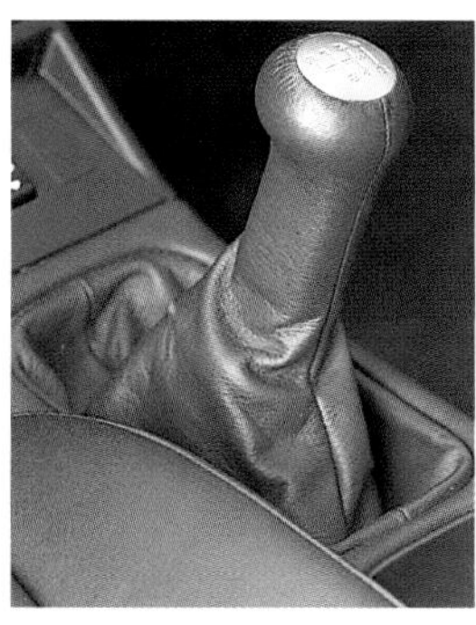

The new six-speed gearbox brought an improved shift and better synchromesh on first and second gear.

exchangers, as well as a central gas mixing unit. This layout improved pressure losses in the system and reduced noise.

From the 1996 model year the engine was upgraded with Varioram induction technology and larger intake and exhaust valves. Maximum power increased to 285bhp at 6100rpm and maximum torque to 340Nm (251lb ft) at 5250rpm.

First seen on the 1995 Carrera RS, Varioram was a Porsche-patented design which altered the length of the inlet pipe according to engine revolutions, so improving the volumetric efficiency at different engine speeds. In the mid-range, it was claimed Varioram increased torque over the 272bhp engine by as much as 40Nm (29lb ft). Fuel consumption and exhaust emissions were also reduced because of the more efficient combustion. Up to 5000rpm the pipes are almost double the length of the pipes in the earlier 993. As engine revolutions increase beyond 5000rpm, a sliding sleeve on each bank of intake pipes, operated by intake vacuum, shortens the intake pipe length in two stages. Above 5800rpm both cylinder banks are inter-connected to ensure best volumetric efficiency.

TRANSMISSION

Two transmission options were offered with the 993 – manual and Tiptronic. As noted earlier, the reworked automatic option proved to be very popular. The shift programme was revised to cope with the increased torque and power of the engine and was enhanced with a feature that enabled sensing of varying road resistance (uphill or downhill). In automatic mode, a down-shift could now be prompted by braking, ensuring the right ratio was available to accelerate away again. Tiptronic was only available on the two-wheel drive models.

Tiptronic S, available as a no-cost option for the 1995 Tiptronic models, gave the driver the choice of shifting in the manual mode either using the floor-mounted lever or using rocker switches integrated into the steering wheel. As with the other Tiptronics, the gear selected was indicated at the base of the speedometer.

Poly-ellipsoid headlamps gave the 911 an altogether different appearance by day and by night. The reflector, rather than the glass lens, produced the required light distribution. The whole lamp unit can be removed by moving a lever inside the luggage compartment.

The manual transmission on the 993 was new and offered six forward speeds. Shifting effort was reduced some 40% on the 964 gearbox by new double-cone synchromesh on first and second gears. As a result of a comprehensive weight reduction effort on the internals, the new gearbox weighed the same as the five-speed 964 unit. Lightening measures included hollow-boring the pinion shaft and fitting the back of the crown wheel with forged pockets. The gearbox housing was a thin-wall aluminium pressure casting with wall thickness reduced by up to 2mm (0.08in) on the previous casing. From the 1995 model year a new hydraulic-assisted clutch system lowered the clutch force and reduced pedal travel.

The Automatic Brake Differential (ABD) option, available for manual 993s, prevented a single wheel spinning under acceleration on differing grip surfaces. The system used the ABS sensors on each rear wheel to detect wheelspin on acceleration. The control unit then applied selective braking through a high-speed hydraulic actuator on the specific rear brake circuit, effectively introducing an intelligent limited slip differential. A control lamp on the combined dial told the driver when this was in operation. The system cut out above 70kph (44mph).

For the start of the 1995 model year an entirely redesigned four-wheel drive model was announced. Claimed to be one of the lightest four-wheel drive systems available, it weighed half that of the 964 variant, while friction losses were reduced by the same amount. The 993 Carrera 4, as a result, came out 30kg (66lb) lighter overall than the 964 version.

ABD was standard on the new Carrera 4, and linked to the drive to the front axle. When a rear wheel slipped, a viscous clutch automatically directed increased drive torque to the front axle. ABD also compensated for the difference in rotation speeds between the front and rear wheels when cornering. An asymmetric rear axle differential lock applied a 25% locking effect to a spinning rear wheel on acceleration and 40% when on over-run. This latter feature was another counter-measure to the traditional lift-off oversteer tendency of the 911, since the lock promoted stabilising understeer should the throttle be abruptly lifted halfway through a bend.

The extent of the improvements on the Carrera 4 were enough for it to enjoy a 0.1sec advantage on 0-100kph (62.5mph) acceleration over the two-wheel drive version, despite a 50kg (110lb) weight penalty. Top speed of the two models was identical.

ELECTRICAL EQUIPMENT & LIGHTING

The new headlamps of the 993 were perhaps its most startling visual feature. They achieved far better lighting – the claimed improvement was approaching 50% – than was available on the 964. Each lamp unit used poly-ellipsoid technology and H1 bulbs for dipped beam coverage. High-beam light intensity was increased using a variable focus reflector. Variable focus lamp design is based on a concept where the focal length of the reflector is calculated for every point on the reflector surface. The reflector, rather than the lens unit, therefore produces the required light distribution. As a result the lens units look completely different from the earlier ones, having a clear glass area where the lens refracting elements used to be. As before, however, individual high-pressure jets kept the glass clean.

Removing the headlamp assemblies was a simple task. A lever inside the luggage compartment released the unit, allowing it to be removed from the front. There were no cables or other clips to be disconnected. This made bulb changing very simple, while the new design also permitted simple changing of the dipped beam direction.

The driving lights, turn indicators and fog lights were located as a unit in the front valence. The fog lights also used ellipsoid technology.

The revised styling at the rear resulted in a narrower reflector band and tail lights. The tail light units were smaller than before since the central reflector now incorporated the reversing as well as the rear fog lights. Teflon film prevented splashed water entering the light units in each rear wing.

SUSPENSION & STEERING

The most significant revision on the 993 over previous 911s was the scrapping of the semi-trailing arm rear suspension and its replacement with a multi-link arrangement. Called an LSA (Lightweight-Stable-Agile) axle by Porsche, this had geometry derived from the Weissach rear axle first used on the front-engined 928.

The Weissach rear geometry provided a degree of roll-steer, with the outer wheel toeing-in (up to 2°) during cornering and reducing the possibility of lift-off oversteer. The most obvious improvements from the driver's perspective were in cornering stability and body roll, while the degree of squat under acceleration was reduced. The 993 indeed proved to be far less susceptible to lift-off oversteer, and more stable during rapid lane changes.

The rear axle looked similar to the dual wishbone layout often used on racing cars. The arms were cast aluminium and fitted inboard to a cast aluminium two-piece sub-frame, which in turn attached through four rubber bushings to the bodyshell. Springing was by coils over gas pressure shock absorbers, with the units attached direct to the bodyshell. The new arrangement provided a much smoother ride, as well as a manufacturing benefit – the whole engine and suspension assembly could be built before installation into the car.

The front suspension was an improvement of the existing MacPherson strut system, with increased castor and negative scrub radius. Almost every front suspension component was redesigned, saving 3kg (6.6lb) on the weight of the whole axle, and improvement of ride comfort was made a priority. The steering action was lighter and a new elastic track rod design reduced the transmission of road vibration back to the steering wheel.

Sport suspension was available as an option and featured shorter, stiffer springs and anti-roll bars together with harder dampers.

BRAKES

The improvements introduced to the 993's brakes began just beyond the pedal, with a new linkage through the vacuum servo that gave a linear increase in braking effort on the master cylinder as the pedal was pressed. Before ABS, such a mechanism might have led to a greater chance of wheel locking, but working in parallel with the pressure-compensating valve to help maintain optimum brake balance, maximum braking effect could now be achieved without excessive pressure on the pedal.

The new ABS 5 system used new control algorithms to cope with difficult road surfaces, such as partially dried or dirty roads. With faster initial response, ABS 5 offered up to 20% shorter braking distances in certain conditions.

The brake discs themselves were larger, increasing in thickness from 28mm (1.10in) to 32mm (1.26in). The diameter of the front discs increased from 298mm (11.7in) to 304mm (12.0in), while the rears were unchanged at 299mm (11.8in). Larger, four-piston, fixed calipers all round resulted in a 45% improvement in the usable surface of the cross-drilled and ventilated discs.

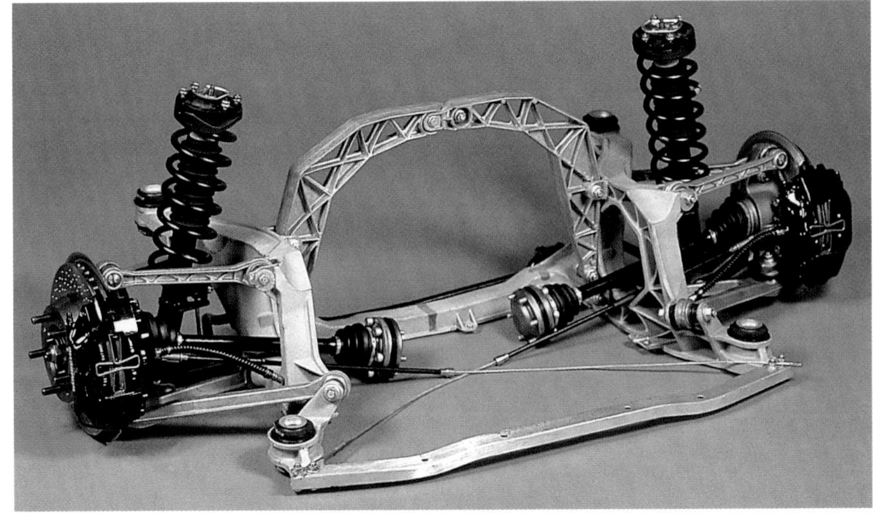

Porsche's Lightweight-Stable-Agile (LSA) design provided the 993 with new multi-link rear suspension – a major change under the surface.

The brakes on the 993 were outstanding, featuring cross-drilled and ventilated discs and four-piston calipers. ABS 5 helped ensure the wheels did not lock up when the pedal was pressed too hard.

The 993 RS continued the theme begun by the 964. Although more refined than the earlier models, the new RS was a supremely accomplished performer, particularly on the race track. The lowered ride height is very evident in this view.

Wheels & Tyres

The low-pressure cast aluminium 'Cup Design 93' wheels were designed to suck hot air away from the brake discs when moving fast and also to conduct heat away through the hub and spokes at lower speeds. Sizes on the standard coupé were 7J × 16in (front) and 9J × 16in (rear), the rims 25mm (1in) wider than those of the 964. Tyre sizes were 205/55ZR16 (front) and 245/45ZR16 (rear). The approved tyres were the Michelin MXX3-WSXX N1, Bridgestone Expedia SO-1 N2, Continental CZ91 NO and Toyo Proxes F15 NO; Pirelli P Zero N1 and Yokohama A008-P could also be fitted. If the older 17in 'Cup' wheels were chosen, these achieved a weight saving of 1.5kg (3.3lb) per wheel.

For the 1996 model year, the Targa featured a new 'concave' five-spoke, two-piece wheel of 17in diameter, but rim sizes remained at 7J and 9J. Tyres were 205/50ZR17 (front) and 255/40ZR17 (rear).

1995-96 Carrera RS

Introduced at the start of 1995, the 993 RS was a considerably improved machine compared to the 1993 limited edition 964 RS 3.8 (see page 106). The two cars did share nearly identical maximum power and torque figures, 300bhp at 6500rpm and 355Nm (262lb ft) at 5400rpm, but torque delivery over the entire range was considerably improved by the first use of Porsche's patented Varioram variable length intake stack system. This system is described in the 'Engine' section of this chapter (see page 131).

As with the older RS 3.8, the capacity increase to 3746cc (228.6cu in) was achieved by enlarging the bore by 2mm (0.08in) to 102mm (4.02in), the stroke remaining at 76.4mm (3.01in). The valve drive mechanism was strengthened to cope with higher maximum revolutions and the intake and exhaust valves increased in diameter, respectively to 51.5mm (2.03in) and 43mm (1.69in).

The RS used the new six-speed 993 transmission with higher ratios on the first three gears. Unlike the earlier RS 3.8, it was equipped with a double mass flywheel to reduce drive-train vibration.

While the ride of the earlier RS models was unquestionably harsh for everyday use, the new 993 RS was more refined, helped by the multi-link rear suspension. The big 8J × 18in and 10J × 18in three-piece wheels, however, led to a rougher ride on normal roads than the regular car's 16in wheels. Tyres were 225/40ZR18 (front) and 265/35ZR18 (rear).

Because some customers were expected to use their cars for fast track work or competition, the bodyshell was seam-welded and the wheel arches were rolled to clear the big tyres. A cross-brace was fitted between the two front strut towers and the spring/damper mountings used ball-joint mountings at their top ends. Stiffer track rods were adopted in the steering linkage (power steering was standard), and ride height was lowered 30mm (1.2in) at the front and 40mm (1.6in) at the rear. The front anti-roll bar was adjustable through five settings and the rear bar by three. The RS combined the automatic brake differential (ABD) for traction control and a limited slip differential (40% lock on acceleration, 65% under deceleration). The brakes were the Turbo's 322mm (12.7in) cross-drilled and ventilated discs with four-piston calipers. ABS 5 was standard.

Externally the new RS featured a lower splitter on the front valence, shaped sill covers and a fixed 'whale-tail' rear spoiler in body colour.

Overall, the RS weighed 1279kg (2820lb), which was 100kg (220lb) lighter than the 1995 993. The savings came from deletion of the usual accessories, such as electric windows and mirrors, central locking, headlamp washers, intermittent wipe control, standard door trims and loudspeakers. The interior lighting system was replaced by a simple light as used on the earlier Speedster, and even the washer bottle for the windshield held only 1.2 litres instead of its usual 6.5 litres. There were no driver or passenger airbags and the only sound insulation was in the engine bay. Thin glass was used and the rear window had no de-mister; the weight saving for the glass alone was 5kg (11lb). An aluminium front bonnet saved 7.5kg (17lb) and replacement of the electric seats by Recaro bucket seats saved 30kg (66lb). The 92-litre fuel tank was standard.

Top speed for the 1995 RS was said to be 172mph

The new Turbo was worth the 12-month wait after the introduction of the 993. The combination of a 408bhp twin-turbo engine, a six-speed gearbox and four-wheel drive ensured awesome performance. Top reading on speedometer (left) increased from 300kph to 320kph (from 180mph to 200mph on US/UK models).

The 993 Turbo featured the traditional 'tea-tray' rear wing – necessary to accommodate the twin intercoolers in the engine compartment – but with down-turned side fences.

There is an engine under there somewhere! Twin air-to-air intercoolers dominated the engine compartment of the Turbo.

(277kph), while 0-100kph (0-62.5mph) acceleration was achieved in just 5.0sec.

The Club Sport derivative (known as the RSR in the UK) could be registered for the road if you were so disposed, but it was aimed at endurance racing (GT2). Costing £71,500 in the UK, £6250 more than the RS, the Club Sport was immediately recognisable from the outside by its more aggressive front spoiler and characteristic bi-plane rear spoiler.

1995-97 TURBO

A Porsche model line-up without a Turbo seems inconceivable, but after the completion of 964 Turbo production in 1994, it was fully 12 months before a 993 with forced induction appeared, in the spring of 1995.

The new 993 Turbo was 60mm (2.36in) wider than the normally aspirated 993, this difference continuing the special look that Turbos have always enjoyed. The front and rear valences were squared off to the ground, with the front opening revised to one large central and two side openings, the latter for the front wheel 'air' spoilers. On the sides, the sill mouldings were given a pronounced flat lower edge and integrated into the wheel arches. On the engine cover, the moving spoiler of the regular car was replaced by a new interpretation of the tea-tray spoiler with down-turned side fences.

Setting off the overall looks of the new Turbo were 18in diameter cast alloy wheels, called 'Technologie-Rad' design by Porsche. Of very lightweight construction, these were a five-spoke design, with each spoke swept back so that that overall impression was of an impeller. The two-piece wheels were friction-welded together during manufacture. The 8J front wheels were fitted with 225/40ZR18 tyres and the 10J rears with 285/30 ZR18 tyres.

Braking was typically sensational on the new Turbo. The marketing literature noted that its new brakes had a maximum braking power of 1941bhp – almost five times engine power. This was calculated in braking from 290kph (180mph) at kerb weight with the driver. In actual terms, this meant the Turbo could brake from 100kph (62.5mph) to a standstill in just 2.61sec. The previous Turbo's giant 322mm (12.7in) discs were carried over and used forced air cooling, while stopping performance at the extremes was enhanced by the next level ABS 5.

The new 993 generation 3.6-litre engine was improved with two KKK K16 turbochargers (the 964 version used a single K27 turbocharger), each with integrated wastegates and two charge air intercoolers. The Bosch M5.2 engine management system controlled air flow in conjunction with the wastegate on the turbochargers. Improved knock control allowed the compression ratio to rise to 8.0:1 from the previous model's 7.5:1 and the engine to run on 95 or 98 RON unleaded fuel. Maximum power was 408bhp at 5750rpm, with maximum torque 540Nm (398lb ft) at 4500rpm. The twin turbo layout gave excellent low-speed torque – a big improvement compared to the 964 Turbo. Even at 2500rpm, there was still 450Nm (332lb ft) available!

The Turbo used a single spark plug per cylinder, but the heads employed the hydraulic valve adjustment of the new range. Four oxygen sensors (up and downstream of the two catalytic converters) combined with the On-Board Diagnostic (OBD) system monitored exhaust emissions and ensured the Turbo met new 1996 US regulations for emissions control.

The new six-speed gearbox was fitted with longer ratios and internals strengthened for the increased engine torque. Excepting the 959, the Turbo came with four-wheel drive for the first time. The new Carrera 4's lightweight system was used with maximum power split being 80/20, biased to the rear. A limited slip differential was standard, while the ABD system ensured traction control up to a speed of 70kph (44mph).

The 993 Turbo had a top speed of 180mph (290kph) and 0-62.5mph (0-100kph) acceleration took just 4.5sec.

This US model Turbo S interior was a product of the factory's Exclusiv customising programme. Special features include the carbon-fibre trim panels, Exclusiv steering wheel, matching leather-trimmed Recaro bucket seats, drilled pedals and reverse-painted instruments.

The GT2 was a no-compromise racer that was available as a 430bhp road rocket for those who wanted a little extra in the overtaking department. Track credits included the FIA GT2 championship in 1996 and second place in 1997.

A car that fails the drug test! This Carrera 4S has had the Porsche Exclusiv custom treatment, including a biplane rear wing and cooling ducts for the front brakes in place of the standard driving lights. The Carrera 4S combined the Turbo's sure-footed handling and exceptional brakes with the much-improved four-wheel drive system and the responsiveness of the normally-aspirated engine.

1995-96 GT2

This is a short indulgence on a car that was built for the track, but of which some 50 were built for the road. The rear-wheel drive 911 GT2 became the equipment of choice in the lower division of endurance racing from 1995. It was a no-compromise racer – with a level of trim to suit – that was about 200kg (441lb) lighter than the 993 Turbo.

The changes compared to the Turbo were extensive in detail. The external changes included large (replaceable) wheel arch flares to accommodate the 235/40ZR18 front (on 9J wheels) and 285/35ZR18 rear (on 11J wheels) tyres, revised and more aggressively styled front and rear valences sculpted to match the flares, and an enormous biplane rear spoiler. The suspension was solid bushed, adjustable and beefed up to meet the demands of racing. The 430bhp engine for the road-legal version was derived from the standard Turbo version, with a remapped engine control unit and maximum boost pressure raised from 0.8 to 0.9 bar. The racing version offered another 50bhp.

The 1998 Evolution model further developed the theme, with reduced weight, detail engine improvements and revised aerodynamics, including a new front spoiler and an even higher biplane rear wing.

1996-97 CARRERA 4S

For the 1996 model year, the Carrera 4S offered the 993 four-wheel drive system in the Turbo's chassis and wider body, with ride height reduced by 15mm (0.6in). The Turbo's fixed tea-tray spoiler was not used because no inter-cooler was fitted. Consequently the less ostentatious movable spoiler was retained as the standard fit. Brakes were the Turbo's 322mm (12.7in) diameter cross-drilled and ventilated discs with four-piston fixed calipers. The Turbo's 8J × 18in and 10J × 18in wheels were fitted with 225/40 front and 285/30 rear tyres.

A high level of equipment for the Carrera 4S included air conditioning, leather, full electronically adjustable front seats and the ten-speaker sound package. The factory noted a top speed of 168mph (270kph) for the 4S compared to the 171mph (275kph) claimed for the regular Coupé, while 0-62.5mph (0-100kph) acceleration was 5.3sec compared to the two-wheel drive Carrera's 5.4sec.

Data Section

PRODUCTION DATA

Model year	Model	Power (bhp DIN@rpm)	Torque (Nm@rpm)	Compression ratio	Weight (kg)	Number built
994 production						
1994	964 Carrera 2/4	250@6100	310@4800	11.3:1	1350/1450	505
	964 Carrera 2/4 US	250@6100	310@4800	11.3:1	1350/1450	456
	964 RS America US	250@6100	310@4100	11.3:1	1350/1450	144
	964 Carrera 2/4 Cab	250@6100	310@4800	11.3:1	1350/1450	315
	964 Carrera 2/4 Cab US	250@6100	310@4800	11.3:1	1350/1450	283
	964 Speedster	250@6100	310@4800	11.3:1	1350	581
	964 Speedster US	250@6100	310@4800	11.3:1	1400	469
	964 Turbo	360@5500	520@4200	7.5:1	1470	471
	964 Turbo US	360@5500	520@4200	7.5:1	1470	466
993 production						
1994	993 Carrera	272@6000	330@5000	11.3:1	1370	7994
	993 Carrera US	272@6000	330@5000	11.3:1	1370	1453
	993 Carrera Cab	272@6000	330@5000	11.3:1	1370	5911
	993 Carrera Cab US	272@6000	330@5000	11.3:1	1370	1285
1995	993 Carrera 2/4	272@6100	330@5000	11.3:1	1370/1420	7018
	993 Carrera US 2/4	272@6100	330@5000	11.3:1	1370/1420	4139
	993 Carrera Cab 2/4	272@6100	330@5000	11.3:1	1370/1420	2878
	993 Carrera Cab US	272@6100	330@5000	11.3:1	1370/1420	3718
	993 Carrera RS	300@6500	355@5400	11.3:1	1279	274
	993 Cup	310@6200	370@5500	11.5:1	1100	110
	993 Turbo	408@5750	540@4500	8.0:1	1575	78
1996	993 Carrera 2/4	285@6100	340@5250	11.3:1	1370/1420	6762
	993 Carrera Targa	285@6100	340@5250	11.3:1	1400	1980
	993 Carrera Cab 2/4	285@6100	340@5250	11.3:1	1370/1420	2066
	993 Carrera US	285@6100	340@5250	11.3:1	1370	3671
	993 Carrera Targa US	285@6100	340@5250	11.3:1	1400	462
	993 Carrera Cab US	285@6100	340@5250	11.3:1	1370/1420	2152
	993 Turbo	408@5750	540@4500	8.0:1	1575	2484
	993 Turbo US	408@5750	540@4500	8.0:1	1575	1357
	993 GT2	430@5750	535@4500	8.0:1	1290	202
1997	993 Carrera 2/4	285@6100	340@5250	11.3:1	1370/1420	5794
	993 Carrera Targa	285@6100	340@5250	11.3:1	1400	1276
	993 Carrera Cab 2/4	285@6100	340@5250	11.3:1	1370/1420	1679
	993 Carrera US	285@6100	340@5250	11.3:1	1370	2972
	993 Carrera Targa US	285@6100	340@5250	11.3:1	1400	567
	993 Carrera Cab US	285@6100	340@5250	11.3:1	1370/1420	2157
	993 Turbo	408@5750	540@4500	8.0:1	1575	972
	993 Turbo US	408@5750	540@4500	8.0:1	1575	1048

Notes
Models denoted US include Canada, Austria and Switzerland. For Tiptronic, add 25kg to weights given for relevant models.

PRODUCTION CHANGES

Dec 1993 (START OF R-SERIES)
New 911 Carrera (993) introduced in Coupé form only; 1994 models also include Carrera 2 Speedster and Carrera 2 Cabriolet in earlier 964 body style. Engine crankshaft strengthened and 1kg heavier, connecting rods lightened (from 0.632kg to 0.520kg), pistons lightened (from 0.657kg to 0.602kg) and elimination of the vibration damper. Hydraulic valve adjustment. Separate exhaust catalytic converters and pipe exits after central mixing chamber. Bosch M2.10 engine management. Battery 75Ah; 115amp/1610watt alternator. New six-speed manual gearbox (Tiptronic optional). Multi-link LSA rear axle suspension system. Fuel tank 74.5 litres (92 litres optional). Drag coefficient, Cd = 0.33. Anti-roll bars (Tiptronic in brackets): 21mm front (22mm), 18mm rear (20mm). Service intervals now 12,000 miles (20,000km). New 993 Cabriolet launched in UK spring 1994 (as was US 993 – as 1995 S series model).

Aug 1994 (START OF S-SERIES)
Tiptronic S with steering wheel shift buttons introduced. October 1994 new Carrera 4 in 993 bodyshell. 993 Carrera RS (and Club Sport) introduced February 1995: 3.8-litre engine (bore 102mm, stroke 76.4mm) with 300bhp (uses Varioram, bigger valves). Battery 36Ah. Gearbox ratios (Club Sport in brackets): first 3.154, second 2.0, third 1.522, fourth 1.242 (1.241), fifth 1.024 (1.031), sixth 0.821 (0.829), reverse 2.857. 240mm clutch, dual mass flywheel. Crown wheel/pinion ratio: 3.444. Reduced shifting effort on first/second compared to 1993 RS3.8. 40%/65% acceleration/ deceleration differential lock. 322mm cross-drilled ventilated disc brakes all round. 360mm steering wheel. Adjustable anti-roll bars (23mm front, 19mm rear). RSR wing adjustable 0-12°.

Aug 1995 (START OF T-SERIES)
Introduction of Targa with new moving roof design. New wheels and tyres (also optional for Coupé/Cabriolet): front 7J x 17in with 205/50ZR17, rear 9J x 17in with 255/40ZR17. Engine in 911 Carrera, Cabriolet, Targa, 4 and 4S upgraded to 285bhp (uses Varioram, bigger valves). Carrera 4S is turbo-bodied Carrera 4. Includes Turbo's brakes, lowered suspension, hollow-spoke wheels. Introduction of 911 GT2 with 430bhp and, from March 1996, 993 Turbo: 408bhp, 3600cc. Two valves/one plug per cylinder; Bosch M5.2 Engine Management; 2 KKK K16 turbochargers with 2 intercoolers; OBD2 diagnostic system; six-speed gearbox with 25% acceleration/40% deceleration locking differential; 18in (8J/10J) aluminium hollow-spoke wheels (also Carrera 4S and elsewhere optional) with 225/40ZR18 front and 285/30ZR18 rear tyres. 322mm cross-drilled ventilated disc brakes all round. Turbo has 22mm/21mm front/rear anti-roll bars.

Aug 1996 (START OF V-SERIES)
Carrera S uses Turbo bodyshell, but with two-wheel drive. Speed-related volume control on standard radio fit (Porsche CR11RDS).

Sep 1997 (START OF W-SERIES)
All new 996 replaces two-wheel drive 993 models. Four-wheel drive and Turbo production continues until approx July 1998. Outline 996 specification: water-cooled boxer six-cylinder engine; 3387cc (bore 96mm, stroke 78mm); compression ratio 11.3:1; four valves per cylinder; four overhead camshafts; max power 300bhp at 6800rpm; max torque 350Nm at 4600rpm; electronic ignition with solid-state distributor (six coils); sequential multi-point injection; variable intake manifold system. Drag coefficient, Cd = 0.33. Data (Tiptronic in brackets): weight, 1320kg (1365kg); length, 4430mm; width, 1765mm; height, 1305mm; wheelbase, 2350mm; track front/rear, 1455mm/1500mm on 17in wheels; fuel tank, 64 litres; 0–62mph, 5.2sec (6.0sec); top speed, 174mph (171mph).

DIMENSIONS

Wheelbase: 2272mm
Track (front/rear): 1405mm/1444mm (RS: 1413mm/ 1452mm; Turbo: 1411mm/1504mm)
Length: 4245mm
Width: 1735mm (Carrera S, 4S & Turbo: 1795mm)
Height: 1300mm (RS: 1270mm; Turbo: 1285mm)
Turning circle: 11.74m

OPTIONS

Ex-factory – in some countries some of these options may have been fitted as standard. Common options without M numbers are as follows: metallic paint, paint to customer choice, leather seats, leather seats with heating, full leather interior (including seats) in series colours, custom colour and/or soft ruffled leather.

M058 Bumpers with impact absorbers; M425 Rear wiper (only for Coupé); M498 Deletion of model designation; M567 Windshield with graduated tint; M650 Electric sunroof; M551 Automatic wind deflector (Cabriolet only); M545 92-litre fuel tank; MP08 Active limited slip differential (manual only); M224 Active brake differential (Tiptronic only); M398 17in Cup design wheels; MP31 Sport suspension with 17in wheels; MP15 Full electric adjustable front seats (left and right); M437 same (left only); M438 same (right only); M383/387 Sports seats (left/right); M586 Lumbar support in seat (left); M513 same (right); MP14 Heated seats (left/right); M454 Automatic speed control; M573 Automatic air conditioning; M659 On-board computer (standard on Tiptronic); M613 Installation for D-Netz cellular (Germany only); M614 Porsche telephone (Motorola) D-Netz (Germany only); M333 Blaupunkt Paris RCR42 radio/cassette (with M490 or M692); Blaupunkt Bremen RCM42 radio cassette; M693 Blaupunkt London RDM42 CD-Radio; M692 CD changer (only with M334 and M490); M490 Hi-Fi loudspeaker system.

1995 RS: driver and passenger airbags; full climate control; RSR spoilers; RSR front strut support; top tinted windshield.

COLOUR SCHEMES

1994
Standard body colours
A1 Black, S8 Riviera Blue, G1 Guards Red, T3 Amaranth Violet, P5 Grand Prix White, X4 Speed Yellow.
Special order body colours
A8 Polar Silver metallic, D3 Iris Blue metallic*, K6 Aventura Green metallic*, F8 Midnight Blue metallic*, Q9 Slate Grey metallic, Z8 Black metallic*. Also any solid or metallic colour to sample (* denotes pearl effect colour).
Interior colours
Midnight Blue, Classic Grey, Chestnut Brown, Black.

IDENTIFICATION

Model year	Model	Engine	Gearbox	Chassis numbers	Engine numbers
964 production					
1994	964 Carrera 2/4	M64/01	G50/G64	WPOZZZ96ZRS40001-0505	62R00001 onwards
	964 Carrera 2/4 US	M64/01	G50/G64	WPOAB296RS420001-0456	62R00001 onwards
	964 RS America US	M64/01	G50/05	WPOAB296RS419001-9144	62R00001 onwards
	964 Carrera 2/4 Cab	M64/01	G50/G64	WPOZZZ96ZRS450001-0315	62R00001 onwards
	964 Carrera 2/4 Cab US	M64/01	G50/G64	WPOCB296RS460001-0283	62R00001 onwards
	964 Speedster	M64/01	G50/03	WPOZZZ96ZRS455001-5581	62R00001 onwards
	964 Speedster US	M64/01	G50/05	WPOCB296RS465001-5469	62R00001 onwards
	964 Turbo	M64/50	G50/52	WPOZZZ96ZRS470001-0471	61R00001 onwards
	964 Turbo US	M64/50	G50/52	WPOAC296RS480001-0466	61R00001 onwards
993 production					
1994	993 Carrera	M64/05	G50/21	WPOZZZ99ZRS310001-6412	63R00001 onwards
	993 Carrera + 718	M64/05	G50/21	WPOZZZ99ZSS310001-1582	63R00001 onwards
	993 Carrera Tiptronic	M64/06	A50/04	As Carrera	63R50001 onwards
	993 Carrera US + 718	M64/07	G50/20	WPOAA299SS320001-1453	64R00001 onwards
	993 Carrera Tiptronic US	M64/08	A50/05	As Carrera US	64R50001 onwards
	993 Cab	M64/05	G50/21	WPOZZZ99ZRS330001-5850	63R00001 onwards
	993 Cab + 718	M64/05	G50/21	WPOZZZ99ZSS330001-0061	63R00001 onwards
	993 Cab US	M64/06	G50/20	WPOCA299RS340001-0061	64R00001 onwards
	993 Cab US + 718	M64/06	G50/20	WPOCA299SS340001-1224	64R00001 onwards
	993 Cup + M001	M64/70	G50/30	WPOZZZ99ZRS398001-8100	63R80001 onwards
1995	993 Carrera	M64/05	G50/21	WPOZZZ99SS310001-7018	63S00001 onwards
	993 Carrera Tiptronic	M64/06	A50/04	As Carrera	63S50001 onwards
	993 Cab	M64/05	G50/21	WPOZZZ99SS330001-2878	63S00001 onwards
	993 Carrera US	M64/07	G50/20	WPOAA299SS320001-4139	64S00001 onwards
	993 Carrera Tiptronic US	M64/08	A50/05	As Carrera US	64S00001 onwards
	993 Cab US	M64/07	G50/20	WPOCA299SS340001-3718	64S00001 onwards
	993 Carrera RS	M64/20	G50/31	WPOZZZ99SS390001-274	63S85001 onwards
	993 Cup	M64/70	G50/30	WPOZZZ99SS398001-8110	63S80001 onwards
	993 Turbo	M64/60	G64/51	WPOZZZ99SS370001-0078	61T00001 onwards
1996	993 Carrera	M64/21	G50/21	WPOZZZ99TS310001-6762	63T00001 onwards
	993 Carrera Tiptronic	M64/22	A50/04	As Carrera	63T50001 onwards
	993 Carrera Targa	M64/21	G50/21	WPOZZZ99TS380001-1980	63T00001 onwards
	993 Carrera Cab	M64/21	G50/21	WPOZZZ99TS330001-2066	63T00001 onwards
	993 Carrera US	M64/23	G50/20	WPOAA299TS32001-3671	64T00001 onwards
	993 Carrera Targa US	M64/23	G50/20	WPOBA299TS385001-5462	64T00001 onwards
	993 Carrera Cab US	M64/23	G50/20	WPOCA299TS340001-2152	64T00001 onwards
	993 Carrera Tiptronic US	M64/24	A50/05	As Carrera US	64T50001 onwards
	993 Turbo	M64/60	G64/51	WPOZZZ99TS370001-2484	61T00001 onwards
	993 Turbo US	M64/60	G64/51	WPOAA299TS375001-6357	61T00001 onwards
	993 GT2	M64/60R	G50/32	WPOZZZ99TS392001-2202	61T00001 onwards
1997	993 Carrera	M64/21	G50/21	WPOZZZ99VS310001-5794	63T00001 onwards
	993 Carrera Tiptronic	M64/22	A50/04	As Carrera	63T50001 onwards
	993 Carrera Targa	M64/21	G50/21	WPOZZZ99VS380001-1276	63T00001 onwards
	993 Carrera Cab	M64/21	G50/21	WPOZZZ99VS330001-1679	63T00001 onwards
	993 Carrera US	M64/23	G50/20	WPOAA299VS32001-4972	64T00001 onwards
	993 Carrera Targa US	M64/23	G50/20	WPOBA299VS385001-567	64T00001 onwards
	993 Carrera Cab US	M64/23	G50/20	WPOCA299VS340001-2157	64T00001 onwards
	993 Carrera Tiptronic US	M64/24	A50/05	As Carrera US	64T50001 onwards
	993 Turbo	M64/60	G64/51	WPOZZZ99VS370001-972	61T00001 onwards
	993 Turbo US	M64/60	G64/51	WPOAA299VS375001-6046	61T00001 onwards

Notes

Chassis numbers These are 17-character VIN industry standard sequences. Consider this example: WPOCA299RS340001 (a US specification 1994 Cabriolet): WPO is the world make code; CA2 is the US VSD code (first letter is body type – A, C or D for Coupé, Cabriolet or Targa; second letter is engine/transmission type – A for two-wheel drive, B for four-wheel drive; third digit is occupant safety system type – 0 for seat belt only, 1 for driver airbag, 2 for driver/passenger airbags; in other markets these three characters were just left ZZZ); 99 is the first two digits of the type; next is the model year letter (R for 1994); S refers to the plant code (Stuttgart); next is the third digit of the type number (3), followed by the body code number.

Engine option From the 1995 model year, a 3746cc engine was an option for the 3.6-litre cars, this enhanced performance version developing 285bhp at 6000rpm. These engines were designated M64/05S (manual) or M64/06S (Tiptronic). For 1996 the enhanced version developed 300bhp at 6500rpm, and designated M64/21S (manual) or M64/22S (Tiptronic).

Miscellaneous The above table makes no distinction between rear-wheel drive and all-wheel drive models (except for Tiptronic, which was available with rear-wheel drive only). Models for Canada, Switzerland and Austria were as US model specification. All manual rear-wheel drive models were available with the optional (M220) limited slip differential. From the US introduction in April 1994, the majority of early models were sold as 1995 models under option M718. Chassis numbers show the letter S for the 1995 model year.

Fabrics
Leatherette for seats, carpets, dash, knee bar, roof liner, A and B pillars, sun visors, window sills front and rear, back-wall top section, steering wheel (leather) and other colour-coded trim. Two-tone interiors with second colour for carpets: Midnight Blue/Marble Grey, Black/Marble Grey, Black/Marble Grey. Leather in Midnight Blue, Classic Grey, Chestnut Brown and Black (except roof liner, A and B pillars, sun visors in leatherette). Special leather in Flamenco Red, Cedar Green, Provence Blue/Midnight Blue*, Provence Blue/Black* (* for dash, knee bar, roof liner, A and B pillars, sun visors, window sills front and rear, back-wall top section in leather, steering wheel). Or leather to customer sample.

Carpets
Midnight Blue, Classic Grey, Chestnut Brown, Black, Marble Grey, Cashmere Beige. Special colours: Flamenco Red, Cedar Green, Provence Blue.

Cabriolet soft-top colours
Classic Grey, Chestnut Brown, Marble Grey, Dark Blue, Black.

1995

Standard body colours
A1 Black, G1 Guards Red, P5 Grand Prix White, S8 Riviera Blue, T3 Amaranth Violet, X4 Speed Yellow.

Special order body colours
A8 Polar Silver metallic, D3 Iris Blue metallic, F8 Midnight Blue metallic, K6 Aventura Green metallic, Q9 Slate Grey metallic, Z8 Black metallic. Plus any paint colour and material to special order.

Interior colours
Black, Cedar Green, Cashmere Beige, Midnight Blue, Classic Grey, Chestnut, Marble Grey.

Fabrics
Leatherette, leather, 'soft ruffled' leather, 'Porsche' cloth.

Carpets
Midnight Blue, Classic Grey, Chestnut Brown, Black, Marble Grey, Cashmere Beige. Special colours: Flamenco Red, Cedar Green, Provence Blue, Rubicon Grey.

Cabriolet soft-top colours
Black, Dark Blue, Classic Grey, Chestnut, Marble Grey.

1996

Standard body colours
A1 Black, G1 Guards Red, J1 Blue Turquoise, P5 Grand Prix White, X4 Speed Yellow.

Special order body colours
A8 Polar Silver metallic, D3 Iris Blue metallic, F8 Midnight Blue metallic, H8 Arena Red metallic, K1 Turquoise metallic, K6 Aventura Green metallic, Z8 Black metallic.

Interior colours
Black, Classic Grey, Midnight Blue, Cashmere Beige, Chestnut. Plus special order colours: Flamenco Red, Cedar Green, Provence Blue, Rubicon Grey.

Fabrics
Leatherette, leather, 'soft ruffled' leather, 'Porsche' cloth.

Carpets
Midnight Blue, Classic Grey, Chestnut Brown, Black, Marble Grey, Cashmere Beige. Special colours: Flamenco Red, Cedar Green, Provence Blue, Rubicon Grey.

Cabriolet soft-top colours
Black, Classic Grey, Marble Grey, Dark Blue, Chestnut.

1997

Standard body colours
A1 Black, G1 Guards Red, J1 Blue Turquoise, G1 Pastel Yellow, Z1 Glacier White.

Special order body colours
E1 Ocean Blue metallic, F1 Zenith Blue metallic, H8 Arena Red metallic, X1 Arctic Silver metallic, Z8 Black metallic.

Interior colours
Black, Classic Grey, Midnight Blue, Cashmere Beige, Chestnut. Plus special leathers in Rubicon Grey, Nephrite (blue/green), Boxster Red (with black Cabriolet soft-tops).

Fabrics
Leatherette, leather, 'Porsche' cloth.

Carpets
Midnight Blue, Classic Grey, Chestnut Brown, Black, Cashmere Beige. Special colours: Rubicon Grey, Nephrite (blue/green), Boxster Red.

Cabriolet soft-top colours
Black, Classic Grey, Dark Blue, Chestnut.

BUYING & DRIVING

The first 911s are now very rare, but have an elegance all of their own. Wood on the dashboard and lots of chrome recall the spirit of the 1960s.

Until a few years ago, any 'elfer' – the German term used to describe 911 enthusiasts – would tell you that the real 911s finished when impact-absorbing bumpers were put on the cars in 1974. I say a few years ago because even the most defensive of the classic brigade have had to admit that progress has at last been made in the 911s of the 1990s. The intervening years saw Porsche develop not so much the raw performance of the 911, but the model's reliability, longevity and most noticeably its driveability. In the late 1970s and early 1980s, the company sought a different type of customer from the small band of the enthusiasts that had bought the pre-1974 models, and this change of strategy saw the emergence of the 911 as the supreme grand tourer. The 1990 Carrera 2 began to recover some of the raw performance, while remarkably retaining the car's outstanding composure. And when the 1994 Carrera came along, the recovery was complete. The wonderful 993 was far and away the best 911 ever.

This short life history, then, allows us to divide the 911 family into four distinct groups from which you can choose to buy. What follows is not a detailed account of what corrosion points or mechanical maladies to look for when buying a 911. Several good books on restoring classic 911s already exist and these will show you what to look for when buying an early model – and if you are serious about these cars you will need to do your homework. This chapter will ask, instead, what you want out of a 911 and suggest some of the more desirable production 911s through some 35 years of production.

The early 911s, up to the end of the 1973 model year, form the first category that you might want to consider. To buy an early 911 means you want a car that has character and one on which you must almost inevitably spend money. If you want a car from this era you probably will not want to drive it every day, but conserve it for use during the summer for club events or on Sunday mornings for adrenalin rushes. You may have your favourite stretch of long and winding road which along part of its length will have a suitably reflective wall or banking that will throw the sound of that glorious, unshrouded air-cooled 'six' back at your ears. We are talking music...

You will know that these early 911s need to be driven properly. You do not lift off in a corner in a 911 – you keep your right foot in there. Early 911s let go very quickly when you unsettle them in a fast bend. But when you get the hang of driving a 911 fast, it is one of the most satisfying driving experiences because it takes a lot of learning.

These classic 911s are, not surprisingly, the most desirable and much of this is due to their rarity, relative simplicity and originality of concept. Most have either been written-off or have rusted away – pre-1976 911s rust very badly. And because they are collectable, the best advice is to research a possible purchase very thoroughly and have a reputable specialist check it out for you. It is very easy to buy a poor car, either because it has been unsafely repaired or inadequately 'restored', or because it is fitted with unoriginal parts. The latter is important because the value of an early car depends upon its originality.

Check the chassis number to ensure that the car is

A Carrera 3.2 makes a great deal of sense for anyone new to Porsches because by this time the whole 911 package was supremely reliable and trouble-free.

what it purports to be – the data in this book will help. The Porsche factory or, outside Germany, the official importer, may be able to help with this research once you find a specific car. A routine service history is not particularly important – what you see is what you buy with any old car – but a prestige history naturally does great things for the desirability of a particular model.

You may fancy wind-in-the-hair driving in an old 911, but old Targas are rarer than old Coupés because fewer have survived. Since the bodyshell was less stiff, most have succumbed to stress-induced corrosion because panels twist, water gets past weakened spot welds, and rust traps are formed. Without the significant stiffening element of the roof, Targas will also not handle as tautly as Coupés – which is why few people race them. So a Targa, unless completely rust-free, is likely to require a lot of work. Furthermore, it is quite normal for older Targas to leak water and create excessive wind noise.

Of the early 911 classics, three particular versions would be my preference. First, any 1965 model (from the first full year of production) captures the character of an early 1960s sports car with its chrome-trimmed instruments and wood rim steering wheel. Unfortunately, these cars are now very rare and, in Europe, their suitability for historic rallying means that any that become available are in danger of being irretrievably converted. Second, the 1966-69 2-litre 911S is a real screamer that handles as positively as a go-kart and sounds terrific. Third, the 1972-3 2.4-litre 911S is the archetypal classic 911. It still needs handling with care, but goes very quickly. With the chin spoiler, the styling is also a little more modern. If you cannot find an S, an E is almost as good if not as 'cammy' – with a T you will always be searching for more power.

Of course, one other early 911 must be considered: the 1972-3 Carrera RS 2.7 is hailed as the most desirable Porsche from the classic era. On the basis that it goes more quickly and costs more than all the other early models, it certainly scores for performance and desirability. But for the classic Porsche buyer, it may seem odd that there appear to be more RSs to choose from than any other early model. This is because all may not be what it seems. It is reasonable to assume that some 1000 'real' RSs survive worldwide out of the original build of approximately 1500, but there are also many fakes.

The prospective buyer of a Carrera RS is strongly advised to seek out either registry secretaries for these models or long-time owners. The value of any RS is directly related to its originality and specification, as well as its provenance and matching serial numbers for the engine and gearbox.

Unfortunately, a large number of RS cars have been restored, particularly in the wake of the late 1980s price boom, using non-lightweight panels or even galvanised panels from the 911SC model. Many cars have been revived or re-constructed from 'remains' amounting to almost nothing, or even from paperwork only. A number of chassis have been re-shelled using a contemporary 911T, E or S. There are a significant number of cars such as these offered for sale all the time: they may look like the real thing, but in truth they cannot be considered 'quality'

The new Carrera 2 and Carrera 4 were supremely refined sports cars – the ultimate grand tourers. Civility was further enhanced when the new 'intelligent' Tiptronic automatic transmission was incorporated onto the Carrera 2.

examples. For instance, an original, unrestored car with a late chassis number, even in a non-lightweight shell, is more worthy of ownership than an early car that has been re-bodied or substantially re-created. By the same token, a good, original, undamaged Touring should be valued more than a 'paperwork' lightweight M471.

Forming a bridge between the classic era and the later, more luxurious models are the 2.7s. These cars had all the looks of the later 911s but none of the longevity, so buying a 1974-75 2.7 Carrera brings the bodyshell liabilities of the classic cars. The early 2.7s did not receive a fully-galvanised body until the 1976 model year, when the shell was guaranteed for six years against rust perforation. And the engine, much stretched from its original 2-litres, was at the limit of its development: 2.7 engines just wear out more quickly than any of the others. The most sought-after 2.7s are those that were fitted with the mechanically-injected engine (911/83) from the 1973 Carrera RS. These were built for the 1974 and 1975 model years only, but were not sold in the US.

The 3-litre Carrera is the first of the contemporary classics for non-US buyers – the Carrera 3.0 had the Turbo's engine without the turbo. With 200bhp, it acquired some of the pep that the 911 had lost after 1973, but it was loaded down with plenty of extra equipment as Porsche sought to widen the appeal of the 911. The 3-litre Carreras, however, are approaching their 20th anniversary and many now show the effects of age, despite their zinc-coated bodyshells. Look for rust around the flexible trim strip that links the front wings, bonnet and the front bumper. Corrosion will also bubble through around the tail-light clusters, where the front wings meet the A-pillar, and around the fuel filler.

It's worth spending a moment discussing how to identify accident damage. On a 911, look for irregular gaps around the doors and compartment lids as a sign of a poor repair. Lift the carpets in the front luggage compartment and look for rippling ahead of the fuel tank, and also check for this giveaway sign in the undertray behind the front seats.

The Carrera 3.0 was a European taster for the car that was to set up Porsche for the 1980s – the 911SC. The SC is the starting point for the second chapter in the story of which 911 to buy. In the SC, introduced for the 1978 model year, the 911 became a world-class sports car with a reputation for supreme engine reliability – the more miles you did, the better the engine became. It was not particularly quick initially, with only 180bhp (DIN) for most markets and even less in the US, but it was solid and could be trusted to work almost more dependably than your hairbrush. Later SCs had more performance: post-1980 models had 204bhp in Europe but stayed at 180bhp in the US, but the latter had more torque.

All 911SCs were galvanised, so barring any badly-repaired accident damage or cars that have lived in harsh climates, you stand a good chance of finding one in sound condition. And I repeat, high mileage does not mean the engine is worn out! Be choosy and look for cars that have the useful factory options fitted from new, such as an electric sunroof, electric windows and a passenger door mirror. The Sport option offered a firmer ride and flamboyant spoilers.

The launch of the Cabriolet in 1983 finally brought proper 'rag-top' motoring to 911 drivers. The Cabrio was an immediate success and resulted in a progressive decline in the popularity of the Targa. Unlike other makes of car, however, there appears to be no clear difference in price – yet – between a Coupé and an equivalent Cabrio. But if the 356 is anything to go by (convertibles *do* command a premium), then buying a 911 Cabrio would be a sound purchase for the future.

Apart from fuel injection tweaks and a few other details, not much happened to the SC during its life

PERFORMANCE AT A GLANCE

Year	Model	Weight (kg)	Power (bhp)	Top speed kph	Top speed mph	0-62mph (sec)	Source
1963	901	1080	130	210	131	8.5*	P.Frère
1964-67	911 (2.0)	1040	130	210	130	8.3*	Motor
1967-69	911S (2.0)	1050	160	220	137	8.0*	Autocar
1968-69	911T (2.0)	1075	110	200	124	8.3	AM&S
1968	911L (2.0)	1075	130	210	131	10.6*	Car
1968	911L US Sporto	1098	130	188	117	10.3*	R&T
1969	911E (2.0)	1020	140	215	134	8.4*	R&T
1969	911E Sporto	1060	140	209	130	9.1*	AMM
1970-71	911T (2.2)	1020	125	205	127	9.5	AM&S
1970-71	911E (2.2)	1020	155	220	137	7.6*	Autosport
1970-71	911S (2.2)	1020	180	220	138	7.0	P.Frère
1972-73	911T (2.4)	1075	130	204	127	8.1/9.5*	Motor
1972-73	911E (2.4)	1050	165	220	138	7.9	Factory
1972-73	911S (2.4)	1050	190	230	144	6.6	P.Frère
1973	Carrera RS M471	975	210	245	152	5.8	P.Frère
1974	Carrera RS 3.0	1063	230	238	148	4.9*	Road Test
1974-75	911	1075	150	210	131	7.9*	R&T
1976-77	911	1123	165	217	135	7.8/7.2*	Motor
1974-77	911S	1105	175	229	142	6.1*	Autocar
1974-77	911S US	1130	165	232	144	7.5*	R&T
1974-75	Carrera 2.7	1075	210	240	150	6.3	AM&S
1974-77	Turbo 3.0	1140	260	250	155	6.0*	Motor
1976-77	Carrera 3.0	1120	200	235	146	6.1*	AM&S
1978-79	911SC	1233	180	227	141	6.5*	Autocar
1978-79	911SC US	1243	180	203	126	6.3*	R&T
1978-79	911 Turbo (3.3)	1300	300	260	162	5.1*	Motor
1980	911SC	1232	188	225	141	7.0	Factory
1981-83	911SC	1160	204	235	146	5.7*	Motor
1984-85	Carrera 3.2	1210	231	245	152	5.6*	Autocar
1984	911SC RS	960	255	255	159	5.0*	AM&S
1987-89	911 Club Sport	1110	231	251	156	5.6*	Autocar
1989-93	Carrera 4	1450	250	260	162	5.7	Factory
1990-93	Carrera 2	1350	250	260	162	5.7	Factory
1990-93	Carrera 2 Tiptronic	1355	250	253	157	6.6/6.2*	Factory/A&M
1991	Carrera 2 RS	1230	260	260	162	5.3	Factory
1991-92	Turbo	1470	320	270	168	5.0	Factory
1992	Turbo S	1290	380	290	180	4.6	Factory
1993	Carrera 2 Speedster	1350	250	260	162	5.7	Factory
1993	Carrera RS 3.8	1210	300	269	168	4.9	Factory
1993-94	Turbo 3.6	1470	360	280	175	4.8	Factory
1994-97	Carrera 3.6	1370	272	270	168	5.4	Factory
1995-98	Carrera 4	1420	272	270	168	5.3	Factory
1994-96	993 Cup	1120	315	280	175	4.7	Factory
1995-96	Carrera RS	1270	300	275	172	5.0	Factory
1995-97	Turbo	1500	408	288	180	4.5	Factory
1996-97	Carrera 3.6	1370	285	274	171	5.4	Factory
1996-97	Carrera S Tiptronic	1365	285	269	168	6.4	Factory
1996-97	Carrera 4	1420	285	274	171	5.3	Factory
1996-97	Carrera 4S	1450	285	269	168	5.3	Factory
1996-97	Carrera S	1400	285	269	168	5.4	Factory
1998	Carrera 3.4	1320	300	278	174	5.2	Factory

Notes

All power figures are DIN. Weights generally tend to quote a specific publication's kerb weight (which usually includes oil and fuel for about 50 miles). Factory figures are the base model with no options, so they are not very realistic! Where 0-62mph time is marked*, this is a 0-60mph time. Magazine source codes: AMM, Australian Motor Manual; A&M, Autocar & Motor (UK); AM&S, Auto Motor & Sport (Germany); R&T, Road & Track (USA).

because Porsche could not decide whether the car was going to be axed. By 1981, Porsche had decided it needed the 911 and two years later we saw the 3.2 Carrera. With more power (231bhp in Europe and ultimately 214bhp in the US), this 911 was the one that Porsche really made money on. There is plenty of choice for the buyer and as a result some good deals. The secret of a good car of this age (and it applies to the SC as well) is a watertight history and proof of originality. This might include all bills and a service history, although I do not subscribe to the belief that an official Porsche history improves value.

The 3.2 Carrera makes a great deal of sense if you are new to Porsche. It is the best value 'contemporary' 911 and mileage is relatively unimportant because the engine is so reliable. The timing chain tensioners, long the 911's Achilles heel, were redesigned and became proverbially 'bullet-proof'.

There was the Sport option which offered the big spoilers and handling package in a normal bodyshell, and was sometimes called the Sport Equipment model in the UK. Then there were the Turbo-bodied models, which were termed Super Sport Equipment. Do not confuse these with the Turbo Sport Equipment in Britain – this was the production Slant-Nose model. In 1987 a new gearbox offered a shorter, more precise shift, together with a lighter clutch pedal and this later G50 gearbox is worth the financial stretch if you can go that far.

The third 'family' for the prospective – and more affluent – 911 buyer is the Carrera 4 and Carrera 2, although some of the classics command similar prices these days. The choice comes down, of course, to whether you want four-wheel-drive or two. The 4 is a wonderfully stable car which transmits its power effortlessly to all the wheels. The Carrera 2 followed the 4 by about a year and replaced the 3.2 Carrera, marking a return to the healthy power-to-weight ratios seen at the start of the 1970s.

The 993 is the 911 every Porsche enthusiast dreams of owning – it combines all the 911's best attributes with significant improvements in handling, ride and refinement. Demand for this fourth generation of the 911 will always be strong, making it doubly important that the car has an unbroken service record and a reliable ownership history. The demand also means that depreciation will be low.

The early two-wheel drive coupés will inevitable be the most affordable, with prices rising for Cabriolets, Carrera 4s and the rare Targas. The best value with Tiptronics will be found in rural areas, rather than in cities, while cars with desirable options like air conditioning, CD players and sport suspension will always sell more quickly.

I have not mentioned the Turbo yet. Perhaps I am saving the best until last? The Turbo is a cult car, the epitome of what Porsche is all about, but the potential buyer has to be extremely careful when looking. The early 3-litre models, despite their weak brakes, are now classics and very scarce. Through the 1980s the Turbo was progressively improved and your choice would inevitably depend on how much money you have. Slant-Nose cars were made from the early 1980s as custom models, but from 1987 this body style became a production variant. They are very desirable – but difficult to park! In the new body style of the Carrera 4, the Turbo is stunning, especially the 3.6-litre version.

Owning a 911 is to possess a landmark in automobile history. If you do not already enjoy this privilege, I hope you can soon.

PORSCHE CLUBS

There are more than 330 Porsche clubs in 33 countries with a total of over 120,000 enthusiasts, so this list covers only the major organisations.

Porsche Club of America PO Box 30100, Alexandria, VA 22310, USA.
Porsche Club of South Australia PO Box 43, Glen Osmond, SA 5064, Australia.
Porsche Club Belgique Steenweg op Leuven 639, B-3071 Kortenberg, Belgium.
Porsche Club Deutschland Adolf Kronerstrasse 18, D-70184 Stuttgart, Germany.
Porsche Club Espana Paseo de la Castellana 62, Madrid 28046, Spain.
Porsche Club de France c/o Texport SA, 29-31 Rue d'Alger BP646, 76007 Rouen, France.
Porsche Club Great Britain Ayton House, Cornbury House, Cotswold Business Village, Moreton-in-Marsh, Gloucestershire GL56 0JA, UK.
Porsche Club Holland Papehof 39, NL 1391 BE, Abcoude, Netherlands.
Porsche Club Hong Kong 227 Prince Edward Road, 1/F Block A, Kowloon, Hong Kong.
Porsche Club Italia Via Guerrazzi 22, 20145 Milano, Italy.
Porsche Owners Club of Japan 16-21 Meguro-Honcho 2-Chome Meguro-ku, Tokyo, 152 Japan.
Nederlandse Porsche Club Huisdreef 1, NL 4851 RA, Ulvenhout, Netherlands.
Porsche Club of New South Wales PO Box 183, Lindfield, NSW 2070, Australia.
Porsche Club New Zealand PO Box 33-1074, Auckalnd 9, NZ.
Porsche Klubb Norge Postboks 83 Lilleaker, N-0216 Oslo, Norway.
Porsche Club South Africa PO Box 72102, Parkview, 2122, South Africa.
Porsche Club Sverige PO Box 34025, S-10026 Stockholm, Sweden.
Porsche Club of Victoria PO Box 911, Kew, Vic 3101, Australia.
Porsche Club of Western Australia PO Box 447, South Perth, Western Australia 6151.

Introduced in September 1997, the 996 marked the fifth generation of Porsches using the 911 title. This universally acclaimed car leads Porsche into the new century.